JOURNALISTIC
FRAUD

JOURNALISTIC FRAUD

HOW THE *NEW YORK TIMES* DISTORTS THE NEWS
AND WHY IT CAN NO LONGER BE TRUSTED

BOB KOHN

WND BOOKS

Nashville

www.WNDBooks.com

Published in Nashville, Tennessee, by WND Books.

Library of Congress Cataloging-in-Publication Data

Kohn, Bob
    Journalistic Fraud : How the New York Times Distorts the News and Why It Can No
Longer Be Trusted / Bob Kohn
    Includes index
    ISBN 0-7852-6104-4
    1. Journalism—Objectivity. 2. New York Times. 3. Mass media—Political aspects—
United States. I. Title
Library of Congress Control Number: 2003090485

Printed in the United States of America

03 04 05 06 07 **BVG** 5 4 3 2 1

To my parents,
Edna and Al Kohn

CONTENTS

PREFACE

Letter to the Editor

The New York Times
229 West 43rd Street
New York, NY 10036

Dear Editors:

This book is ultimately addressed to you, the editors of the *New York Times*, as well as its publisher, each of the board members of the New York Times Company, and the eight trustees of the 1997 Sulzberger Trust who, by contract, control the destiny of what has been for well over a hundred years the greatest newspaper in the world—a privilege that is now mortally threatened by the actions of its current publisher.

I've never met Arthur O. Sulzberger Jr., the current publisher of the *New York Times*. In fact, I hadn't even really heard of him until three months after I began writing this book. I'm certain he is a thoughtful, caring, talented person who thinks he is making the right decisions for the institution over which he, by birthright, has been given plenary control. But no one is immune from error, and Sulzberger, in my view, as documented here, is making the blunder of a generation.

I have been an avid reader of the *New York Times* ever since a daily subscription was offered to me at a discount in the 1960s when I was a pupil in the New York public school system at P.S. 169 in Queens. I would today consider myself a typical reader of the *Times*, though my political beliefs are far to the right of the *Times*' editorial page—which, in the minds of many, might mean I am a moderate.

For many years, I have enjoyed my morning coffee with the breadth of wonders presented in the *New York Times*, from its extensive coverage of international news to always interesting articles on the arts, media, business, and the latest developments in science and technology—though, in recent years, I've been skipping each day's editorial page offerings because I can no longer stomach them.

But it is not the editorial pages of the *Times* that have prompted me to write this book. While traveling with my wife through New England last summer, my vacation was punctuated each morning with a copy of the *New York Times*. With my daily task being merely to navigate us to the next used bookstore, diner, or motel, leisure provided me with that rare pleasure of slowly perusing the morning paper—even during the work week—wringing out as much information and entertainment that the *Times* may afford a happy tourist while at breakfast. What I found, however, was something more disturbing than entertaining.

Quite simply, I began to notice a fundamental change in the way in which the *Times* has been reporting *the news*. I'm not referring to the substance or tone of its editorial views, but to the way the paper has been expressing those views—specifically, to the way the *Times* has waged editorial crusades, not on the paper's editorial pages, but within "objective" news stories appearing on the front page and other news pages. With my wife at the wheel, I started memorializing my observations in my Palm Pilot. By the time we got home, I had twenty pages of notes and a determination to carry on. I continued to read the *Times* carefully each morning, very carefully, and organized my observations on a new laptop computer. After many trips to libraries, including a visit to the New York Public Library, the result was this book.

Suffice it to say that it pains me to watch the *New York Times* lose the reputation that so many honest journalists have worked so hard to build over its 152-year history. It is not an overstatement to say that if the current publishing policies of the *Times* continue, the "newspaper of record" will become indistinguishable from the "tabloid" publications the *Times* seems fond of deriding.

I state this not as an expert but as a consumer, and I know there are many who are beginning to feel the same way. According to published reports, even some of the reporters and columnists who work at the *Times* are becoming increasingly concerned about the changes we are witnessing.

One need not be an insider or a professional critic to take note of the changes threatening the demise of the *Times*. I am not an historian or journalist, and I have not interviewed anyone for this book. The criticism presented here is derived solely from the pages of the newspaper, combined with my training as a lawyer and the education of journalism classes I took in school.

Though the criticism in this book may in some places be severe, I've worked to carefully document every fact. As for the tone, I've tried not to be too academic, striving for the balance of gravity and passion typifying that of the editorial pages of the *Times*—no less objective, no more "mean-spirited."

I am just a guy who reads the *Times* carefully each morning, and I believe I am speaking on behalf of tens of thousands of like-minded readers. Many of us had hoped to be reading the *Times* during our retirement, enjoying the well-written prose on a variety of political and cultural happenings with our morning cups of coffee.

It is the sad prospect of losing that little pleasure that has driven me to complete this book. It is my earnest hope that those to whom this preface is addressed will read this as they would a customer complaint letter. The response I hope to evoke, however, is not a refund of my money but a genuine change in the editorial attitude of the publisher, drawing the *Times* back to the reverence for impartiality it demonstrated over half a century ago. Only in that way will fervent fans be able to imbibe their daily dose of the *Times*, comforted by the thought that the same pleasure may be enjoyed by their children some day.

I am not suggesting that the *Times* change its editorial views—its editors are free to crusade against all the "wrongs" they believe are fit to print on their editorial pages. I'm just suggesting that the editors of the *Times* limit their crusading to their editorial pages and leave the news gathering and reporting function to those who appreciate their responsibility to report accurately that which happens—to report the news "impartially, without fear or favor."

Unfortunately, I have no insight into the likelihood that this advice will be heeded. I can only hope the following pages will provide the spark of understanding necessary to reverse the steady decline in the *Times'* reputation and value as a credible source of news.

"The only end in writing," said Dr. Samuel Johnson, "is to enable the reader better to enjoy life, or better able to endure it." If little else, it is hoped this book will enable frustrated readers of the *Times* to better tolerate their few minutes each morning with the ailing "Grey Lady."

Sincerely,
Bob Kohn
June 6, 2003

ONE

Bias, Slander, and Fraud

For more than a century, men and women of
The Times have jealously guarded the paper's integrity.
Whatever else we contribute, our first duty is to
make sure the integrity of The Times is not
blemished during our stewardship.

*— From "Code of Conduct for the News and Editorial
Departments of the* New York Times*" (January 2003)*

$\mathfrak{T}$imes have changed, and with it, regrettably, so has the *Times*. What
was once considered the "newspaper of record"—a moniker reportedly
coined by an early advertising manager for the *New York Times*—is
quickly losing its reputation as a reliable source of news.

The aim of this book is to convince the publisher of the *Times* to reverse the
ideologically tainted news reporting practices that are destroying the integrity
of his newspaper. The means is simple: By providing examples taken directly
from within the four corners of the news pages, this book exposes the pronounced liberal bias that pervades the news pages of the *New York Times*. This
book does not concern the political positions taken in the editorials or opinion
columns of the *Times*. Nor is it about *media bias*, insofar as that term has been

used to describe perceptions of an overall liberal bias in the mainstream media. This book is about *editorial opinion disguised as objective news* and what can be done to stop it.

The crux of this book is best illustrated by a joke that has been circulating around the Internet:

> The Pope was visiting Washington, D.C. and President Bush took him out for an afternoon on the Potomac, sailing on the presidential yacht. They were admiring the sights when, all of a sudden, the Pope's hat—his white zucchetto—blew off his head and out into the water. The secret service guys started to launch a boat, but Bush waved them off, saying, "Wait, wait. I'll take care of this. Don't worry."
>
> Bush then stepped off the yacht onto the surface of the water and walked out to the Holy Father's little hat, bent over and picked it up, then walked back to the yacht and climbed aboard. He handed the hat to the Pope amid stunned silence.
>
> The next morning, the *New York Times* carried a story, with front-page photos, of the event. The banner headline read: "BUSH CAN'T SWIM."

The revelations of "frequent acts of journalistic fraud"—upon the discovery in May 2003 that a *Times* staff reporter, Jayson Blair, engaged in fabrications and plagiarism that may have polluted hundreds of the paper's news articles— brought to light what may be the underlying cause of the journalistic fraud addressed in the following pages. As the *Times* scrambled to defend its reputation in the aftermath of its startling disclosure, facts about the circumstances leading up to the scandal began to surface. Commentators in the media, including respected journalists and academicians, began to accuse the top managers of the *Times*' newsroom of arrogance, hypocrisy, and incompetence.

One would expect that these unfortunate events would have humbled the publisher and resulted in an earnest effort to uproot the offending practices. While the Blair scandal led to a high-level management shakeup, there are no signs of any real institutional change on the horizon. On the day the *Times* announced the resignation of Howell Raines as executive editor, the *Wall Street Journal* reported on the debacle with views from those inside and outside of the *Times*. "There is an endemic cultural issue at the Times that is not a Howell creation," said veteran *Times* reporter Linda Greenhouse in "AMID TURMOIL, TOP

EDITOR RESIGNS AT THE NEW YORK TIMES" (June 6, 2003). "[I]t's a culture where speaking the truth to power has never been particularly welcomed."

In an editorial entitled "Turmoil at the Times" (June 6, 2003), the editors of the *Wall Street Journal* honed in on the broader questions of credibility still facing the *Times*:

> [O]ur view is that what we have been seeing on the front page [of the *Times*] in recent years is less straightforward reporting and more advocacy journalism. In this sense, the scandal over Jayson Blair's fabrications is symptomatic of a broader credibility problem that won't vanish merely because Mr. Raines does.

Yet, Arthur O. Sulzberger Jr., the publisher of the *Times*, has since made it clear that readers can expect no real change in the paper's strategic vision. When asked by the *New York Observer* ("SULZBERGER JR. VOWS TO RIGHT TIMES' COURSE," June 16, 2003) about the future of the front page after Raines' departure, Sulzberger "bristled." "That's strategy," Mr. Sulzberger said. "Things that are strategic don't change with people."

Despite the managerial shuffle, the *Times'* practice of distorting its news pages to reflect its ideological opinions goes on, and the reputation of the *New York Times* as a credible source of news has gone into a tailspin.

Much has been published on the subject of liberal media bias. Bernard Goldberg, a veteran reporter for CBS News, courageously blew the whistle on his colleagues in his book *Bias* (Regnery, 2001). In that bestselling exposé, Goldberg revealed in stunning detail how liberal bias pervades television newsrooms, not by virtue of a "well-orchestrated, vast left wing conspiracy," but by a common view of the world held by those who occupy America's newsrooms.

Ann Coulter, in her book *Slander* (Crown, 2002), enlarges upon what Goldberg called "liberal hate speech" and demonstrates how the liberal media acts like a classic propagandist, using name-calling to advance their political agenda. "Progress cannot be made on serious issues," she says, "because one side is making arguments and the other side is throwing eggs."

But again, this book is not concerned with name-calling or what the *Times* says on its editorial page. Nor does it concern "the media," which Eric

Alterman, in his book *What Liberal Media?* (Basic Books, 2003), found to be "on the whole" more conservative than liberal. Though, arguably, purveyors of conservative commentary, such as Rush Limbaugh, have as much influence on public opinion as their liberal counterparts, such as the editorial pages of the *New York Times*, Alterman misses the point.

Though conservatives may strongly disagree with editorials published by the *Times* or with liberal columns, or other forms of liberal commentary, they don't fundamentally object to them for what they are—as long as such commentary is properly represented or labeled as such. What they object to is commentary that is misrepresented as "objective" news reporting. They object to how news organizations use their *news* pages to convey the same *opinions* that appear on their editorial pages.

Thus, the true debate is not about *media bias*, but about *news bias*. Alterman fools no one by trying to refute evidence of liberal bias by cleverly changing the playing field—from a discussion of "the news" to a discussion of "the media." You can't take a lead front-page story in the *New York Times*, place it alongside a Rush Limbaugh monologue, and then call them both "journalism" for the purposes of weighing whether the media is biased. The Rush Limbaugh program is pure commentary and analysis—never represented as objective news— and is therefore, by nature, biased. Under no circumstances could the same be said of lead stories appearing on the front page of the *New York Times*, and to suggest otherwise is to fundamentally misunderstand the difference between telling the truth and telling a lie.

This book makes no claim that "the media" as a whole has a liberal bias. It more modestly intends to demonstrate, systematically, that a liberal bias pervades the news pages of the *New York Times*. In other words, what this book takes aim at is not the *slander*, but the *journalistic fraud*: what Goldberg called "passing off editorial opinion as straight news" and what Coulter, from the reverse perspective, called "ostensibly objective news coated with smears."

It is not about the *media*, but the *news*—purportedly "hard" news, "objective" news, "straight" news—and how that news is distorted for the purpose of influencing public opinion, aligning it with the liberal views of the *Times*. This book also explores how the integrity of the *Times* is being destroyed under the stewardship of its current publisher and what can be done to save a great American institution from his folly.

A Tradition of Impartiality

It had been the long-standing tradition of the *New York Times* to strive for impartiality in its news reporting. When Adolph S. Ochs purchased the *Times* in 1896, the *Times* was widely considered to be an organ of the Democratic party. To reassure Republicans of the paper's political objectivity, Ochs published one of the only statements ever to have appeared in his paper over his name:

> It will be the aim of the *Times* . . . to give the news impartially, without fear or favor, regardless of party, sect or interests involved.

Adolph S. Och's son-in-law, Arthur Hays Sulzberger, who succeeded Ochs as publisher (serving from 1935 to 1961), continued the *Times*' tradition of impartiality, through at least the early 1950s.

Sulzberger reconfirmed his father-in-law's promise—to report "the news impartially, without fear or favor." That promise, he once wrote, "continues to be the role of the *Times* in the community." On the division between reporting the news and publishing editorial opinions, Sulzberger added:

> We are anxious to see wrongs corrected, and we attempt to make our position very clear in such matters on our editorial page. But we believe that no matter how we view the world, our responsibility lies in reporting accurately that which happens.

Sometime before the end of Sulzberger's reign as publisher in 1961, the *Times* began to abandon its tradition of impartiality. In 1969, Herman H. Dinsmore, a 50-year veteran of the newspaper business—as a reporter, editor, and college professor—published the book *All the News that Fits: A Critical Analysis of the News and Editorial Content of The New York Times* (Arlington House, 1969). Dinsmore joined the foreign desk of the *New York Times* in 1929, rising to the position of editor of its international edition from 1951 through 1960. After thirty years as a reporter and senior editor for the *New York Times*, Dinsmore retired to teach journalism at the Columbia Graduate School of Journalism. He, like Bernard Goldberg, knew firsthand what he was talking about.

Reflecting on the transformation of the *Times* from a "great newspaper" prior to the end of World War II to what it had become by the end of the 1960s, Dinsmore unabashedly introduced his 1969 book with the following blunt disclosure:

> The *New York Times* today is deliberately pitched to the so-called liberal point of view, both in its news and editorial columns.

His book proceeded to expose the worldview of his colleagues, the paper's editors of that time, and provided specific evidence of the bias employed by the *Times* during the 1950s and 1960s. As just one example, the book makes a serious and convincing case that the *New York Times,* through a series of editorials and news articles, was influential in bringing Fidel Castro and his Communist regime to power in Cuba.

It was a *Times* reporter in Havana who reported that Fidel Castro's Cuba was "free, honest, and democratic" as thousands suffered and died in Castro's political prisons. Similarly, in the 1930s, Walter Duranty, a *Times* correspondent in the Soviet Union, assured readers that there was "no actual starvation" in the Ukraine while Stalin was mounting his campaign to "collectivize" the farms in the region. The West later discovered that Stalin's actions resulted in a famine that claimed the lives of millions of people. For his deceptions, Duranty won a Pulitzer Prize, an award that has been challenged and is now under review by the Pulitzer board.

In terms of their human dimensions, these distortions of the truth tower over the startling but relatively minor accounts of lies and plagiarism by *Times* reporter Jayson Blair. Yet, the *Times* calls this most recent affair "a low point in the 152-year history of the newspaper." No doubt Blair's actions represented "a profound betrayal of trust," as the paper's mea culpa stated, but the journalistic fraud regularly engaged in by the *Times* goes far beyond the unethical conduct of a solitary reporter whose transgressions are merely symptomatic of a more endemic problem.

While the *Times* engaged in damage control in response to the Blair scandal, it failed to address the journalistic fraud that had long been spreading through its news pages like a virus. The *New York Times* may have emerged from the intensive care necessitated by the lapses of this one reporter, but its ultimate credibility will depend on whether its publisher recognizes the full extent of the problem and, by addressing its causes, implements its cure.

THE CHANGING TIMES

On May 22, 2001, Arthur Ochs Sulzberger Jr., the grandson of A.H. Sulzberger and current publisher of the *New York Times*, announced the appointment of Howell Raines as the new executive editor of the paper, effective September 6, 2001. For nearly nine years prior to that appointment, Raines had been the *Times'* editorial page editor, what may be considered the chief opinion officer of the *New York Times*. Now, as executive editor, Raines assumed the role of chief news officer, responsible for reporting the news, with the news division's staff of about 1,200 people worldwide at his disposal.

Upon the announcement of Raines' appointment to head the news division, Arthur Sulzberger Jr. wrote in an internal memo to the *Times'* staff:

> What to say about Howell? Well, most of you know him as our esteemed fire-breathing, take-no-prisoners editorial page editor.

Howell Raines is what the *Times* would call an "unabashed liberal." A profile of Raines in the *New Yorker* entitled "THE HOWELL DOCTRINE" (June 10, 2002) stated:

> [Arthur Sulzberger Jr.] knew that Raines, like him, took liberal positions on affirmative action, capital punishment, abortion rights, health insurance, welfare, the environment, and the role of an activist government. Sulzberger said that he saw the editorial-page editor and the executive editor as partners in the *Times'* future.

In an autobiographical book published in 1993, *Fly Fishing Through the Midlife Crisis* (William Morrow & Co.), Raines wrote about his disgust for President Ronald Reagan:

> In 1981, shortly before the inauguration of Ronald Reagan, my family and I arrived in Washington. . . . I had arrived in our nation's capital during a historic ascendancy of greed and hard-heartedness. . . .
>
> Then one day in the summer of 1981 I found myself at the L.L. Bean store in Freeport, Maine. I was a correspondent in the White House in those days,

and my work—which consisted of reporting on President Reagan's success in making life harder for citizens who were not born rich, white, and healthy—saddened me. . . .

Reagan couldn't tie his shoelaces if his life depended on it.

Even after he assumed his post as head of the news division, Raines continued to wear his extreme left wing political views on his collar. On November 30, 2001, Raines appeared on C-SPAN's "Washington Journal," hosted by Brian Lamb. Regarding President Clinton and his policies, particularly the ill-fated attempt to introduce socialized medicine in the United States, Raines said, "We had editorially supported virtually every aspect of his program, and were particularly evangelical, I would say, about his medical care reform package."

On August 6, 2002, Raines appeared on "The Charlie Rose Show," broadcast on PBS. When asked how history would judge Bill Clinton, Raines steered clear of the fact that Clinton was only the second president in U.S. history to be impeached, and replied:

Huge political talent. Huge political vision and I suspect—none of us, I can't predict who's going to win the next election, much less what history is going to say about anyone. But I think President Clinton's role in modernizing the Democratic party around a set of economic ideas and also holding onto the principles of social justice. And presiding over the greatest prosperity in human history. Those would seem to me to have to be central to his legacy.

Shortly before Raines assumed control of the newsroom, a few solitary words of concern were being expressed about the propriety of Raines' selection as chief editor of the *Times* news division. In a piece published in the *Washington Post*, "A LIBERAL BIAS?" (August 29, 2001), columnist Robert J. Samuelson wrote:

We in the press are routinely self-righteous, holding others—politicians, public officials and corporate executives—to exacting standards of truthfulness, performance and conflict of interest. But we often refuse to impose comparable standards on ourselves, leading some (or much) of the public to see us as hypocritical. A troubling example involves the recent promotion of Howell Raines from editorial page editor of the *New York Times* to executive editor. . . .

In many ways, he seems superbly qualified. Raines, 58, has been a *Times* bureau chief in both London and Washington. In 1992, he won a Pulitzer Prize. But what ought to disqualify him is his job as editorial page editor, where he proclaimed the *Times'* liberal views. Every editor and reporter holds private views; the difference is that Raines' opinions are now highly public. His page took stands on dozens of local, national and international issues. It was pro-choice, pro-gun control and pro-campaign finance "reform." Last year, it endorsed Al Gore. In general, it has been critical of President Bush, especially his tax cut.

Does anyone believe that, in his new job, Raines will instantly purge himself of these and other views? And because they are so public, Raines' positions compromise the *Times'* ability to act and appear fair-minded. Many critics already believe that the news columns of the *Times* are animated—and distorted—by the same values as its editorials. Making the chief of the editorial page the chief of the news columns will not quiet those suspicions. But asked about possible conflicts, publisher Arthur Ochs Sulzberger Jr.—who selected Raines—dismissed them with a short statement: "The brilliant and honorable tenure of Max Frankel as executive editor of the *Times* (1986-94), following his years as editorial page editor (1977-86), stands as a testament that a great journalist knows the difference between these two roles. Howell is certainly a great journalist." In other words: Get lost.

Concerns that Raines would aggressively use the news division to advance the editorial positions he had driven in his previous position were soon confirmed.

The bias had gotten so bad that, within a year after assuming control of the news division, Raines found himself dealing with a minor revolt among the rank and file news reporters at the *Times'*. The *Times* reporters were becoming gravely concerned that Raines' use of the front page to crusade editorial causes was beginning to reflect poorly upon the reputation of the professional reporters associated with the paper. Some of these reporters even began talking to other members of the press about their disenchantment with Raines' aggressive use of the front page for editorial purposes.

As we have seen, critics have long charged the *Times* with bias, but if the *Times'* own staff was taking notice, something very unusual was happening.

From all appearances, when Raines took charge of the news division, he simply pushed the accelerator pedal to the floor. As a result, the exploitation of the news division for advancing the editorial positions of the *Times* had become brazen and obvious.

On September 11, 2001, with the attacks against the World Trade Center towers and the Pentagon, the nation found itself suddenly at war. Soon after launching its military response against the Al Qaeda terrorist organization and factions in Afghanistan accused of aiding them, the Bush administration considered the unthinkable consequences of weapons of mass destruction finding their way into the hands of terrorists. Given that one potential source of such weapons was Iraq, President Bush quickly pressed the United Nations to resume its inspections of Iraq for weapons of mass destruction and suggested that if Iraq balked at those efforts, force may be necessary to open Iraq's borders to UN inspectors or to disarm the regime.

To no one's surprise, the *New York Times* immediately declared its opposition to the use of military force against Iraq, beginning with an editorial entitled "THE WRONG TIME TO FIGHT IRAQ" (November 26, 2001). What few saw coming, however, was how Howell Raines was about to set in motion one of the most extensive crusades against an administration's wartime policy ever to appear on the front pages of any newspaper.

Over the following several months, the *Times* rolled out an unprecedented series of *news articles* calculated to advance the *Times'* political agenda and oppose the Bush administration policies on Iraq. (This remarkable use of the front page of the *Times* to crusade for the paper's editorial views is more fully described in Chapter Nine.) The more Bush talked about potential military action against Iraq, the more vociferous the *Times'* opposition became—on both its editorial pages and its news pages.

The campaign against Bush administration policies on Iraq conducted by the news division reached a crescendo in August 2002 when an especially egregious front-page story in the *Times* prompted Pulitzer Prize-winning columnist Charles Krauthammer to declare in the *Washington Post* (August 18, 2002):

> Not since William Randolph Hearst famously cabled his correspondent in Cuba, "You furnish the pictures and I'll furnish the war," has a newspaper so blatantly devoted its front pages to editorializing about a coming American war as has

Howell Raines' *New York Times*. Hearst was for the Spanish-American War. Raines (for those who have been incommunicado for the last year) opposes war with Iraq.

Krauthammer, in that column, went on to expose how the *Times*—in a front-page article entitled "REPUBLICANS BREAK WITH BUSH ON IRAQ" (August 16, 2002)—distorted the views of former Secretary of State Henry Kissinger to sensationalize a fabricated rift between Dr. Kissinger and President Bush on Iraq policy. (The details of this story are set forth in Chapter Five.) The *Times* later printed a half-hearted retraction, but its front-page campaign against the way the United States was carrying out the war on terrorism continued.

A few weeks later, Raines and Sulzberger were the subjects of a taped interview sponsored by the journalism department at the University of California, Berkeley. The forum, held on November 18, 2002 and later broadcast on C-SPAN, was entitled "Business and Editorial Policies of the New York Times."

Mark Danner, a U.C. Berkeley journalism professor, and occasional op-ed writer for the *Times*, confronted Raines with Krauthammer's column. While the professor read Krauthammer's first paragraph aloud, Raines shifted nervously in his seat; the audience anxiously awaited his reply.

Without missing a beat, Raines made Ann Coulter's case for her. Rather than intelligently replying to the criticism, he grabbed a figurative grade A egg and threw it at Krauthammer:

> I can't explain why Charles took leave of his senses. He'd be the best witness on that.

The ad hominem attack was poignant in the way it alluded to Krauthammer's former profession: he was a psychiatrist—a slap that many of Krauthammer's friends and associates would not miss. Clearly not happy with that response, the journalism professor pressed further:

> How do you stop from over-compensating, as it were, when you get that kind of criticism? That is, the Krauthammer quote was just the tip of the iceberg. It was a great stir, and that the perception has persisted that the *Times* is conducting a campaign against the war at least in conservative circles. Indeed, you can sit here and say here's Arthur Sulzberger, he eats lunch every week with

the editorial page editor, and they're against the war, and here is Howell Raines, and he was editorial editor an eye-blink ago, and they're publishing these leaks in the paper, and so and so. How do you stop the conservative criticism from hitting some way what you're publishing?

Raines was getting visibly uncomfortable. The suggestion that he was employing his news division to conduct an editorial campaign was apparently getting under his skin. But Raines knew the drill well and prudently stuck to his strategy by grabbing hold of several more eggs and tossing them, albeit indiscriminately, in the hope they would somehow strike the right target:

> One, you put any kind of criticism in an intellectual framework. The latter connections that you just ran through is from a *Weekly Standard* editorial. . . . The *Weekly Standard* is a publication that was founded to promote Rupert Murdoch's political ideology in the United States. So, when one hears that vein of criticism one considers the source, and I don't mean that as an insult.

The first problem with this is, while Krauthammer does write for the *Weekly Standard*, the article he wrote criticizing the *Times* was actually published by the *Washington Post*. Raines might have been a little more careful about where he aimed his eggs.

As to Raines' misdirected remark about Murdoch, if the *Weekly Standard*, a magazine that consists almost entirely of editorial content—which positions nothing its editors or any of its writers profess as objective news—can be dismissed as merely a means of promoting its owner's ideology, what, using the same logic, can be said about the *New York Times*?

The thought may not have occurred to Raines that the *New York Times* has been strictly controlled and operated to promote the political ideology of the Ochs/Sulzberger family. The "newspaper of record" remains very much a mouthpiece for the Sulzberger family. That family, for generations, has maintained the contractual right to elect nine out of thirteen members of the board of directors of the New York Times Company, which assures them the right to appoint the company's chairman and CEO and the publisher of the *New York Times* newspaper. Arthur Sulzberger Jr., who is the chairman of the company and the current publisher of the *Times*, is one of eight Ochs/Sulzberger family members who get to select those nine board members. The family holds this right for as long as they desire to maintain it.

Later on in the Berkeley interview, Sulzberger reinforced how much his family continues to influence the paper:

> It wasn't until I got the job as publisher that I really began to see how the Ochs/Sulzberger values are inculcated in the *New York Times*.

Slowly, but surely, both media watchers and common readers of the *Times* began to notice something odd was happening. Since the 1960s, the *Times* has been a stalwart promoter of the liberal agenda, but now—with its blatant use of its news division to advocate that agenda—it was becoming obvious to even casual readers that the reputation of the *Times* as an accurate source of news was in jeopardy. Had Sulzberger and Raines taken leave of *their* senses? Worse was yet to come.

THE AGENDA IS EVERYTHING

In the midst of its campaign to oppose military action against Iraq, the *Times* began to wage another crusade on its front pages. This time, the *New York Times* had set its sights on a 300-member golf club. Beginning in July 2002, the *Times* published over forty articles and editorials over a four-month period criticizing the Augusta National Golf Club, host of the Masters golf tournament, for not admitting women as members.

In an editorial entitled "AMERICA'S ALL MALE GOLFING SOCIETY" (November 18, 2002), the *Times* called upon Tiger Woods to boycott the Masters tournament. When Tiger refused to submit, the *Times* turned its turret toward CBS, who had the broadcast rights to the Masters tournament.

But, instead of writing an editorial calling for CBS to boycott the Masters, the *Times* reserved room on its front page to report to the world what CBS had *not* done: "CBS STAYING SILENT IN DEBATE ON WOMEN JOINING AUGUSTA" (November 25, 2002). The next day, a coy *Times* editorial staff responded to this "news" with an editorial entitled "THE MASTERS BUSINESS" (November 26, 2002), which called on CBS to boycott the 2003 Masters tournament.

The *Times'* behavior on this occasion was loudly criticized. What was striking and different about this criticism, however, was that much of it originated not from conservative critics, but from within the *Times'* own staff of reporters.

An article published in *Newsweek* magazine entitled "THE CHANGING TIMES" by Seth Mnookin (December 9, 2002) broke the news about the turmoil within the ranks of the *New York Times*. *Newsweek* published the following remarkable statement by an unnamed *Times* staffer in reference to the November 25 article on CBS:

> That was shocking. It makes it hard for us to have credibility on other issues. We don't run articles that just say so-and-so is staying silent. We run articles when something important actually happens.

The *Newsweek* article revealed a growing recognition, especially among news reporters, that the *Times* was losing its reputation by disguising its editorial positions in the form of front-page news stories. Another *Times* staffer suggested to *Newsweek* that the "chorus of complaints" among the *Times* staffers was growing so loud that Raines was "in danger of losing the building"—i.e., many *Times* reporters were apparently ready to quit over the issue.

Then, a few days later, all hell broke loose when news surfaced that the *Times* refused to print two pieces written by its sports columnists—a column by Pulitzer Prize-winning columnist Dave Anderson and a column by *Times* sportswriter Harvey Araton—because they disagreed with the views expressed in the *Times'* editorial pages on the Augusta National matter.

The online edition of *Newsweek* (December 4, 2002) reported the story as follows:

> Newspapers are supposed to foster healthy debate, raise conflicting points of view and present all sides of a story. Aren't they? It's a question employees at the *New York Times* are asking after the *New York Daily News'* Paul Colford reported that *Times* editors recently spiked two sports columns that disagreed with the paper's editorial stance on Augusta National's ban on female members. The paper's thinking seemed to run something like this: we're against

this horrible discrimination, and we're going to resort to censorship to make our point.

The same day, *Times* managing editor, Gerald M. Boyd, circulated an internal memorandum—which was immediately leaked by a *Times* employee to the Internet—defending the paper's position on both its coverage of the Augusta National question and its spiking of the two sports columns. As to its 33-article crusade against the golf club: "There is only one word for our vigor in pursuing a story—whether in Afghanistan or Augusta. Call it journalism." And the censorship of its sports columnists? "Recently we spiked two sports columns that touched on the Augusta issue. We were not concerned with which 'side' the writers were on. A well-reported, well-reasoned column can come down on any side, with our welcome."

It's doubtful that the *Times'* own front-page articles on the Augusta issue could have met that very test. What's more, the *Times'* managing editor failed to adequately apply that test to the two spiked columns. As to the first, it was rejected merely because it disagreed with the *Times'* editorial page:

> One of the columns focused centrally on disputing *The Times'* editorials about Augusta. Part of our strict separation between the news and editorial pages entails not attacking each other. Intramural quarreling of that kind is unseemly and self-absorbed.

As to the second, Boyd took a slap at his own columnist, asserting that his logic did not meet the *Times'* "standard":

> The other spiked column tried to draw a connection between the Augusta issue and the elimination of women's softball from the Olympics. The logic did not meet our standards; that would have been true regardless of which "side" the writer had taken on Augusta.

Boyd was "silent" on whether the writings of other regular *Times'* columnists—such as Maureen Dowd, Paul Krugman, and Frank Rich—have their logic scrutinized against the same "standard."

Criticism of the *Times* spread quickly. *Slate* columnist Jack Shafer wrote (December 6, 2002):

> Did *New York Times* Managing Editor Gerald Boyd read Richard Nixon's memoir *RN* before penning his memo to the staff defending his decision to spike sports columns by Dave Anderson and Harvey Araton that dared to take issue with a Nov. 18 *Times* editorial? The hubba-hubba self-congratulation and extreme defensiveness of the memo sounds like something Nixon might have composed to blot out the din of anti-war protesters chanting outside the White House gates.

The same day, the National Society of Newspaper Columnists issued the following statement:

> While the *Times* may well be taking a principled stand on the issue of whether women should be admitted to Augusta National Golf Club, it should also recognize the important principle that a newspaper informs its readers best when it provides a diversity of opinion.

An article published in the online edition of *Editor & Publisher* magazine entitled "EDITORS WEIGH IN ON 'NY TIMES' AUGUSTA ISSUE" (December 6, 2002) reported that "most editors at a cross-section of major newspapers said they would not object to a columnist who criticized the paper's editorial position, saying columnists are hired specifically to tell readers what they think." One editor stated, "Our columnists have such wide latitude it would never be a consideration here. They can do what they want. It has never been an issue for us."

This last statement was from Leonard Downie Jr., executive editor of the *Washington Post*, the newspaper that the *Times* considers to be one of its main rivals. Perhaps this quote, or the overwhelming negative accumulation of editorial opinion, was the proverbial straw; within hours, the *Times* backed down and agreed to run the two spiked columns in the following Sunday edition of the *Times*. Apparently, the "logic" of the columns now met the *Times'* "standards."

The *Times'* use of its news division to crusade for its editorial causes continued unabated. In April 2003, the *Times* stepped up its war against Augusta National, even as U.S. troops were advancing on Baghdad. Not only was the *Times* quick to criticize CBS for daring to cover the 2003 Masters tournament, the *Times* did not hesitate to ridicule CBS for *how* they covered it ("CBS Is Planning to Stress Golf, Not Protests," April 7, 2003). Meanwhile, the *Times* never called upon its own sportswriters to boycott coverage of the 2003 Masters tournament. On the contrary, *Times* sports columnists began writing pieces aligned with the *Times'* editorial views, criticizing the Augusta National Golf Club for maintaining its policy against women membership.

One *Times* Sports page staffer told Sridhar Pappu of the *New York Observer* in "Off the Record" (May 11, 2003), "Howell [Raines] and Gerald [Boyd] are running our department right now, it's pretty clear."

As much as the *Times* had been keen to celebrate those who resigned as members of Augusta National in protest of the club's membership policies ("Former Top Executive at CBS Resigns from Augusta," December 3, 2002), it has been reluctant to criticize, at least publicly, John F. Akers (former CEO of IBM), a member of Augusta National and also, since 1985, a member of the board of directors of the New York Times Company.

The Low Point

On Sunday, May 11, 2003, the *New York Times* used the real estate of a lead front-page article to announce a stunning admission that would cast a long shadow over the trustworthiness of the once venerable institution:

Times Reporter Who Resigned Leaves Long Trail of Deception
A staff reporter for The New York Times committed frequent acts of journalistic fraud while covering significant news events in recent months, an investigation by Times journalists has found. The widespread fabrication and plagiarism represent a profound betrayal of trust and a low point in the 152-year history of the newspaper.

The four-page, 14,420-word article was billed as an accounting of the dozens of known journalistic deceptions perpetrated by 27-year-old *Times* reporter Jayson Blair, who had worked for the paper for nearly four years. Blair had resigned just ten days earlier, shortly after he was first confronted with evidence that he had plagiarized the work of another journalist. The article laid out in excruciating detail how, in at least thirty-six fabricated stories and possibly hundreds more, Blair made up quotes, copied material written by other journalists, and wrote stories under the pretense of being on the scenes of the events when he was really in his apartment in Brooklyn.

The article primarily addressed *what* happened, but to many it fell short by failing to address the question on everyone's mind: *how* could it have happened? Even an "Editor's Note" accompanying the story failed to provide an adequate explanation. Written presumably by Howell Raines, the short note simply explained why the *Times* was running the cover story and closed with a terse apology to the paper's readers.

ULTIMATE RESPONSIBILITY

Since the Blair scandal broke, highly respected journalists and commentators, with no apparent axe to grind, had become increasingly critical of the *Times*. Typical of the criticism was the following comment published in the *Newsday* article "REPORT DETAILS REPORTER'S FRAUD" (May 11, 2003):

> "This is the worse thing that can happen to a newspaper," said Paul Levinson, chairman of the communication and media studies department at Fordham University. "Howell Raines should have been keeping a more careful eye on these things." After reviewing the Times report, Levinson described it as "self-serving" and failing to disclose "that the Times did something wrong. . . . They need to do a lot more."

Bob Steele, director of the ethics program at The Poynter Institute, a journalism school, told the *New York Post* ("TIMES TRICKSTER FALLS SICK," May 12, 2003), "I am very disappointed that the New York Times' checks and balances system didn't work."

Andrew Sullivan formulated perhaps the most ironic and damning analogy of all (AndrewSullivan.com, May 12, 2003):

> How does a reporter whose former editor had written a memo demanding that he be removed from writing for the Times altogether get reassigned *with-*

out his subsequent editor being informed of his record? Forget the affirmative action dimension. This is just recklessly bad management. It reminds me of the Catholic Church reassigning priests to new parishes without telling the parishioners of the priests' past. It smacks of a newsroom in which everyone is running scared of the big guy's favorite new hire, and so no one is able to stop a disaster from happening until it's too late. . . .

The New York Times' reputation is not the responsibility of new hires in their twenties. It's the responsibility of the editors, just as the responsibility for bad priests lies ultimately with the cardinals and bishops who hire them. In this instance, Raines is the Times' Cardinal Law. His imperial meddling, diversity obsessions, and mercurial management style all made Blair possible.

Raines was losing respect from all quarters, but most important, he was losing the respect of his staff and perhaps all hope of ever regaining that respect. As the *New York Daily News* reported in "STAFF TRUST ELUDING RAINES" (May 16, 2003):

> [I]t is clear that the everyday behavior of Raines—widely viewed as arrogant and aloof, even by those who admired his work as a reporter and editorial page editor—has supplanted Blair as the hot topic inside and outside the Times.

Anger at Raines in the newsroom had been festering for over a year. "From the moment Howell Raines was appointed executive editor of *The New York Times*, there was tension in the newsroom," Seth Mnookin reported in *Newsweek* ("TIMES BOMB," May 26, 2003). One of the first to publicly write about Raines' management style was columnist John Ellis. Nearly a year before the Blair scandal broke, Ellis described on his web-log (JohnEllis.Blogspot.com, May 11, 2002) what he called the "Raines regime":

> The Rainesian management model resembles a kind of anti-network; in which an ever-smaller number of people are engaged in the guidance and definition of the enterprise. As the network narrows, the center (Raines and his management team) grows in importance. At its worst, this kind of management leads to the Sun God management system, in which The Great Leader is

surrounded by adoring sycophants. Raines is a prime candidate to fall into this trap, since his ego needs greatly exceed his management skills.

According to Mnookin:

> Newsroom staffers also felt as if Raines led the staff on crusades, obsessing about stories—like the ban on women at the Augusta National Golf Club, host to the Masters—in a way that caused the paper to make news instead of break it. (Sources at the paper say Raines nominated the paper's Augusta coverage for a 2002 Pulitzer—which shocked some *Times* staffers, because the paper had come under fire for spiking two sports columns that took issue with the paper's editorial stance on the subject.)

The institutional penchant for putting ideological passion above journalistic integrity can be traced right up to the paper's publisher and CEO. Arthur Sulzberger Jr., the man who "saw the editorial page editor and the executive editor as partners in the *Times'* future," was quoted some years ago as having said, "Diversity is the most important issue facing our paper." As the Blair scandal has painfully demonstrated, Sulzberger lost sight of the priorities of his stewardship: The most important issue facing the *New York Times* must, at all times and under all circumstances, be the *truth*. The *Times'* obsession with race—along with its other obsessions, like those against the death penalty, against the membership requirements of a 300-member golf club, and against the policies, any policies it seems, of the Bush administration—have supplanted the paper's dedication to integrity in its news reporting.

AN OPPORTUNITY FOR CHANGE

On June 5, 2003, the *Times* announced that Howell Raines and Gerald Boyd had resigned. Though their resignations provide a ray of hope for a new era of responsible news reporting, it remains to be seen whether the tyranny of political ideology over the *Times'* newsroom will really end with the Raines regime. We know that, even during the extraordinary aftermath of the Blair revelations, when Sulzberger, Raines, and Boyd were expressing contrition and asking forgiveness—from their staff, their readers, and the gods of journalism—the paper continued its quixotic war against an imagined evil.

For example, on Tuesday, May 14, 2003, the day Raines stood before his reporters and accepted blame for journalistic fraud, the *Times'* front page carried a "news" article—"BUSH'S SUPPORT STRONG DESPITE TAX CUT DOUBTS"—that was a masterpiece of distortion. While reporting that the public was having "persistent reservations" about the president's tax cut proposal, the results of the poll actually showed that over twice as many people believed a tax cut would be good for the economy as those who believed it would be bad. None of the questions asked in the poll concerned whether the public had any "doubts" or "reservations" about the president's tax cut proposal.

Later in the week, in "KEEPERS OF BUSH IMAGE LIFT STAGECRAFT TO NEW HEIGHTS" (May 16, 2003), the *Times* used its front page to essentially accuse President Bush of wasting taxpayer money on public appearances and suggest that the president's policies have more form than substance.

The publisher's contrition over the Blair scandal seems entirely focused on the ethics of its reporters' news gathering activities, with not even a scant recognition of its broader credibility problem: the plunge in the reliability of the paper's news pages stemming from its zeal for advocacy journalism. We may now be sure of the whereabouts of the *Times'* reporters when they file their stories, but can we really trust we are getting fair and balanced reports? What has been practiced with impunity for years by the *New York Times*—the persistent publication of liberal views disguised as objective news—is still practiced with impunity, and there are no signs that any of the repercussions arising from the Blair scandal will result in a change in the behavior of the news reporters and their editors, at least insofar as objective reporting is concerned. Sadly, fairness and accuracy in reporting no longer seem a part of the *Times'* DNA.

FOCUS ON TECHNIQUE

Three hundred sixty-five days a year—day in and day out, year after year—not only on the editorial pages, but disguised as objective news, the *Times* has accumulated such a work of "propaganda," as Coulter calls it, that the editors of the Soviet *Pravda* must have marveled at not only the chutzpa of the editors of America's "newspaper of record" but also the technique those editors have employed to exert its influence.

This book is largely about that technique. We will not attempt to merely restate the evidence that Coulter so painstakingly compiled. Nor do we have any insider evidence of bias that made Goldberg's book so credible and riveting. I am just an ordinary consumer who reads the *Times* carefully every day. Using evidence derived primarily from within the four corners of the newspaper, we take here a slightly different tack on how the media can, and specifically the *New York Times* does, distort the news.

We make little reference to the editorials written by the *Times* or to any of the propaganda pieces gracing its op-ed pages (i.e., the page opposite the *Times'* editorial page, containing opinion articles by columnists and others). We have no issue with editorial opinion when it is labeled as such. The public knows these pieces are biased and can give them the authority they may merit. They may be slanderous, but they are not fraudulent.

Nor do we take issue with the *Times'* articles identified as "News Analysis," even though they often appear on the front pages of the *Times* and are formatted like objective news stories. Some of these "News Analysis" pieces are labeled "Economic Analysis" or "Military Analysis," providing them with a false air of objectivity. When they appear on the Internet or on wireless devices, it is often impossible to distinguish them from straight news stories. (The nytimes.com website includes the phrase "News Analysis," but it appears above the headline rather than in the story, and it is in light grey, barely noticeable. When they appear on many other websites such as *Yahoo! News* or on wireless devices, the "News Analysis" label is completely missing.) Though having the appearance of straight news stories, these "News Analysis" pieces (whether they are labeled "News Analysis," "Economic Analysis," or "Military Analysis") are nothing more than thinly disguised editorial opinions of the *Times'* reporters and editors.

To briefly illustrate the political nature of these "News Analysis" pieces, consider the opening sentence of the "News Analysis" published in the *Times* ("TESTING OF A PRESIDENT; UNCERTAINTY AT NEXT STEP," December 13, 1998) days before the congressional vote to impeach President Clinton, an outcome the *Times* was marshalling all of its influential resources to defeat:

WASHINGTON, Dec. 12—A touch of dignity and a heavy dose of uncertainty surround the capital today, as what seems to be the only city in America that takes impeachment seriously looks toward a House vote on articles calling for President Clinton to be removed from office.

This "news analysis" of the country's reaction to the impeachment charges—i.e., that no one outside of Washington was taking the charges seriously—apparently failed to take into account a "straight" news story appearing in the *Times* just two days earlier under the headline "CITIZENS LEFT AND RIGHT BATTLE AT THE GRASS ROOTS" (December 10, 1998), which suggested exactly the opposite in its first paragraph:

> On one level, the battle over the impeachment of William Jefferson Clinton is being played out in the House Judiciary Committee hearing room and in other Washington power alleys. But it is also being fought at a grass-roots level all over the country, with both those who fervently want the President impeached and those who just as fervently want him left alone trying to find ways to give weight to their wishes.
>
> Some of these people are egged on by conservative and liberal lobbying groups, but a great deal of the outcry is arising unbidden.

Whether they contain informed analysis or not, their appearance and placement on the front pages of the *Times* make it unlikely that the public recognizes these "News Analysis" stories for what they really are: a clever way to sneak editorial opinions onto the front page where they can be easily mistaken for straight news. Nevertheless, they are labeled in such a way that makes it clear—to informed readers—they *do not* represent "objective news." For this reason, we have no more concern with these "News Analysis" pieces than we do opinions properly labeled as editorials. These pieces may be biased and intentionally misleading, but the public knows, or should know, that they do not constitute objective news.

THE POWER OF PASSING OFF OPINION AS NEWS

Sneaking editorial opinions onto the front page by identifying them as "news analysis" is, to be sure, one way to couch editorial opinion as straight news, but the deception on which this book zeros in—one far more pervasive and perni-cious than the antics of Jayson Blair—is the direct manipulation of the "straight" news story. We will examine precisely how the *Times* passes off editorial opinion as straight news—parsing the fraud to get an insight into the variety and nature of the techniques employed by the *Times*. We will also arrive at a better under-standing of the power these techniques have over public opinion.

The particular power this *passing off* has on influencing readers is founded upon the following principle: The lacing of editorial opinion into what has the appearance of a straight news story lends a level of credibility to the opinion that is normally reserved for objective news.

The enhanced credibility afforded the editorial opinion when it is disguised as objective news makes the use of this deception a much more effective means of influencing the public than the mere expression of opinion in editorials and op-ed pieces.

However, the effectiveness of the deception (i.e., its usefulness as a means of influencing people) is limited by the extent to which people believe that the news, as reported by the *Times,* is impartial. In other words, the ability of the *Times* to leverage its news pages for the purpose of conveying an editorial agenda is a function of the paper's reputation for impartial reporting. The greater the reputation the paper has for impartial reporting, the more effective will be the slanting of that news as a means of influencing public opinion.

Until recently, the *Times'* reputation for impartial reporting "without fear or favor" had been legendary. Since at least as early as the 1960s, criticism of the *Times* as an arm of the Democratic party was largely limited to conservatives and conservative media watch groups. More recently, however, even the average Joe has noticed the left-wing editorial crusades masquerading as news on the front pages of the *New York Times*.

Opinion polls consistently confirm the public's conviction that the news is slanted (even 57 percent of Democrats believe so, according to a recent poll by the Pew Research Center, which also reported that 56 percent of Independents and 69 percent of Republicans are convinced the press is biased). Bernard Goldberg's *Bias* and Ann Coulter's *Slander,* both of which, ironically, reached No. 1 on the *New York Times* bestseller list, have blown the lid off any remain-ing notion that the press is objective.

The *Times* is beginning to lose its reputation overseas as well. Andrew

Sullivan, in his column for the *Sunday Times of London* (November 17, 2002) made this observation about media bias in the U.S.:

> The classic American examples are *National Public Radio* and the *New York Times*. Virtually no Republicans work in either organization. The news stories reflect, in the case of NPR, a benevolent, well-meaning but thoroughly liberal view of the world. In the case of the *New York Times*, the news stories do exactly what they do in the [London] *Guardian*: they are designed, edited, and written to promote a political agenda.

The *Times*' ability to leverage its news division will continue to fade as the paper's reputation for objectivity continues to decline. Should the *Times* choose to continue using its news division to influence public opinion, it will have to adopt a more subtle means of deception.

STYLE GUIDE FOR LIBERAL BIAS

Reporters for the *New York Times,* it seems, are expected not only to convey the liberal viewpoint on all political issues reported but also to impede the expression of the conservative viewpoint. This message was finally and formally revealed publicly when a *Times* op-ed page writer, when listing the reasons for the political losses suffered by the Democratic party in the 2002 midterm elections, admitted the following (Paul Krugman, November 8, 2002):

> Talk radio and Fox News let the hard right get its message out to its supporters.

Being appalled at how other news outlets would "let" conservative messages be conveyed to the public, the *Times* editors are evidently committed to not "let" the same happen in *their* news organization.

Reporters for the *Times* should find the techniques detailed in this book particularly useful in currying the favor of their editors. In fact, viewed perversely, this book provides step-by-step instructions on how to disguise liberal opinions as objective news, a practice that has been raised to an art form by the

New York Times and one that reporters can effectively learn by carefully study-ing their example.

A style guide for liberal bias, this book might also serve as a textbook at the Columbia School of Journalism if the professors there would not find it redun-dant. At worst, recent graduates may find it a useful reference in their daily search for the truth and for a means of twisting it to meet the political demands of their editors.

We also expect lay readers, even those who have already come to appreciate the works of Bernard Goldberg and Ann Coulter, will use this book as a tool for better understanding what they read in the *New York Times*.

Conservatives, for example, might replace their quality time with the *Times'* crossword puzzle with a new kind of daily game: exposing the fraud themselves by parsing the "straight" news stories on the front page and identifying each clever technique employed that day to influence public opinion. The bias is sometimes so laughably obvious that readers may often find this game more entertaining (and certainly easier) than completing the crossword puzzle.

If readers merely acquire a greater understanding of how the *Times* uses the news to influence public opinion, this book has served a valuable purpose. The *Times* has raised the practice of slanting the news to an art form, a brand of fraud having a subtlety the likes of which even a Jayson Blair might respect and a technique of propaganda that only a Soviet apologist could fully appreciate. It deserves to be studied, and studied carefully.

TWO

The Purpose of a Newspaper

To give the news impartially, without fear or favor,
regardless of party, sect or interests involved.

—*Adolph S. Ochs, publisher of the* New York Times, *1896-1935*

There was a time when publishers of newspapers believed they were in the business of reporting the news. Publishers once dedicated themselves to the journalistic ideals of reporting the news as accurately as possible, without a hint of bias, letting the readers draw their own conclusions.

Though news editors would express their opinions on subjects, such expressions would be reserved for the editorial pages, with editorial opinions clearly identified as such. Never would an editorial be passed off in the form of a straight news story.

This basic principle of journalism was unambiguously embodied in the code of journalistic ethics adopted in 1923 by the American Society of Newspaper Editors: "Sound practice makes clear distinction between news reports and expressions of opinion. News reports should be free from opinion or bias of any kind."

As they still do today, newspapers typically adopted style guides, distributed to the newspaper's staff, which outlined the principles under which the paper's reporters and editors were expected to perform. For example, the *Style Guide of the Detroit News* (The Evening News Association, 1924) reflected the publisher's dedication to fair and unbiased reporting:

> The hardest lesson the journalist must learn is the development of the impersonal viewpoint. He must learn to write what he sees and hears, clearly and accurately, with never a tinge of bias. His own views, his personal feelings and his friendships should have nothing to do with what he writes in a story.

Journalism textbooks published in the first half of the 20th century reflected the journalistic ethics of the time. One such textbook, Bastian's *Editing The Day's News* (Macmillan, 1923), put it this way:

> A news article should tell what happened in the simplest, briefest, most attractive and accurate manner possible; it should draw no conclusions, make no gratuitous accusations, indulge in no speculation, give no opinions.

The difference between a news article and an editorial was a simple matter in those days. According to this 1923 text: "The news columns inform; the editorial columns comment, interpret, and furnish guidance to public opinion."

The day Adolph S. Ochs took control of the *New York Times* in 1896, he published the following declaration of principles:

> It will be my earnest aim that *The New-York Times* give the news, all the news, in concise and attractive form, in language that is parliamentary in good society, and give it as early, if not earlier, than can be learned through any other reliable medium; to give the news impartially, without fear or favor, regardless of party, sect or interests involved; to make the columns of *The New-York Times* a forum for the consideration of all questions of public importance, and to that end to invite intelligent discussion from all shades of opinion.

Och's son-in-law assumed the position of publisher of the *Times* in 1935. In a letter to the daughter of a *Times* executive, who wanted a comment for a school theme on freedom of the press, Arthur Hays Sulzberger memorialized his concurrence with the tradition of impartiality established by his predecessor:

After Adolph S. Ochs took over *The Times* in 1896, he published one of what I believe to be the only two statements that ever appeared in this paper over his name in which he dedicated this property "to give all the news impartially, without fear or favor." That continues to be the role of *The Times* in the community.

Regarding the use of news columns for editorial purposes, Mr. Sulzberger, grandfather of the current publisher, was similarly straightforward: "We do not crusade in our news columns."

A Break from the Past

Such quaint notions of accurate, impersonal, and impartial news reporting—reporting which draws no conclusions, makes no gratuitous accusations, indulges in no speculation, gives no opinions, does no crusading—no longer apply to today's news organization, whose very purpose has undergone a fundamental change.

Today, it seems, newspapers are in the business of identifying solutions to society's problems and influencing public opinion to agree with those solutions. News gathering and reporting are no longer the ends of the newspaper; they have become merely a means to an end.

Over the course of the past fifty years, the line between the editorial opinion and the news article has become increasingly blurred. Today, the two are nearly indistinguishable. Though maintaining some stylistic differences, the editorial opinion and the news article have the same purpose and often work in tandem to maximize the newspaper publisher's influence over public opinion.

The profession has become very open about these changes. In 1975, when the American Society of Newspaper Editors assembled to rewrite the code of ethics that served them for nearly fifty years, they took their original canon—"*News reports should be free from opinion or bias of any kind*"—and turned it on its ear with the following: "Distinguish between advocacy and news reporting. Analysis and commentary should be labeled and not misrepresent fact or context."

No longer did the society stress that news be free from opinion or bias of any kind. The focus shifted away from how news reports should be written to how "analysis and commentary" should be labeled. The straightforward canon established in the 1920s was replaced with the rather vague, *"Distinguish between advocacy and news reporting."*

Those in the profession—whose day-to-day tools of trade are words and their meaning—fully understood the future they were forging. In 1975, members of the press were feeling good about themselves, having accomplished in the prior year the exposure of the Watergate scandal and the resignation of President Richard M. Nixon. News editors were getting comfortable with their new role, and the message they sent to their fellow editors and reporters was now clear: straight news articles need no longer be "free from opinion or bias of any kind." And while the new ethics code elsewhere demands that the deliberate distortion of facts is *"never* permissible," it merely *recommends* that analysis and commentary *"should* be labeled."

In today's journalism textbooks you will find little that approximates the ideals of journalism to which publishers of a century ago were dedicated. Instead, while they do devote some consideration to the ethical problems of today's journalist (e.g., when and under what circumstances journalists may accept gifts), the new textbooks devote substantial discussion to what they call *"the problem* of objectivity," "multi-cultural reporting," and news "framing" (i.e., selecting the viewpoint, or perspective, from which you tell a story).

One journalism textbook, Baker's *Newsthinking* (Allyn & Bacon, 2001), actually instructs:

> Rule Number 1: There are no rules. . . . Rule Number 1 makes it clear that if any rules or policies have to exist, they can be broken—crushed whenever the news requires it.

Jayson Blair's alma mater, the Merrill College of Journalism at the University of Maryland, would probably distance themselves from such a principle, but the scandal brought about by their notorious alumnus has been, according to the school's dean, "like a bad dream." One can only hope that the affair will serve as a wake-up call to the nation's journalism schools.

In June 1997, twenty-five prominent journalists, who had come to believe that their profession was doing more to damage the public interest than to serve it, gathered at the Harvard Faculty Club to discuss what was wrong with today's journalism and what they could do to change it. Dubbing themselves the "Committee of Concerned Journalists," the group set out to examine the role of news reporters in a free society and to establish a new set of principles for professional journalists. Over the following three years, with the assistance of a team of university researchers, the group conducted a series of public forums and private surveys, including input from over 1,200 journalists, in what they characterized as "the most sustained, systematic, and comprehensive examination ever conducted by journalists of newsgathering and its responsibilities."

The results of this effort were reported in a book by Bill Kovach and Tom Rosenstiel, *The Elements of Journalism* (Three Rivers Press, 2001). To no one's surprise, except perhaps the American public, one of the book's most astounding conclusions was stated in no uncertain terms: "It is worth restating the point to make it clear. Being impartial or neutral is not a core principle of journalism."

Mr. Kovach, the co-author of that statement, had served as a reporter and editor for the *New York Times* for eighteen years, including a stint as the *Times'* Washington Bureau Chief.

In the taped interview at U.C. Berkeley (November 18, 2002), referenced in the previous chapter, Arthur Sulzberger Jr. left no doubt that the *New York Times* has indeed assumed what Jack Shafer of *Slate* has called "the journalistic role as party of opposition."

Sulzberger: We're actually engaged, for the first time in my memory, in ongoing national debate as to whether or not this country should go to war, and those debates, at least in my experience, which is heavily-flavored by the Vietnam War experience—which, was my growing up—those debates always seem to take place after Americans are already in combat, not before.

I think, whether you think we should go to war, whether you think we shouldn't go to war, or whether you feel you don't have the information you need to make either of those decisions, what is healthy here is that we are having this debate.

That's our job. That's Howell's and my job, and other journalists, is to ensure that that debate is open, is honest, that we can marshal the facts we need to let the American citizens decide what's the best course of action.

Mark Danner: I don't get the impression though that most Americans really feel that—and obviously this isn't the *Times'* fault—that the debate has been full, open and thorough.

Sulzberger: I think that's right. It has not been. Speaking as an American as well as a newspaper publisher, I'd love to have this administration more engaged in that discussion and the debate.

Howell Raines: Mark, with respect, I think you are missing something here. If there is an absence of debate in the country, if the Congress is not standing up to the administration in an adversarial way on issues of national importance, that's a news story—that condition is part of what we report.

Thus, the publisher of the *New York Times* and the head of his news division made it clear that reporting accurately what happens is not enough: The paper has a duty to report *what does not happen*. That Congress is not being adversarial enough against the White House is not merely an opinion for an editorial; it is front-page news. That Tiger Woods and CBS have refused to boycott the Masters tournament is front-page news. In other words, anyone who fails to act in accordance with the views of the editors of the *New York Times* is fodder for a front-page crusade.

The rationalization for this new definition of "news" is precisely as Sulzberger explained: The job of the news division is to ensure a healthy "debate" on issues the *Times'* editors believe are of national importance— whether the issue is how the president of the United States is conducting a war or how a 300-member golf club maintains its membership policy. The news division, it appears, is to report on what others have not said or done on issues of importance to the editors of the *Times*.

It is notable that, in its coverage of these "debates," the *Times* will stand for no internal dissension. When the *Times* embarks upon a crusade, the op-ed pages, the news pages, and all other sections of the paper, including the sports pages, must follow in lock-step the lead established by the *Times*, editorial staff (unless news of its censorship leaks and someone raises a public stink about it).

Modern journalism begins with the *New York Times*. A book entitled *The New York Times Manual of Style and Usage* (Three Rivers Press, 1999) presents its authors' views on the proper mechanics of usage and grammar for a modern newspaper—for example, whether the word *martini* should be capitalized in a news story (no, say the authors). In a few entries, the authors touch upon policy, but they are reticent to moralize, saying, "A style book cannot also be a journalism text or policy handbook."

Where the authors do address policy, they embrace a traditional view. According to the entry on *fairness and impartiality*: "The news columns take no sides and play no favorites in what they cover or what they omit."

As we have seen, the *Times* pays mere lip service to the ideals of the profession published in its own style manual. If the editors of the *Times* believe public debate on an issue has not been "adversarial" enough, the *Times* will treat that as news and will report what does *not* happen. If the *Times* ever truly had a tradition of separating its editorial views from its duty to accurately report what happens, that duty has been, as the Bard would say, "more honored in the breach than in the observance."

INFLUENCING PUBLIC OPINION

At the dawn of the new millennium, the transformation of mainstream journalism is now complete. The aim of today's newspaper is not merely to gather and impart the news but to influence public opinion. News gathering and reporting have become merely a means to that end. The tools of propaganda have found a new home.

Any means to persuade the public to agree with the views of the newspaper's editors is justified by the reasonableness of their views and their good intentions. The most powerful means of influencing public opinion—passing off an editorial as a straight news story—is a practice that has become both acceptable and common.

It should be no great surprise to anyone that the influence over public opinion exerted by the *New York Times*—the "newspaper of record"—exceeds that of any other newspaper or news organization in the world.

"As the *Times* goes, so goes a large part of the nation's press," wrote Herman Dinsmore, former *Times* news editor, over thirty years ago. Since that time, the influence the *Times* exerts over the news media has been dramatically enhanced by the speed and breadth of modern networks of digital telecommunication.

Articles that appear in the *Times* are syndicated to hundreds of newspapers across the country and around the world. Every evening, articles, editorials, photos, and other features to be published in the *Times* the following day are transmitted electronically to over 650 newspapers that subscribe to the New York Times News Service; these articles and features then appear in the pages of local newspapers alongside articles written by reporters for those local papers. The *Times* itself owns over 15 other regional newspapers, including the *Boston Globe*, all of which echo the articles and commentary appearing in the *New York Times*.

By this means, what the editors of the *Times* think is news becomes news in all of these local newspapers. And how the *Times* slants the news is automatically repeated verbatim in these other newspapers. The *Times* even offers condensed versions of the top twenty stories from each day's edition, reducing the likelihood that their news service subscribers will alter the *Times'* slant where shorter versions of their most important stories are selected for local use.

Moreover, by letting their affiliates know which stories merit front-page placement and which merit high prominence on the front page, the *Times* makes it easier for hundreds of newspapers to mirror the relative weight that the editors of the *Times* believe their stories merit. By 7:30 P.M. eastern standard time, the *Times* transmits to its subscribers a precise description of the layout of the front page of the next day's *Times*, including story placement, photo placement, and the size of each headline. Local papers have the freedom, of course, to make their own decisions on where and how these *Times* stories are positioned in their papers (e.g., on the front page or on page 16), or they may replace a *Times* article with one written by a local reporter. But the tone handed down from Mt. Olympus remains.

It is important to note that, while this "sound chamber" in which the *Times'* slant reverberates is very loud, the chamber itself is very, very small and manageable. There are fewer than 70 daily newspapers in the U.S. operating in major metropolitan areas, nearly all of which subscribe to the Times News Service. The total number of daily newspapers in the U.S. is fewer than 1,000, and most of those are owned by fewer than 20 other companies.

Whether they subscribe to the Times News Service or not, virtually all other newspapers look to the *Times* to determine what is important. The editors and reporters of the *Times* determine what is news and what is newsworthy. They determine what is a story and what is not a story. They determine the essence of a story, what to feature or highlight in the leading sentence and headline, and what experts to turn to for authoritative context. *Slate* editor Michael Kinsley explained in a column defending the paper after the Jayson Blair disaster, "Even if you don't read the *Times* yourself, you get your news from journalists at other media who do. The *Times* sets the news agenda that everyone else follows" (May 21, 2003). The *Times* even sets the agendas at the television news networks. One writer for *Newsweek* magazine, in "THE GREY LADY APPLIES ROUGE AND LIP GLOSS" (September 15, 1997), described the *Times'* influence over network news the following way:

> The *Times* is special, not so much for the paper itself as for its effect on everybody else. Preeminent among a tiny handful of papers including the *Wall Street Journal* and the *Washington Post* (*Newsweek's* sister publication), the *Times* sets the agenda for what the network-news divisions and a host of other news outlets do.

And the influence of the *Times* is not limited to the news. Other news organizations look to the *Times* for guidance on their editorial views as well. Bernard Goldberg, a thirty-year veteran of CBS News, put it this way in his original *Wall Street Journal* piece "NETWORKS NEED A REALITY CHECK" (February 13, 1996):

> One thing to remember about network news is that it steals just about everything from print. So if the *New York Times* is against the flat tax, and the *Washington Post* is against the flat tax, the networks can't, and won't, be far behind.

The arguments, nomenclature, and tone formulated by the editors of the *Times* are posted on the editorial and op-ed pages of the "newspaper of record," and regional editors and network anchors, like lemmings, readily pass along the prefabricated opinion to millions of readers and viewers.

The old joke applies: Peter Jennings is not a "yes man." If the *Times* says "no!" Peter Jennings says "no!"

THE TIPPING POINT

Aristotle observed, "The least deviation from the truth is multiplied later a thousand-fold." In today's dot-com-speak, Aristotle was reflecting upon the *tipping point*. Once the *Times* sets an opinion in motion—especially one wrapped in the credibility of a straight, front-page news story—the slant ultimately manifests itself in popular beliefs or misconceptions.

Coulter documented a series of misconceptions that have been woven into the fabric of American public opinion by the liberal media: for example, that "Republicans are dumb" and "Democrats are smart"; that Republicans represent "the rich" while the Democrats represent "working families"; that an organized group called the "religious right" actually exists, and so on.

Once firmly established in the public's mind, these misconceptions may be called upon by the media, or the politicians who benefit from them, like a propagandist calls upon established stereotypes to arouse the passions or influence the votes of an Orwellian public.

When the *Times* feels particularly confident that a recent propaganda campaign has been successful, it immediately commissions a public opinion poll. As we shall see later, if the findings are to their liking, the poll numbers invariably make front-page headlines. If not to their liking, they spin the survey results with an interpretation in line with their political agenda and report a blatant distortion of the poll in the headline, lead, and body of a "straight" news story, almost always on the front page.

When the *Times* is skeptical of government plans to engage in a military conflict to protect the interests of the American public or secure the nation against weapons of mass destruction, because of its risks and "serious economic impact" (as it did in an editorial on July 30, 2002), it runs a "news" article on its front page (as it did that same day), flush with sympathetic quotes regarding the "profound effect" such plans would have on the nation's economy.

By masterfully using the front page of the *New York Times* as a tool of propaganda, which in turn is geometrically enhanced by the waves of influence reverberating through the journalist community, a few liberal-minded individuals at the *New York Times* are at one of the most powerful wheels of influence of modern times.

As referees of the truth, these people affect our understanding of our institutions, our leaders, and ourselves. They mislead our thoughts, our actions, and our votes. As a result, many of us hold opinions colored with falsehoods without knowing how we even arrived at them.

It is worth considering, however, the extent to which these referees of the truth will be able to maintain their influence over public opinion. Already, there are signs of cracks in their domination of political influence, not from causes within but from evolutions in other mediums of expression over which the *Times* has little control.

"Talk radio," with Rush Limbaugh clutching the lead microphone, has—as *Times* op-ed writer Paul Krugman put it (November 8, 2002)—"let the hard right get its message out." The repeal by the Federal Communications Commission of the "Fairness Doctrine" in 1987 released radio stations from the obligation of having to offer opposing viewpoints. No longer obliged to carefully regulate the opinions expressed over their broadcast facilities, radio stations quickly discovered an audience hungry for the expression of views and values not given attention in the pages of the *New York Times* and elsewhere in the mainstream media.

As we have seen, however, with the ongoing struggle against the three hundred evil men in Augusta, when the *Times* orders up a crusade, it can be a tenacious fighter. "Call it journalism," to use the words of the *Times'* managing editor. Though there have been no sightings of a full-fledged campaign by the *Times* to influence the return of the Fairness Doctrine, we are beginning to hear the rumblings of one.

A plank in the last Democratic presidential platform called for the readoption of the Fairness Doctrine, but hopes for that were dashed, at least temporarily, with Al Gore's defeat in the 2000 presidential election. However, within days after that election the *Times* published an editorial ("THE PUBLIC DUTIES OF BROADCASTERS," November 11, 2002) urging the FCC to review its decision to scrap the Fairness Doctrine.

Such half-hearted attacks on freedom of speech are not likely to bring about the demise of talk radio. Nevertheless, the *Times* has been busy on another front in its war against the First Amendment—at least the part that doesn't concern freedom of the press. In contrast with its losing battle to regulate speech by radio talk show hosts, the *Times* has had some recent success in opposing the freedom of speech of another group it fears: the American citizen.

ELIMINATING THE COMPETITION

Over the past five years, the *New York Times,* in concert with the *Washington Post,* has published an editorial vigorously supporting what they call "campaign finance reform" an average of once every five days. That's more than once a week, fifty-two weeks a year, over five years. The threats of thermo-nuclear war, global warming, world hunger, and Newt Gingrich have all taken a back seat to what the *Times* clearly sees as by far the most important issue of our time.

At the heart of these editorials is what amounts to a vitriolic attack on the use of "soft-money" contributions in our political system. Soft-money is the money donated by individuals or organizations to politicians, political parties, or other groups for the purpose of financing the campaign of a particular candidate for public office or the promotion or advertising of an opinion on an issue of public importance. (By contrast, "hard-money" is the maximum amount of money the law permits individuals or organizations to directly contribute to a particular candidate for public office.)

The organizations or groups to whom the money is contributed—such as political parties (e.g., the Democrat and Republican parties, at national, state, and local levels) and trade or political associations (e.g., Common Cause, the Sierra Club, NAACP, Association of Trial Lawyers of America, the National Organization for Women, and the American Civil Liberties Union, on the left, and the National Rifle Association, National Right to Life Committee, and similar organizations on the right)—are specialists in the art and science of how to spend these contributions to further the opinions of those who made the contributions. In other words, political parties and these advocacy groups specialize in helping individuals exercise their rights of free speech.

Using a loud speaker in New York's Times Square, which requires a government permit, is not going to be a very effective way of exercising your freedom of speech, at least if your intention is to influence a significant amount of people. The odds of getting a letter to the editor published in the *New York Times* is slim, and a single appearance of a single letter is not going to put a dent in the drumbeat of opinion being expressed against you by organizations like the *Times.*

Accordingly, individuals who are like-minded on an issue seek to pool their resources and provide them to organizations that specialize in helping them get their views expressed to others above the din and outside the control of today's media. These organizations use their expertise to create newspaper, magazine, radio, and television advertisements and use the pooled resources of their "soft-money" contributors to finance the placement and broadcast of these ads.

Plainly, an individual's own use of his own money to finance advertisements in the media to influence others is a protected exercise of free speech under the First Amendment. Why would the same money contributed to an organization that would help that individual find a more practical way to express his views be treated any differently?

Opponents of soft-money contributions answer that the pooling of soft-money, by many individuals desiring to express their views together, causes the corruption of our politicians. That is, it causes our elected officials to cast their votes based solely upon the views of those who made significant campaign contributions, rather than following their own political views or those of the people who cast votes for them.

No concrete evidence, however, has been presented to support the view that there is widespread corruption in the U.S. Congress. The only criminal case in recent memory that has lead to the conviction of a member of Congress (namely, James Traficant Jr. D-Ohio) arose out of the congressman's accepting relatively minor gifts and favors from a constituent. But even then, no charge was made that the congressman cast any vote in favor of or against any legislation that directly or indirectly benefited the constituent or that a vote was cast a certain way at the constituent's behest.

No member of Congress has stepped forward to admit that he is corrupt or that he has cast any vote on any grounds other than his own political views or those of his constituents. (This includes Senator Torrecelli D-New Jersey., who resigned from his re-election campaign in disgrace after accusations of accepting personal gifts from a campaign contributor.) Nor has any charge of that nature been directed against any single sitting or former member of Congress.

Whatever you may think of our recent presidents, no serious charge has been brought against any of them for taking a particular action, one way or the other, solely on the basis of the size of a particular campaign contribution. (One exception may be President Clinton's pardon of billionaire Mark Rich, who fled the U.S. to avoid punishment for tax evasion. Rich's ex-wife made sizable contributions to Bill and Hillary Clinton's election campaigns and to the Democratic party; that affair, apparently, was not serious enough to taint Howell Raines' view of the Clinton legacy.)

Surely, many politicians have voted in favor of laws that were also favored by those who have contributed to their campaigns, but this is not a sign of corruption. Rather, it is a healthy indication of representative democracy at work.

Yet, one of the most common misconceptions in the minds of the American public today is that virtually all politicians are corrupt. With no evidence to support it, where does a belief in widespread political corruption come from?

You need look no further than five years of editorials, appearing at least once a week, in the *New York Times*, making broad and baseless accusations of corruption against the 535 basically honest men and women serving in Congress, and one in the presidency, in whom 280 million people have invested their trust.

The *Times*' extended diatribe against soft-money and its connection to a perception of widespread political corruption—a perception completely manufactured by the *Times*, the *Washington Post*, and other media accomplices—has gone virtually unchallenged.

Moreover, the *Times*' efforts have not been limited to its editorial pages. The opinions of the *Times* on campaign reform have been disguised countless times in the form of straight news stories, both on its front pages and in its other news pages. What started out as a vague, unsupported opinion by a staff of intelligent editors skilled in the art of bias has, from its gestation on the front page of the *Times*, percolated throughout American public opinion to become what it is now: nearly a self-evident truth.

Indeed, Senator Mitch McConnell (R-Kentucky), in March 2002, courageously went to the floor of the U.S. Senate and stated the plain truth: "In short, I believe that the appearance of corruption is whatever the *New York Times* says it is."

THE WORLD'S LARGEST SOFT-MONEY OPERATION

With so little evidence to back its claims, why has the *New York Times* been so obsessed with forcing the elimination of soft-money contributions to political and issue campaigns?

To answer this question, consider what the *Times* has become. With the transformation into an organization whose main purpose is to influence public opinion, the *Times* itself has become the world's largest soft-money operation.

Recall, soft-money is *money contributed by individuals to organizations who specialize in using the media to express an opinion.* These organizations use their expertise to help individuals exercise their right of free speech. In today's world, access to such organizations and the ability to freely contribute money to them, hard or soft, is essential if the First Amendment is to have any practical meaning to the average citizen.

In 1976, in the case of *Buckley v. Valeo,* which concerned the constitutionality of the limitations on the campaign contribution enacted by Congress at that time, the Supreme Court addressed the point directly:

> A restriction on the amount of money a person or group can spend on political communication during a campaign necessarily reduces the quantity of expression by restricting the number of issues discussed, the depth of their exploration, and the size of the audience reached. This is because virtually every means of communicating ideas in today's mass society requires the expenditure of money.

In the over twenty-five years since the writing of that opinion, the expenditure of money required to effectively communicate ideas—to communicate them above the noise level of today's mass media—has increased enormously. Arguably, with the *Times* becoming increasingly passionate about exerting its influence on public opinion and public policy, even more money is required to express views that are contrary to those of the *Times.*

So people who desire to express their opinion to a large audience find that, given today's world of mass media, the only practical means of doing so is to pool their resources. Organizations who specialize in expressing opinions in the media aggregate the resources of individuals, helping them get their opinions heard above the din. Ideally, these organizations would like to have as much influence on public opinion as possible, with the intent of getting those views adopted as public policy.

If the organization just described sounds like the *New York Times* itself, it should be no surprise. The *Times* is an organization that specializes in using the media to influence public opinion. It, too, wants its opinions adopted as public policy, and for that purpose they would like to have as much influence on public opinion as possible.

In other words, the *New York Times* is no different from political parties or trade associations who pool and spend soft-money for the purpose of using the media to influence public opinion.

The only difference between the *Times* and these other soft-money organizations, such as the Republican party or the National Rifle Association, is scale. The *New York Times* is a public company worth about $7.3 billion, with annual revenues over $3 billion and profits over $200 million. No other political organization or trade association in America can come close to employing the amount of soft-money the *Times* has at its disposal for influencing public opinion.

Moreover, no other organization has at its complete disposal the front page, the internal news pages, *and* the editorial pages of the *New York Times,* plus that of the *Boston Globe* and over 15 other regional papers, and the pages of the over 650 news organizations that subscribe to the New York Times News Service. If you wished to run an advertisement in the *New York Times*, something that would cost you about $75,000 for a full page, the *Times* could refuse to run the ad if its content does not meet its "standards."

Of course, the thesis of this book is that neither advertisements in the *Times* nor the contents of its editorial pages, however far and wide they may reverberate through the journalism community, will ever achieve the influential power of opinions disguised as straight news articles appearing on the front page and other news pages. Most importantly, that is something to which no one but the *Times* has access.

Thus, the *Times* is nothing but a large corporate soft-money operation, which uses its $3 billion dollars a year in revenue, and plenary access to its journalistic resources, to influence public opinion.

THE *TIMES'* SOFT-MONEY VS. YOUR SOFT-MONEY

When individuals pool their resources and provide soft-money to an organization as a practical means of attempting to influence public opinion, they are acting—perhaps on a smaller scale, but in principle—no differently from the *Times*, with one important exception: they are doing it in *competition* with the *Times*.

It is this competition the *Times* seems determined to eliminate—soft-money that is used to express views that are different from their own. The *Times*, it appears, just doesn't want *your* soft-money to compete with *their* soft-money in the arena of influencing public opinion.

Thus, beginning about 1996, it appears that the *New York Times* made a fateful decision: Use $3 billion a year in resources to influence public opinion, lawmakers, and ultimately public policy to eliminate or drastically limit the rights of individuals who wish to act collectively to influence public opinion. At the same time, make sure the *Times* is exempt from any such limitation.

After five years and about $15 billion dollars in soft-money, its editorial efforts have been remarkably successful. On the misconceptions front, the expression "soft-money" is now part of the American lexicon.

Consequently, with no evidence that the public's exercise of its First Amendment rights cause public corruption, the *Times* cheerfully reported to an indifferent public the most sweeping federal legislation against freedom of speech ever passed by Congress: the signing on March 28, 2002, of the McCain-Feingold Bill on campaign financing.

Just before the bill's passage, a lone senator courageously stepped out onto the floor of the United States Senate and tried to explain what was happening. Senator McConnell put it this way:

> Mr. President, I would like to begin by citing the ultimate campaign reform—the First Amendment to the Constitution:
>
> "Congress shall make no law…abridging the freedom of speech, or of the press. . . ."
>
> I referred to the freedom of the press because it is the robust exercise of that freedom which has brought us here today to assault the freedom of speech. . . .
>
> Why is the press—the institution that has unlimited free speech—so interested in restricting the speech of everyone else? Let's take a closer look.
>
> The unconstitutional issue ad restrictions in this bill purport to limit advertising within proximity to an election. However, it does not—interestingly enough—apply to newspaper ads. So, the already-powerful corporations that control the news—and in many instances, the public policy—in America will get more power and more money under this new law. One has to wonder why that blatant conflict of interest has not been more discussed in a debate about the appearance of conflict.

Senator McConnell grossly understated the enormity of the victory that Congress was about to hand the *Times*, but that triumph could only have been a small relief to the *Times*, who still have their work cut out for them.

Should the Supreme Court overturn the legislation, you can be sure the justices who vote to support the First Amendment will be vilified in front page headlines: "MR. CHIEF JUSTICE REHNQUIST CAN'T SWIM." Whether the justices will knuckle under to the enormous pressure soon to be aimed at them from the front pages will be an interesting test of the integrity of the High Court.

BRAVE NEW WORLD

The time is long past when publishers of newspapers believed they were in the business of reporting the news, when journalistic ethics demanded that news reports "be free from opinion or bias of any kind," when news articles strictly informed, reserving commentary for editorial columns.

Now, in the 21st century, the purpose of a newspaper is to identify solutions to society's problems and to influence public opinion to agree with those views. Ann Coulter stated this more colorfully: "Liberals, explicitly view the dissemination of news in America as a vehicle for left-wing indoctrination." Whichever way this point may be expressed, we would be kidding ourselves to deny its truth.

At the end of the day, before the paper hits the presses, the *New York Times* is all about influence. The publisher and editors of the *Times* have made no apologies for infusing their editorial views into their news pages. The integrity of the paper, jealously guarded for over half a century, has recently been blemished with distorted reporting, made worse by editorial attacks on the First Amendment rights of millions of American citizens.

In an ugly manifestation of their arrogance, the *Times* seems convinced that their opinions are correct and their solutions should be adopted as public policy. That would seem to be the only explanation for the unscrupulous means they have chosen to exercise their influence. The ends, it would appear, justify the means.

The balance of this book focuses on just one of the means to that end: *How to influence public opinion by passing off an editorial opinion as a straight news story.* In the next chapter, we will begin by exploring how the first sentence of a seemingly straight news story can be manipulated to reflect the opinion of the organization that published it.

THREE

Distorting the Lead

I have six honest serving men;
They taught me all I knew;
Their names are *Where* and *What* and *When*;
And *How* and *Why* and *Who*.

— *Rudyard Kipling*

Rudyard Kipling memorialized the standard for writing the basic news lead in the verse set forth above. Kipling lived in simpler times, when honesty was something the public expected from public institutions such as news organizations.

In this chapter, we will review the basics of news writing and explore how the *lead*, or introductory sentence, of a straight news story can be manipulated to reflect the political slant of the newspaper.

THE INVERTED PYRAMID

At the dawn of the 20th century, professional journalism came of age when news reporters and their editors began to widely embrace what has become known in journalism as the *inverted pyramid*.

The difference between a news article and other forms of composition—such as the novel, short story, poem, or essay—is that, unlike the news article, these other forms of writing usually begin with minor or incidental details and, toward their end, build to a climax. By contrast, the news writer reverses this plan, opening the news story with the climax and then adding layers of detail in a descending order of importance.

Compare the typical "pyramid" format on the left with the "inverted pyramid" style of the modern newspaper on the right:

Chronological Style
Pyramid

Jane Smith, 18, daughter of Leslie Smith of 100 Main Street, got into her car Monday morning and began driving down Main Street on her way to school.

At about 10 A.M., she pulled up alongside the car of David Wells, 19, of 50 Water Street in Middleton, who was waiting at the stoplight on the corner of Ocean and Maple Street.

When the light turned green, the two cars began racing down the street, each reaching a speed of about 50 miles per hour. When Jane's car reached Temple Avenue, she spotted 3-year-old Bobby Jones running out into the middle of the street.

Swerving to avoid the young boy, she lost control of the car, which jumped the sidewalk and hit a tree. When the ambulance workers arrived, they found her body twisted in the wreckage. The girl was rushed to Community Hospital where she was treated for multiple injuries.

Newspaper Style
Inverted Pyramid

A young girl was critically injured Monday morning near the corner of Main Street and Temple Avenue when her speeding car struck a tree after swerving to avoid hitting a toddler who ran into the middle of Main, according to police.

The injured girl, Jane Smith, 18, daughter of Leslie Smith of 100 Main, is being treated for multiple injuries at Community Hospital. Doctors described her condition as critical and could give no assurances that the girl would survive. No one else was injured in the accident.

Jane was driving to school Monday morning when the accident occurred. At about 10 A.M., while driving down Main Street, she pulled up alongside the car of David Wells, 19, of 50 Water Street in Middleton, who was waiting at the stoplight on the corner of Ocean and Maple Street.

When the light turned green, the two cars began racing down the street, each reaching a speed of about 50 miles per

Doctors described her condition as critical and could give no assurances that the girl would survive. No one else was injured in the accident.

hour. When Jane's car reached Temple Avenue, she spotted 3-year-old Bobby Jones running out into the middle of the street. Swerving to avoid the young boy, she lost control of the car, which jumped the sidewalk and hit a tree.

When the ambulance workers arrived, they found her body twisted in the wreckage and rushed her to the hospital.

The inverted pyramid style of writing—providing the essence of the story first and adding detail in a descending order of importance—was an important newswriting innovation for several reasons.

First, it facilitates the grasp of the news by a busy reader confronted with more information than he has the time or interest to absorb. If the most important information, or climax, of the story is placed at the beginning, the reader can quickly learn the gist and, if interested, can continue on to the details. He should not have to read the article to its conclusion to learn the essence of the story.

From a purely mechanical perspective, placing the essence of the story in the lead sentence facilitates the writing of the headline. As we will further explore in the next chapter, a headline consists of the minimum number of key words or their synonyms necessary to succinctly express the content of the story. If the lead of the story is complete, an editor should not have to look beyond its first sentence or paragraph to compose a proper headline.

A news story following the inverted pyramid form also facilitates page makeup. In laying out the pages of the newspaper, the makeup editor often finds it necessary to cut the length of an article to fit it within the space available. If the least important details are at the end of the story, he can cut the story short without affecting its essence. In our example, everything after the first paragraph in the story on the right can be cut without affecting the story's core. By contrast, to preserve the essence of the story on the left, cutting could not be done without extensive rewriting, an impracticality for a makeup editor on a deadline.

If the essence of the story is its climax, then a proper inverted pyramid places the story's climax in the lead or opening sentence. The most important elements of a well-written news article thus appear in the lead, the very first sentence of the story.

For the same reason, the most important element of the lead should receive the most emphasis, and the place to provide that emphasis is at the very beginning of the lead.

WRITING THE LEAD

When a newsworthy event occurs, a reporter should begin to think in terms of the following six questions:

1. *Who* was involved?

2. *What* happened?

3. *When* did it happen?

4. *Where* did it happen?

5. *Why* did it happen?

6. *How* did it happen?

These are journalism's five *W*s and *H*. They are the questions a reader wants to have answered when learning of a particular incident. A good news story will answer all six questions, insofar as they are answerable at the time the story is written. For the reasons explained above, a good news story will also attempt to answer these questions at the very beginning, usually in the very first sentence—what we have been calling the *lead sentence*.

The *lead* is the first part of a news story that provides the gist or outline of the most important elements of the story in the fewest possible words. (Elsewhere in this book, we refer to something called the *lead story*—meaning the most prominent story appearing on the front page of a particular edition of a paper, usually the story that appears in the upper right hand column of the front page. This should not be confused with the *lead sentence* of a particular story. However, the word *lead*, in both instances, denotes "most important".)

Take the following example of a good lead:

> A young girl was critically injured Monday morning near the corner of Main Street and Temple Avenue when her speeding car struck a tree after swerving to avoid hitting a toddler who ran into the middle of Main, according to police.

It answers all six of the questions, the five Ws (i.e., *Who, What, When, Where,* and *Why*) and the *H* (i.e., *How*). The closing phrase, "according to police," is known as the *attribution*, which is best placed at the end of the lead.

> (*Who?*) A young girl (*What?*) was critically injured (*When?*) Monday morning (*Where?*) near the corner of Main Street and Temple Avenue (*How?*) when her speeding car struck a tree (*Why?*) after swerving to avoid hitting a toddler who ran into the middle of Main, (*Attribution*) according to police.

It is not, however, enough that the lead sentence answer as many of these six questions as the story demands, or even all six. The answers must be arranged in the lead as to give proper emphasis to those that are most important.

As we have said, the most important news element of the story is given emphasis by placing it at the beginning of a sentence. Thus the writer selects the *W* or the *H* that is most important and opens the lead with it.

For example, if, in the above story, the most important element were the cause (i.e., the *Why*) of the accident—the errant toddler—the lead might read as follows:

> A 3-year-old boy running into the middle of Main Street led to the critical injuries of a young girl whose car hit a tree after swerving to avoid him, according to police.

This particular "cause" may well be the most important element of the story if, for example, a spate of errant toddlers had caused similar accidents prior to this incident. Alternatively, the cause could be attributed to the two speeding cars racing down the street. But since it was the driver who was critically injured, and whose fate remains in the balance, the *Who*, rather than the *Why*, is probably the most important element at this stage of the news coverage.

Determining the most important element of a lead is an exercise of journalistic judgment. How the reporter and editor exercise that judgment depends on the circumstances.

For the most part, the first few words of a straight news article normally contain the *What* of the story. The *Who* of the story might begin the lead where it is a well-known political figure, celebrity, notorious criminal, or fatality. Opening the lead with the *Where* is generally reserved for bombings, earthquakes, or other catastrophes, or actions taken by countries, states, cities, or communities. The *When* rarely opens the lead, but commonly the word "today" will immediately follow the *What* or the *Who*. When the lead is already packed with the other *W*s, the *Why* may be relegated to the second or third paragraph of the article.

While reasonable minds may come to different results, a good journalist will ferret out sufficient facts during his investigation, and a full factual backdrop will invariably point him to the most important element of the lead. If, in our example, the reporter should discover through investigation that an unusual number of accidents had recently occurred near the intersection where the accident took place, his discovery about the *Where* might lead to a more enlightening cause of many of the recent accidents. Thus, the *Where*, or a previously unknown *Why*, may deserve emphasis and therefore become the proper subject of the opening few words of the lead sentence.

SLANTING THE LEAD

In the days when accurate and impersonal news reporting was considered a virtue, it was a basic tenet of journalism that:

> A plain statement of fact is the best introduction to a news story.

That is a direct quote from a bulletin on press style, written by the co-founder of the *Associated Press*, Melville E. Stone, in the early 1920s to his news correspondents. Stone continued:

> Introductions must be impartial.
> It is possible to take almost any set of statements and present them in such

a way as to convey any one of several shades of meaning. This may depend merely on the order of presentation.

Associated Press stories must be accurate and accuracy involves not only the truthfulness of individual statements but the co-relation of these statements in such a way as to convey to the reader a fair and unbiased impression of the story as a whole.

An account of a court proceeding, a political debate, or any other event which involves conflicting claims or interests, should not be introduced by singling out a particular phase of the story which is limited to one side of the controversy, simply because that is the most striking feature. Such a form of introduction tends to place emphasis on one side of the case, giving bias to the entire story.

Thus, the reporters of the *Associated Press* were trained with what their common sense would otherwise have dictated: *impartiality* may depend upon context, and *accuracy* not only involves the truthfulness of the statements made but how they are placed (or omitted).

By reversing the common sense approach of the 1920s, we can construct a very useful recipe for slanting the lead sentence of virtually every straight news story. The result could be considered a useful set of guidelines on writing news leads for the *New York Times*:

1. Introductions to even the straightest news stories may be made partial to the editorial views of the publisher.

2. It is possible to take almost any set of statements and present them in such a way as to convey any one of several shades of meaning. This may depend merely on the order of presentation.

3. Individual statements must be truthfully reported, but the co-relation of these statements may be arranged in such a way as to convey to the reader the impression of the story we want the reader to have.

4. An account of a court proceeding, a political debate, or any other event which involves conflicting claims or interests should be introduced by singling out a particular phase of the story which is limited to one side of the controversy. Such a form of introduction tends to place emphasis on one side of the case, giving bias to the entire story.

Let's take a look at one example that will serve to illustrate these guidelines. When the president of the United States accomplishes an objective, such as signing a bill into law, the journalist has a choice: he may write a lead that constitutes "a plain statement of fact," expressing several of the five Ws and perhaps the H, or he may write an introduction that is "partial to the editorial views of the publisher."

If the president is a Republican and a plain statement of the facts would make him look good, the path is clear: convey to the reader the impression of the story we want the reader to have. For example, when a Republican president signs a bill into law, one effective tactic is to arrange the lead in such a way as to convey the impression that the president was responsible for the problems leading up to the need for the legislation.

If you read the headline "BUSH SIGNS BILL AIMED AT FRAUD IN CORPORATIONS," you might expect the lead to read like this:

> WASHINGTON, July XX—President Bush today signed a sweeping corporate-fraud bill that . . .

Thus begins "a plain statement of fact" about what the president did that day. To the extent there is a political backdrop to the president's action, or questions about its consequences, a newspaper can speculate with a "News Analysis" piece; or it can leave that task to those who control the editorial or op-ed pages of the paper.

But the notion that "a plain statement of fact is the best introduction to a news story" is not consistent with the mission of the modern newspaper, which is to influence public opinion. To properly influence the reader, you must spin the story before you report the news.

For example, a front-page "straight" news story in the *New York Times* under the headline "BUSH SIGNS BILL AIMED AT FRAUD IN CORPORATIONS" (July 31, 2002) opened with the following *editorial* observation in the most emphatic position of the lead:

> WASHINGTON, July 30—In a sign of how profoundly the nation's business scandals and volatile stock market have rocked his administration, President Bush signed a sweeping corporate fraud bill today . . .

Given what we have said about writing news leads, one might struggle to determine which of the *W* or *H* the above introduction was supposed to represent. The "sign" the *Times* referred to was certainly not the *Who, When, Where,* or *How.* That leaves the *What* and the *Why.*

The *What* of the story is clearly the bill that Bush signed into law, leaving us with the *Why.* Is the *Times* saying that President Bush is signing a bill into law *because* his administration has been rocked by business scandals and a volatile stock market?

The truth of the matter is that virtually all of the activity that lead to these business scandals—the false reporting of financial statements by a handful of corporations and the failure of the SEC and Justice Department to discover these activities—occurred during the eight years of the Clinton administration. The extensive and swift enforcement actions by the Bush administration—including several laudable instances where members of the administration refused to respond to attempts by certain corporate officers to gain the benefits of influence—have been primarily responsible for the discovery, disclosure, and prosecution of these fraudulent activities.

Nevertheless, in one strategically placed statement of opinion by the *Times* (i.e., its opinion of *why* Bush signed the legislation) in the introduction to the lead sentence of a "straight" news story about a simple but important legislative accomplishment, the *Times* placed the blame on Bush and not his predecessor. Rather than "rocking the legacy of the Clinton administration" or "a sign that Bush is cleaning up the mess left by his predecessor," Bush's accomplishment was redirected into a sign of how *his* administration had been "rocked" by scandal.

If that were not enough, in editorial after editorial, the *Times* continually implores one party or the other, usually the Republican party, to act in a "bi-partisan" way and to enter "compromises" to bring about legislation for the public good. After Bush did just that—reached such laudable compromises to achieve a worthy bi-partisan goal—the *Times* saw fit to single out another phrase in the lead to serve their ideological war with the president.

Making compromises is the bread and butter of federal lawmaking—certainly no bill in the history of the nation was signed by a president that didn't contain some compromises by both the president and members of the opposing party. In fact, there were central provisions in the corporate fraud bill that Democrats who voted for the bill had opposed several weeks earlier.

Nevertheless, to emphasize that Bush made important compromises without noting the compromises made by his opposition, the *Times* gave further bias to the entire story by closing the lead with a flourish:

> WASHINGTON, July 30 — In a sign of how profoundly the nation's business scandals and volatile stock market have rocked his administration, President Bush signed a sweeping corporate-fraud bill today *with central provisions that he opposed just three weeks ago.* (emphasis added)

Thus, before the reader learns the contents of the law, and how the sausage was finally made, we begin with the notion that the president not only deserves no credit for the legislative accomplishment but also is signing the legislation with profound reluctance.

Certainly, the Pulitzer people should begin polishing up another prize for this artful work of journalism. If the rest of the story were a straight account of the contents of the legislation, it would be difficult to read it without inferring a bias against the president.

Thus, we see, introductions to even the straightest news stories may be made partial to the editorial views of the publisher and editors of a paper. You can manipulate the story just by choosing which aspect of the facts—the *who, what, when, where, why* or *how* of the story—to emphasize.

Let's now take a closer look at some of the specific techniques employed by the *Times* to slant the lead sentence of a story with liberal bias. The two questions in a lead that most easily afford an opportunity to inject the liberal bias are the *Who* and the *Why* of the story. Let's first explore the *Who*.

SLANTING THE *WHO*

The *Who* is not always but is very often the most important fact in a story. Where the *Who* is important, it should be emphasized. Emphasis, as we have said, is usually accomplished by placing what requires emphasis in the lead sentence of the story and, where appropriate, at the very beginning of the lead.

Nevertheless, a most effective technique of injecting a liberal bias in a story is to manipulate the *Who*. Proper emphasis of the *Who* may be achieved by observing the following rule:

Emphasize the *Who* if

1. the *Who* is a Republican and the *What* is bad news, or

2. the *Who* is a Democrat and the *What* is good news.

For example, in a relatively straightforward story about a plan by the Republican administration to vaccinate health care and emergency workers against smallpox, the lead could be written this way:

WASHINGTON, July XX—The Bush administration plans to vaccinate roughly a half million health care and emergency workers against smallpox as a precaution against a bioterrorist attack.

The problem with this lead sentence is that it makes the Republican look good. The workers who would benefit from a vaccination program of this kind would be expected to warmly welcome it, but scoring points for Republicans when they are helping "workers" is not in the liberal playbook. Remember, the Republicans must be identified with "the rich," never "workers."

The choice is simple: either do not report the story at all, or, if that's not possible, slant the lead to reduce the political mileage the Republicans might gain from the report.

In this case, simply blunt the positive effect by downplaying the *Who* in this story. Ask yourself the following: do we have to give the Bush administration credit for this at all?

Take a look at how the *New York Times* dealt with the problem one Sunday morning under the headline "U.S. TO VACCINATE 500,000 WORKERS AGAINST SMALLPOX" (July 7, 2002). It was the lead story, appearing on the front page, in the upper right corner, the most prominent position of the paper; but the editors of the *Times* just couldn't bring themselves to give credit to Bush, especially where the benefit was slated to go to "workers." The lead read as follows:

WASHINGTON, July 6—The federal government will soon vaccinate roughly a half million health care and emergency workers against smallpox as a precaution against a bioterrorist attack, federal officials said.

It wasn't "Bush" or the "Bush administration" conducting the vaccinations; it was the "federal government." Moreover, the attribution was given to "federal officials," not "Bush administration officials." To determine the identity of this "federal official," you had to turn to page 16 where you would find a quote from an advisor to Tommy G. Thompson, Bush's secretary of health and human services.

Looking at the story objectively, the *Who* in the story was actually misplaced. The *Who* that needed to be emphasized by the *Times* were those who were going to receive the vaccinations, not those who devised the plan. Thus, the lead, as properly written, should have been:

WASHINGTON, July XX—Roughly a half million health care and emergency workers will soon be vaccinated against smallpox by the U.S. government as a precaution against a bioterrorist attack, Bush administration officials said.

Oops. That should be "federal officials said." If we were writing this during the Clinton years, of course, we would change this to "Clinton administration officials said." Better yet, to place the Democrat in the story in the most favorable light, you would emphasize the *Why* and closely associate it with the *Who,* as follows:

WASHINGTON, Dec. XX—As a precaution against a bioterrorist attack, President Clinton has authorized the vaccination of roughly a half million health care and emergency workers against smallpox, cabinet officials announced.

Let's now compare the above story with an actual story reported by the *Times* during the Clinton years (December 27, 1998):

CLINTON PLANS $25 MILLION INITIATIVE ON INFECTIOUS DISEASES
WASHINGTON, Dec. 26—President Clinton will soon propose a $25 million initiative to combat the spread of infectious diseases, including virulent

new strains of microbes that resist treatment by antibiotics and other drugs, Administration officials said today.

Compare that to a *Times* story on how the Bush administration planned to instruct state governments on the immunization plan (September 23, 2002):

U.S. PLAN TO MEET SMALLPOX THREAT

WASHINGTON, Sept. 23—Federal health officials today instructed states to be prepared to vaccinate as many as 1 million people in 10 days in the event of a biological attack using smallpox.

The editors of the *Times* seem well aware of the influence this subtle means of injecting bias into a straight news story has on public opinion over time. If they didn't believe it works, they would not be so consistent in its application.

Conversely, when the story can be perceived as adverse to the Republican occupying the White House, the paper will emphasize the *Who* by name. For example, when implementation of the "U.S." plan to vaccinate 500,000 health care workers showed signs of trouble, it suddenly became "President Bush's plan." IN "MANY BALKING AT VACCINATION FOR SMALLPOX" (February 7, 2003), the *Times* crafted the following lead sentence for its front page:

President Bush's plan to vaccinate 500,000 health care workers against smallpox is getting off to a slow start as hundreds of hospitals and thousands of nurses across the country say that they will not participate.

It is worth noting that this "news" was not derived from information gathered from independent sources but was merely the conclusion reached by the *Times* from "a nationwide survey" conducted by the *Times'* staffers (assuming we can trust, after the Blair scandal, that the reporters actually made the phone calls). The administration responded that the program was "still very much in the early stages." The article provided no information about how the survey was conducted or what questions were asked of the hospitals with whom the *Times* said it conferred.

The following lead was published as the lead news story on the front page of the *Times* (July 1, 2002) under the headline "BUSH SLASHING AID FOR E.P.A. CLEANUP AT TOXIC SITES":

WASHINGTON, June 30—The Bush Administration has designated 33 toxic waste sites in 18 states for cuts in financing under the Superfund cleanup program, according to a new report by the inspector general of the Environmental Protection Agency.

The cuts, imposed because the cleanup fund is hundreds of millions of dollars short of the amount needed to keep the program on schedule, mean that work is likely to grind to a halt on some of the most seriously polluted sites in the country, confronting the surrounding communities with new uncertainty over when the work will resume, how quickly it will proceed and who will pay for it.

Of course, the real story here was not the *Who* but the *Why:* "because the cleanup fund is hundreds of millions of dollars short of the amount needed to keep the program on schedule." Anyone who has taken a basic civics course knows that it is Congress who authorizes funds; the executive branch can only administer the spending of the funds.

Here, since the funds allocated by Congress were inadequate to do the work on schedule, the administration was required to make the necessary scheduling decisions regarding the allocation of federal resources. To do otherwise, like spending more money than allocated by Congress, would be a violation of the U.S. Constitution. If a Republican president ever exceeded congressional spending limits on military, you could be sure to read about it on the front page of the *Times*.

The headline and lead sentence upon which it was based brilliantly misled the public into thinking that Bush was making the cuts when in fact the blame rested with Congress. An accurate, simple statement of the truth would have been:

WASHINGTON, June XX—The inspector general of the Environmental Protection Agency reported to Congress today that, because the Superfund cleanup program is hundreds of millions of dollars short of the funding necessary to keep the program on schedule, the federal government will be forced to postpone work on the cleanup of 33 waste sites in 18 states.

The headline derived from such a lead would properly be: "E.P.A. TELLS CONGRESS IT LACKS FUNDING FOR TOXIC CLEANUP."

But there was even more going on in this story. Later, we explore how a paper can slant a story by the omission of a key fact. Here, the story failed to state that the Bush administration's proposed spending on the Superfund had actually increased—rising from $1.27 billion in 2002 to $1.3 billion in 2003. Had that fact been reported, the article could not have supported the headline "BUSH SLASHING AID FOR E.P.A. CLEANUP AT TOXIC SITES." Rather the headline might have read, in the least favorable light to the administration, "E.P.A.: BUSH FUNDING INCREASE FAILS TO KEEP PACE WITH TOXIC CLEANUP."

Moreover, buried in the seventh paragraph of the article was the fact that the funding shortfall was really not a shortfall but merely the difference between what bureaucrats at the EPA regional offices were requesting and what the Superfund managers were able to allocate under budget constraints—i.e., under the law. The reasonableness of the funding demands of the regional offices was a question that was neither asked nor answered in the article.

Perhaps the real story, if it had been reported fairly, would not have warranted front-page coverage; but the *Times* must keep in mind the political needs of the next Democratic candidate for president, such as a better headline for use in campaign ads that attack "Bush's record on the environment." So the *Times* delivered what the doctor ordered: "BUSH SLASHING AID FOR E.P.A. CLEANUP AT TOXIC SITES."

The truth was that the Bush administration had been unusually creative in proceeding with the cleanup of toxic waste sites in the face of tightened budgets. A month after the foregoing story appeared on the front page of the *Times*, the following story was buried on page 12, under the headline "SUPERFUND MAKES RARE DEAL WITH FLORIDA" (July 31, 2002):

> WASHINGTON, July 30—Short of money and struggling to end delays in cleaning up toxic waste sites, the federal Superfund program has entered an unusual arrangement with Florida in which the state will pay for work at a toxic site that would normally be handled by the federal government.

Thus, it seems the *Times* could not bring itself to suggest that the Bush administration was even remotely involved in the effort to clean up the toxic waste site. To avoid the unacceptable alignment of "Bush" and "cleaning up toxic waste," it actually had to spin the *Who* of the story that entered into the arrangement with the state of Florida.

The *Times* continued:

The arrangement illustrates just how tight Superfund money has become, forcing Washington to seek creative approaches to help finance even a relatively small project.

To use the name "Bush" in the same sentence as the word "creative" would also be unacceptable, so the reporter ascribed the creativity to "Washington."

Again, these are not isolated examples; the *Times* employs the technique continually. The following lead was published on the front page of the *Times* (August 13, 2002) under the headline "CHILD-SMUGGLING RING BROKEN UP BY THE U.S. IMMIGRATION AGENCY":

> WASHINGTON, Aug. 12—Federal officials said today that they had broken up a huge child-smuggling ring that preyed on illegal immigrants desperate to be reunited with their children.

The word "Bush" not only fails to appear in the lead sentence, it does not appear in the article at all. It would seem strange to the editors of the *Times* to associate Republicans with the protection of children against exploitation. To mention "President Bush" or the "Bush administration" would have done just that.

Consider a front-page article on how the Bush administration ordered a product recall that virtually shut down the nation's largest processor of donated human tissue on the grounds that their products were not safe for patients. Under the passive-voiced headline "RECALL IS ORDERED AT LARGE SUPPLIER OF IMPLANT TISSUE" (August 15, 2002), the following lead appeared:

> The Food and Drug Administration yesterday shut down a substantial part of the CryoLife Corporation, the nation's largest processor of donated human tissue on the grounds that the company could not adequately assure that its soft-tissue products were free of deadly bacteria and fungi.

To suggest that President Bush or his administration would take severe action against a "corporation" to protect "the public" or "consumers" is not something the *Times'* editors could countenance. Thus, the word "Bush" does not appear in the headline, the subhead, the sub-subhead, the lead, or anywhere else in the article.

Let's take a look at the reverse case, where the *Times* omitted the name "Clinton" to protect the former president. The lead story on the front page (September 19, 2002) read as follows:

U.S. FAILED TO ACT ON WARNINGS IN '98 OF PLANE ATTACK

WASHINGTON, Sept. 18—The United States intelligence community was told in 1998 that Arab terrorists were planning to fly a bomb-laden aircraft into the World Trade Center, but the F.B.I. and the Federal Aviation Administration did not take the threat seriously, a Congressional investigation into the Sept. 11 attacks found.

The 1998 intelligence report from the Central Intelligence Agency was just one of several warnings the United States received, but did not seriously analyze, in the years leading up to the Sept. 11 attacks that were detailed today at a Congressional hearing.

In other words, the Clinton administration was aware that Al Qaeda was planning an attack involving an aircraft flying into the World Trade Center three years before it happened. That President Clinton squandered the opportunity to prevent the devastating events of September 11 should have been no surprise to the *Times*. It had been widely reported that James Woolsey, the CIA director at that time, found it almost impossible to get an appointment to see President Clinton. When a private plane crashed on the White House grounds, there were jokes at the CIA that it was Woolsey trying to get a meeting with the president.

Nevertheless, because of the way the article was written, the story went virtually unnoticed and unreported by other news outlets. Imagine if the story had been written in a way that explicitly identified the *Who*:

CLINTON TEAM FAILED TO ACT ON WARNINGS OF A PLANE ATTACK

WASHINGTON, Sept. XX—The Clinton administration was aware in 1998 that Arab terrorists were planning to fly a bomb-laden aircraft into the World Trade Center, but the F.B.I. and the Federal Aviation Administration did not take seriously the threats reported by the Central Intelligence Agency, a Congressional investigation into the Sept. 11 attacks found.

The 1998 intelligence report from the C.I.A. was just one of several warnings the Clinton administration received, but did not seriously analyze, in the years leading up to the Sept. 11 attacks that were detailed today at a Congressional hearing.

Had the story actually been written this way, all hell would have broken loose in a media frenzy that might have resulted in an irrecoverable blow to the Clinton legacy. Fortunately, the *Times'* editors had the presence of mind to ensure that out of the 1,500 words in the story the name "Clinton" was not among them. The editing is even more brilliant than it appears: if the reader didn't connect for himself the year 1998 with the Clinton administration, the implication is that that the Bush administration made the blunder.

The Bush administration, however, didn't fail to make the connection and immediately decided to back a congressional investigation into the intelligence failures. But here is how the *Times* reported the story the next day:

WHITE HOUSE, IN SHIFT, BACKS INQUIRY ON 9/11
WASHINGTON, Sept. 18—The White House gave in today to growing Congressional demands for an independent investigation of last year's terrorist attacks, setting the stage for a comprehensive inquiry into the failures and vulnerabilities that made the hijackings possible.

By slanting the story as the Bush administration's "giving in" as part of a "shift" in position (connoting indecision or discomfort) and again failing to report the connection between the Clinton administration and the security failures discovered (but not reported) the day before, the lead implies that the Bush administration was shaken by the report and reversed course as a move to defend its own failures.

The truth was that the Bush administration changed its position because it became comfortable with the prospect of a potential investigation. There was now clear evidence that the blame for the intelligence failures leading to September 11 could be laid at the doorstep of President Clinton. (That's not a terribly noble reason to support the investigation, but it was the nub of the story.) Nevertheless, you wouldn't necessarily see it that way after reading the ten slanted column-inches of text on the *Times'* front page.

A persistent reader will find, where the article continued on page 10 of the paper, the following:

If an independent commission is empaneled, the agencies would be back under heavy scrutiny, undergoing far more searching and possibly more critical examination that could threaten the reputations of senior officials from both the Bush and Clinton administrations.

Here, you finally find the first and only use of the word "Clinton" in an article concerning intelligence blunders that occurred largely during the Clinton administration. Not surprisingly, however, the suggestion is that only the reputations of "senior officials" from the Clinton administration, not the reputation of President Clinton himself, could be threatened by a critical examination of those failures.

This technique has been used in earnest when reporting the administration's war on terror. During a week in which Senator Tom Daschle (D-South Dakota) and former Vice President Al Gore had been harshly criticizing the Bush administration for not making progress against the Al Qaeda terrorist organization, the Bush administration announced that it had captured Al Qaeda's chief of operations in the Persian Gulf—a significant achievement against Al Qaeda and, given the timing, a humiliating turn of events for the Democrats. It would have been humiliating for the *Times,* too, but there are ways to deflect the damage and avoid discomfort.

Turning to their favorite ploy—slanting the *Who*—the *Times* brilliantly minimized the political damage in the lead front-page story under the following headline, "A MAJOR SUSPECT IN QAEDA ATTACKS IS IN U.S. CUSTODY":

WASHINGTON, Nov. 21—A senior leader of Al Qaeda described as its chief of operations in the Persian Gulf has been captured, American officials said today.

Attributing the news to "Bush administration" officials would have given Bush credit in a way that would have been too obvious. The word "Bush" does not appear in the headline, lead paragraph, or even in any of the six paragraphs above the fold of the front page. Finally, below the fold, in the seventh paragraph of the article, the *Times* mentions the name "Bush," but only in this back-handed fashion:

His capture they said is a relief to American intelligence agencies at a time when the Bush administration has been criticized for having failed to apprehend the terror network's most notorious leaders, including Mr. bin Laden.

Had Al Gore been president, would there be any doubt about how the *Who* in the lead would have been slanted?

> WASHINGTON, Nov. XX—In a triumph of the Gore administration's prowess in the prosecution of the war on terrorism, the White House announced today the capture of a senior leader of Al Qaeda described no less as its chief of operations in the Persian Gulf.

And the headline? "GORE TEAM CAPTURES MAJOR AL QAEDA SUSPECT."
On the morning of the 2002 midterm elections, the *Times* had no choice but to report the following news:

> U.S. IS REPORTED TO KILL A LEADER OF QAEDA IN YEMEN
> WASHINGTON, Nov. 4—The Central Intelligence Agency, using a missile fired by an unmanned Predator aircraft, killed a senior leader of Al Qaeda and five low-level associates traveling by car in Yemen on Sunday, American officials said today.

But to have closed the lead sentence with the attribution "Bush administration officials said today" would only have strengthened President Bush's record on the war against terrorism. To do so on the day of an election that would determine control over Congress would undermine everything the *Times* had done to disparage Bush's wartime record during the prior weeks and months. In fact, the word "Bush" did not appear at all in this 991-word story. For some reason, the headline of the story was changed in a later edition to "C.I.A. IS REPORTED TO KILL A LEADER OF QAEDA IN YEMEN," but no mention of Bush or his administration was added.

On Sunday, March 2, 2003, the *Times* reported the capture of an Islamist militant who had been described as the "CEO" of Al Qaeda in a lead front-page article under the headline "PAKISTANIS ARREST QAEDA FIGURE SEEN AS PLANNER OF 9/11." Elsewhere, the arrest was characterized as a "tremendous blow" to Al Qaeda and a milestone victory for the Bush administration in the war against terrorism—but not in the lead "news" story of the *New York Times*. As to be expected, the phrase "Bush administration" is not mentioned in the lead sentence, the headline, the subhead, nor anywhere else in the *Times* article:

ISLAMABAD, Pakistan, March 1—Khalid Shaikh Mohammed, suspected of planning the Sept. 11 attacks on New York and Washington and one of the F.B.I.'s most wanted terrorists, was detained by Pakistani authorities this morning and is now in American custody, officials said.

By contrast, directly opposite the above story, appearing on the front page of the same issue was an article entitled "TURKISH DEPUTIES REFUSE TO ACCEPT AMERICAN TROOPS" (March 2, 2003). The subhead read "A BLOW TO BUSH'S PLANS," and the lead, of course, emphasized the "blow" over the plain facts of what happened:

ANKARA, Turkey, March 1—The Turkish Parliament today dealt a heavy blow to the Bush administration's plans for a northern front against Iraq, narrowly rejecting a measure that would have allowed thousands of American troops to use the country as a base for an attack.

A few days later, the *Times* reported that an opportunity to capture Khalid Shaikh Mohammed was bungled in 1996 by "American officials" (i.e., the Clinton administration). According to the *Times*, the "United States," not the Clinton administration, "missed their best opportunity to prevent the Sept. 11 strikes on New York and Washington." The article, buried on page 12 under the headline "QAEDA AIDE SLIPPED AWAY LONG BEFORE SEPT. 11 ATTACK" (March 8, 2003), did not open with a traditional lead that reported the news, but cleverly employed the guilt-by-association technique, naming "President Bush" before reporting the intelligence failure:

WASHINGTON, March 7—President Bush has hailed the arrest of Khalid Shaikh Mohammed as a watershed event in the war against terrorism.

Yet, the United States actually came tantalizingly close to catching Mr. Mohammed seven years ago, after his involvement in a botched terror operation in the Philippines, but long before he planned and executed Al Qaeda's deadly plot to attack the World Trade Center and government targets in Washington.

Buried in the eighteenth paragraph of this 1,400-word story, the *Times* revealed that a Pentagon plan to capture Khalid Shaikh Mohammed in 1996 was rejected by the "Deputies Committee, an interagency group during the Clinton administration that was made up of the second highest ranking officials from major departments and agencies, including Justice, Defense, State and N.S.C." Against the advice of the CIA, which feared that notifying the Qatar government would lead to Mr. Mohammed's fleeing Qatar and CIA surveillance, the Deputies Committee instructed the FBI to meet with Qatar officials to discuss the matter. Shortly after that meeting, Mr. Mohammed slipped away, as the CIA had feared.

Using the same style of lead writing employed by the *Times* on events involving the Bush administration, we can construct a lead sentence that would better summarize the news reported in the article and place emphasis on the import of the story:

> WASHINGTON, March XX—Missing the United States' best opportunity to prevent the Sept. 11 attacks on New York and Washington, seven years ago the Clinton administration allowed Khalid Shaikh Mohammed to slip from U.S. surveillance and escape capture by rejecting a Pentagon plan to seize him while he was residing in Qatar.
>
> Against the advice of the C.I.A., President Clinton's Deputies Committee . . .

Thus, in another classic manipulation of the *Who* to protect the Clinton legacy, a straight news lead was discarded in favor of a lead that downplayed the newsworthiness of the story, and no reference was made to the former president under whose watch the chance was blown. Instead, President Bush was gratuitously mentioned in the lead sentence of a story that had absolutely nothing to do with either him or the national security failures revealed in the article.

We can include more examples of the technique but hope these few have sufficiently illustrated the art and clearly demonstrated how the *New York Times* manipulates the *Who* in straight news stories to advance its political ideology.

Do not think for a moment that the *Times* does not know exactly what it is doing here. Its writers and editors appear to be keenly aware of the subtle effects that the use and omission of words have on influencing public opinion. As evidence of this self-awareness, consider the following article (September 25, 2002):

PRESIDENT'S VOCABULARY NOW OMITS GORE'S NAME
WASHINGTON, Sept. 24—Perhaps it is a dislike so pure that he dares not speak its name. Perhaps President Bush considers a hissing match with his 2000

presidential opponent beneath him. Or perhaps, as the White House insisted, the president meant absolutely nothing by a noticeable omission.

Whatever the reason, Mr. Bush avoided saying the words "Al Gore" today, even when pressed about his reaction to a speech that Mr. Gore made on Monday criticizing the White House's willingness to go it alone in Iraq.

One need not be a student of psychology to recognize how revealing that opening line is. Perhaps it is a dislike of George W. Bush that is so pure that the *Times* can't speak his name—at least when reporting news that reflects favorably on the president. Whatever the reason, the *Times* has reduced the technique of slanting the *Who* to an art form. Now let's explore how they slant the *Why*.

SLANTING THE *WHY*

Sometimes the *Why* rather than the *Who* or the *What*—i.e., the cause, rather than the perpetrator, the people affected, or the result—is the most important feature of the story.

In a typical story about a car accident, determining the cause can be a relatively straightforward matter: "A toddler ran out into the road." Consequently, we have become accustomed to reading the cause of events in a news story as though it were objective fact. Yet, determining the cause of an event is not an exact science, even in the case of an auto accident. In the political arena, the cause is rarely a matter of simple *fact*. On the contrary, it is almost always a matter of *opinion*.

Featuring the *Why* of a story, or slanting it to reflect the paper's political ideology, is a most ingenious way of lacing an opinion into a seemingly straight news story. A reporter can make considerable mileage out of "reporting" an opinion of the cause of an event as though it were a fact. If there is no *Why* to report, the paper can fabricate one that is consistent with its editorial views. Alternatively, if the story has an objective *Why*, the paper can change it to suit its needs.

The ingenious use of the editorial *Why* to spin a story before reporting the news is applied liberally—in both senses of the word—on the front pages of the *New York Times*. One example occurred in a *Times* story covering an address to the nation by President Bush, who, in response to the need to provide greater security against the threat of homeland terrorist attacks, called for the creation of a new cabinet department.

The most prominent story on the front page of the *Times* under the headline "BUSH, AS TERROR INQUIRY SWIRLS, SEEKS CABINET POST ON SECURITY" (Friday, June 7, 2002) actually began this way:

> WASHINGTON, June 6—Responding to widespread criticism of the government's handling of terrorist threats, President Bush called tonight for the creation of a new Cabinet department for domestic defense that would combine 22 federal agencies into a single one aimed at preventing future attacks against the United States.

Notice how—at the very beginning of the lead, where it receives the most emphasis—the participial phrase ("Responding to widespread criticism") is used, before reporting the news, to present the *Times'* editorial spin of the *Why.*

In a story about the president of the United States moving to create a $37 billion cabinet department in the largest realignment of federal agencies since the end of World War II, one might report a number of good *Whys,* or reasons, which may have justified such a move. If the president were a Democrat, the reason might have something to do with national security. Since the president is a Republican, the reason is more likely to be purely political: the President was merely "responding to criticism" of his handling of the war on terror—not just ordinary criticism, but "widespread criticism." It would have been inconsistent for the "newspaper of record" to also report that, according to the *Times'* own polls, over 80 percent of the public approved of the way President Bush was carrying out the war on terror.

The point is this: A news organization can always disparage a Republican by suggesting that his actions were politically motivated or put a Republican on the defensive by reporting that his actions were in response to criticism. It helps if that criticism was generated on your editorial page; in that way, you cannot be accused of lying about the existence of the criticism.

Another example of this technique surfaced in the lead sentence of a lead front-page article run under the headline "BUSH, IN SHAKE UP OF CABINET, OUSTS TREASURY LEADER" (December 7, 2002):

WASHINGTON, Dec. 6—Wrestling with a shaky economy and criticism that his administration projects a muddled message on how to respond, President Bush today dismissed his Treasury secretary, Paul H. O'Neill, and the director of his National Economic Council, Lawrence B. Lindsey.

Isn't the pattern obvious?

Taking a parting shot at the *Times'* use of the opening phrase technique to pre-spin the news to support its friends, let's see how the *Times* minimized potential political damage to Al Gore arising from the disclosure that one of his aides performed lobbying work for Enron during Gore's 2000 election campaign. The lead of the article, which ran under the headline "SENATOR RELEASES DOCUMENTS ON GORE AIDE'S ENRON TIES" (November 13, 2002), began as follows:

WASHINGTON, Nov. 12—In a parting shot at Democrats today, Senator Fred D. Thompson released documents . . .

Do we really need to read this story any further?

SLANTING THE *WHAT*

The *What* is more important than the *Who* when the event would be significant no matter who the individuals involved are. Much of this book is devoted to the means by which the editorial views of a newspaper are injected into a story to slant its *What*, including the distortion or omission of key facts, the direct injection of opinion, and the abuse of public opinion polls, among other techniques. But what if there was no *What*?

We already touched upon the extensive advocacy campaign waged by both the editorial and news divisions of the *New York Times* to pressure the Augusta National Golf Club to abandon its long-standing policy against the admission of women as members and to influence Tiger Woods to boycott the Masters golf tournament until the club acquiesces to the *Times'* demand.

Turning to the fact that CBS had not abandoned its plans to televise the tournament, the *Times* was apparently pessimistic that an editorial would effectively influence CBS. So, in its thirty-third article on the subject in just four months, the *Times* ran a front-page story under the headline "CBS STAYING SILENT IN DEBATE ON WOMEN JOINING AUGUSTA" (November 25, 2002). The lead read as follows:

> Ever since the Augusta National Golf Club, host of the Masters tournament, came under attack for its refusal to admit women as members, CBS has been silent on the issue, apparently hoping that the complaints of one women's group will be smothered by public indifference or by a backlash against what some women shrug off as an archaic feminist principle.

The *What* of the story was CBS's silence. In other words, the *Times* reported the "news" that *nothing happened*. It then speculated on what it thought CBS was "apparently" thinking.

Manufacturing the *What* of a story is tantamount to manufacturing the story itself. This technique, and the crusading that can be accomplished with it, is explored at greater length in Chapter Nine. Suffice it to say here, nothing seems to deter the modern newspaper from doing what it deems necessary to advance the paper's political ideology. Of course, if a story already has a *What*, reporters and editors, as we shall see, seem to be given leave to spin it with one of the other techniques to press forward the editorial views of the publisher.

SLANTING THE *WHERE*

Though infrequently employed to serve a bias, the *Where* may also be used to slant a story. In the following example, the *Times* used the location of a speech by President Bush, and the presence of his primary Democratic opponent, to suggest the president's proposals were politically motivated.

In an article entitled "BUSH APPEALS FOR HIS DOMESTIC SECURITY PLAN OVER DEMOCRATS'" (August 16, 2002), the *Times* seized on the *Where* to undermine the *What* of the story—the substance of a presidential speech on homeland security:

> MOUNT RUSHMORE NATIONAL MEMORIAL, S.D., Aug. 15—
> President Bush placed himself against the backdrop of one of America's most famous national monuments today to press for Senate approval of a new

Department of Homeland Security, even as Senator Tom Daschle, the Democrat from South Dakota who has stood in the way of the president's version of the plan, sat right up front.

In the next paragraph, the paper did a brilliant job of undermining the president's message by not only accusing Bush of playing politics but also suggesting his trip might be in violation of campaign finance laws—using the *Where* to make the point all the more poignant.

> Mr. Bush's three-hour visit on a brilliant summery day to Mr. Daschle's home state was billed by the White House as a policy event, meaning that taxpayers, not the Republican party, picked up the president's travel bill. But the past presidents carved into the cliffs looking down on the scene—George Washington, Abraham Lincoln, Thomas Jefferson and Theodore Roosevelt—would have recognized a morning laden with politics.

It is axiomatic that when a Democrat or liberal makes a speech in support of a policy or specific piece of legislation, one can lend credibility to the effort by calling it a "policy" speech. When a Republican or conservative makes a similar speech, the effort can be undermined by labeling it as "political." Here, the towering figures of four of our greatest presidents were invoked to bring force to the newspaper's charge that Bush's effort was politically motivated. Expressing such a charge in the paper's editorial page is fair game, but not in a straight news story.

The story also made use of another *Times* technique of injecting bias: contrasting an event as it was "billed" (i.e., a "policy" event) with how the *Times* chose to characterize it (i.e., an event "laden with politics").

Thus, with a little creativity, even the *Where* may be used to undermine the *What* and ridicule the *Who* of the story to advance the ideological objectives of the paper.

SLANTING THE *WHEN*

What has been said of the *Where* may also be said of the *When*. It generally may be disposed of in two words, as in the following example:

WASHINGTON, Sept. 18—The United States intelligence community was told [*When?*] in 1998 that Arab terrorists were planning to fly a bomb-laden aircraft into the World Trade Center, but the F.B.I. and the Federal Aviation Administration did not take the threat seriously, a Congressional investigation into the Sept. 11 attacks found.

This article, which ran under the headline "U.S. FAILED TO ACT ON WARNINGS IN '98 OF A PLANE ATTACK" (September 19, 2002), has already provided us with an example of how the *Who* of the story—the Clinton administration—was suppressed so as to minimize the embarrassment to President Clinton. By the same token, it could be said that the story was distorted by omitting the *context* of the *When*—the year 1998 was when Clinton was president and the FBI and the Federal Aviation Administration were part of his administration.

The same can be said of the many articles published in the *Times* about the Enron scandal, where virtually all of the illegal activity that lead to the downfall of Enron Corporation occurred during the eight years of the Clinton administration. It is mildly ironic how Howell Raines could call the Reagan years an "historical ascendancy of greed and hard-heartedness" without making the same observation about the Clinton years.

There are other creative ways to use the *When* of a story to support a political end. For example, on March 27, 2002, President Bush signed into law the McCain-Feingold Campaign Finance Reform Bill. It was a bill, as we have seen, for which the *Times* had employed its vast soft-money machine to ensure its passage. It was also a bill that contained many provisions that troubled President Bush, not the least of which was its blatant violation of the First Amendment. The *Times*, however, was triumphant and did not miss the opportunity to stick the bill into the face of its chief foe when that opportunity presented itself on the day he signed the bill.

In a classic example of emphasizing the *When* of the story for political purposes, the *Times* ran the following lead under the headline "PRESIDENT SIGNS BILL ON CAMPAIGN GIFTS; BEGINS MONEY TOUR" (March 28, 2002):

President Bush signed a major overhaul of the nation's campaign finance system into law without ceremony today, then almost immediately left Washington on Air Force One for a two-day, three-state trip to raise nearly $4 million for Republican candidates and his party.

Thus, as with the *Where*, the timing of an event or activity may provide an opportunity for a newspaper to slant a story to support its ideological agenda—here, to cast a routine presidential fund-raising trip as a hypocritical defiance of the law he just signed and as an embarrassing junket "on Air Force One."

SLANTING THE *HOW*

In the typical story, the *How* is rarely the most important fact—such as how the president flies to a fund-raising event (i.e., "on Air Force One"), but, once in a while, even the *How* may afford an opportunity for a newspaper to take a shot at an ideological opponent.

By slanting the *How*, the *Times* took another shot at the president in the wake of an astounding diplomatic success: when the United Nations Security Council unanimously supported an effort by the Bush administration for passage of a tough UN resolution to disarm Saddam Hussein. The question of how the Bush administration accomplished the unanimous vote naturally arose, and a reporter wrote an intelligent 1,400-word front-page story (November 9, 2002) detailing the extraordinary three-month effort by Secretary of State Colin Powell to negotiate a resolution that finally achieved the unanimous UN acceptance.

However, the article opened with how Powell obtained his first victory: persuading Vice President Dick Cheney and Defense Secretary Donald Rumsfeld (and presumably President Bush, though that was never stated in the article) that the administration needed the support of the United Nations before taking military action against Iraq.

WASHINGTON, Nov. 8—In late August, from the Situation Room at the White House, Secretary of State Colin L. Powell made one of the most important presentations of his tenure, arguing via video screen to President Bush at his ranch in Texas that the administration needed to go to the United Nations for another round of weapons inspections in Iraq.

Also in the room were Vice President Dick Cheney and Defense Secretary

Donald H. Rumsfeld, who had made little secret of their disdain for his line of action. Yet when Secretary Powell completed his argument, both supported him, an administration official said.

That lead provided the opportunity for the following crafty headline:

HOW POWELL LINED UP VOTES, STARTING WITH HIS PRESIDENT'S

Portraying Secretary Powell as "lining up" the president along with other nations of the Security Council—as a basketball coach might line up his players—is a slant calculated to belittle both the president's role in the matter and Powell's weight of argument.

In contrast with the headline, the article itself did no such thing. It made no reference to the president's decision to back Powell's proposed course of action, though that seemed to be implied when it reported Powell's "victory" in gaining the support of Cheney and Rumsfeld, as the first step toward securing the unanimous support of the Security Council. Given the strong nature of Cheney's and Rumsfeld's initial opposition to Powell's proposed course, it would seem that the matter was given a very thorough consideration by the president and his national security staff, who seemed to have demonstrated a remarkable degree of deliberation and open-mindedness.

To have reflected upon the *How* in this way, however, would have exhibited a competency that should never be conveyed about a Republican administration on the front page of the *New York Times*. Modern copy editors seem to be on the lookout for an opportunity to slant even a truly objective story with a biased headline. Our next chapter will explore the use of biased headlines in more detail.

FOUR

Distorting the Headline

The function of the head is to tell the facts,
not to give the writer's comments on the facts.

—*Style Guide of the Detroit News* (1924)

In the days when professional publishers of newspapers believed they were in the business of reporting the news rather than influencing public opinion, the rules for writing headlines paralleled the rules for writing the straight news story.

According to the *Style Guide of the Detroit News* (1924):

> The head is an advertisement, and like all good advertisements, it should be honest, holding out no promise that the story does not fulfill. It should be based on the facts as set forth in the story and nothing else. The head should be a bulletin or summary of the important facts, not a mere label. It is usually best to base the head on the lead of the story. . . . The function of the head is to tell the facts, not to give the writer's comments on the facts.

Though news reporters rarely write the headlines—a task usually reserved for copy editors and headline writers—the news reporter maintains great influence over the headline by virtue of the fact that a good headline is a summary of the lead sentence. If the lead is biased, a biased headline is sure to follow.

Biased headlines are important. Most people don't read newspapers; they scan them—that is, they read the headlines, and when a headline piques their interest, they may go on to read the lead sentence of the story. The lead might entice one to read on, but only a small percentage of people who read a headline go on to read the whole article.

Thus, the vast majority of people who read newspapers gain their understanding of the news by glancing at the headlines and subheads. To influence the headlines is to influence public opinion.

Furthermore, a slanted headline, like a slanted lead, will influence how people absorb what they read in the rest of the article. For example, a headline and lead slanted against the president will predispose the reader against the president when reading and interpreting the facts presented in the rest of the story, even if those facts are presented in a straightforward and balanced way.

In the previous chapter, we saw how a lead may be slanted by manipulating the *Who*. Let's look at how those leads affected the headlines.

- What could have been "BUSH TO VACCINATE 500,000 WORKERS AGAINST SMALLPOX" was reported by the *Times* as "U.S. TO VACCINATE 500,000 WORKERS AGAINST SMALLPOX."

- What should have been "BUSH FUNDING INCREASE FAILS TO KEEP PACE WITH TOXIC CLEANUP" was reported by the *Times* as "BUSH SLASHING AID FOR E.P.A. CLEANUP AT TOXIC SITES."

- What the *Times* reported on page 12 as "SUPERFUND MAKES A RARE DEAL WITH FLORIDA" could have been the front page story "BUSH E.P.A. TAKES CREATIVE APPROACH TO TOXIC CLEANUP."

- What could have been "BUSH TEAM BREAKS UP CHILD-SMUGGLING RING" was reported as "CHILD-SMUGGLING RING BROKEN UP BY THE U.S. IMMIGRATION AGENCY."

- What was reported as "A MAJOR SUSPECT IN QAEDA ATTACKS IS IN U.S. CUSTODY" could have been "BUSH DEALS BLOW TO AL QAEDA; PERSIAN GULF CHIEF IN CUSTODY."

DISTORTING A HEADLINE TO HYPE THE PAPER'S VIEWS

When the editors of the *New York Times* want to send a message, nothing seems to deter them from distorting their headlines to achieve their editorial objectives. For example, the *Times* was getting a little impatient both with the conservative government of Israel, which has taken a hard line against Palestinian terrorist organizations, and with the Bush administration, which approached the Middle East with a strategy different from that of the Clinton administration, whose policies many believed exacerbated the violence in the region.

So, in an article reporting on U.S. reaction to an Israeli incursion into Gaza in retaliation for a suicide bombing attack on Israeli citizens (April 18, 2001), the *Times* took the opportunity to stand in place of the Bush administration to announce its own stance on the Israeli action. The unusual three-column-wide headline read:

POWELL ASSAILS ISRAEL FOR GAZA INCURSION

The lead sentence of the article read as follows:

> WASHINGTON, Apr. 17—Secretary of State Colin L. Powell, employing the harshest language against Israel since the Bush administration took office, assailed Israel today for using "excessive and disproportionate" force in seizing a part of Palestinian-ruled territory in Gaza, and urged its forces to withdraw.

The article did not quote anyone to support the *Times'* characterization of Powell's statement as "harsh" or as "assailing" Israel's action. On the contrary, about two-thirds down, the article says:

> While criticism of Israel was the strongest since Mr. Bush has been in office, administration officials took pains to say that the language was carefully moderated.

Moderation is about the only way you could characterize Secretary Powell's only extended quote in the article:

77

"We call upon both sides to respect the agreements they have signed," General Powell continued. For the Palestinians, he said, that meant renouncing terrorism and bringing all Palestinian military forces under control. "For the Israelis," he added, "this includes respecting their commitment to withdraw from Gaza, according to the terms of the agreement signed by Israel and the Palestinians. There can be no military solution to this conflict."

Ignoring the obvious pains taken by Secretary Powell and the State Department to use moderate language, the *Times* was determined to send its own message to express its displeasure with the conservative government of Israel. Thus, the *Times* sent Israel a wakeup call by hyping the Bush administration's moderate statement and shouting it through the megaphone of a front-page slant.

DISTORTING A HEADLINE TO DOWNPLAY A STORY

When the *Times* publishes an article that detracts from its political agenda, it appears quite willing to distort the headline to mute the story. On January 30, 2003, the leaders of eight European nations—the Czech Republic, Denmark, Hungary, Italy, Poland, Portugal, Spain, and the United Kingdom—joined together and published an open letter supporting the United States' strategy to disarm Saddam Hussein. The letter was published in the *Wall Street Journal* and in the leading newspaper in each signatory's country.

In a strong rebuke to France and Germany, who had been presumed to speak for a Europe united against U.S. strategy on Iraq, the letter thanked the U.S. for its past "bravery, generosity and farsightedness" in standing against the tyrannies of nazism and communism and urged other European nations to join them in backing the Bush administration's policies on Iraq. A ninth nation, Slovakia, signed the letter the following day.

In any newspaper that prides itself for its international reporting, the story for such an unprecedented action should be front-page news, and its headline should be easy to write: "EIGHT EUROPEAN NATIONS DECLARE STRONG SUPPORT FOR BUSH ON IRAQ." How else could you describe what happened? The *Times* copy editors found an alternative.

Perhaps it was because the *Wall Street Journal* had the scoop; perhaps the *Times* just couldn't bring itself to so publicly embarrass its own editorial writers, and their French and German allies, in their war against the Bush administration. Whatever the reason, the result was predictable: the *Times* buried the news on page 10, wrote a lead sentence that opened with a blatant attack on America's strongest ally, and printed a headline designed to ensure that virtually no one would read the story (January 31, 2003):

EUROPEAN LEADERS DIVIDE BETWEEN HAWKS AND DOVES
LONDON, Jan. 30—Assuming a somewhat frayed mantle as global diplomat, Prime Minister Tony Blair flew to the United States tonight to meet President Bush, bearing an unusual pledge of support from nine European leaders but leaving a Continent ever more divided over the need for war against Iraq.

Even before the lead disparaged Tony Blair's authority as a diplomat, the headline labeled as "hawks" those who stepped forward to recognize and appreciate America's historic role in guaranteeing peace and freedom on the European continent. According to the *Times*, those who stand by America, especially those willing to declare their support so publicly, are the bad guys. Moreover, these bad guys, with their letter, now leave Europe "ever more divided" than before.

Those who got their news primarily from the *Times* had been conditioned to believe that European leaders were united against the U.S., and that the U.S. was "going it alone," on the question of military action against Iraq. The letter, however, demonstrated the truth, which the *Times* had refused to acknowledge, even after the letter's publication in ten of the world's leading newspapers: that France and Germany, who had been attempting to thwart U.S. policy at every turn, were deeply out of touch with the rest of the Europe. That included Russia, at the time, if you take into account the story buried on page 9 of the same issue: "RUSSIA SOFTENS OPPOSITION TO MILITARY ACTION IN IRAQ" (January 31, 2003).

In other words, the Bush administration was building the very coalition the *Times* had been suggesting was requisite to military action against Iraq, and therefore burying the story behind personal attacks, a tenth-page placement, and a muted headline seemed necessary to preserve the *Times*' continued stance against U.S. foreign policy.

As U.S. troops rolled into Baghdad in April 2003, Iraqi citizens streamed into the streets in celebration, toppling a statue of Saddam Hussein in a scene that symbolized the fall of the Iraqi dictator's thirty-year grip on Iraq. The next day, newspapers across the country reported the momentous event with headlines reflecting the moment, such as the following which graced the front page of *USA Today* (April 10, 2003):

BAGHDAD FALLS
JUBILANT CROWDS SWARM U.S. TROOPS AS 3-WEEK WAR TOPPLES
REGIME; 'GAME IS OVER,' IRAQI DIPLOMAT SAYS

That same day, the editors of the *New York Times* must have been under sedation when they offered up their version of the story:

U.S. FORCES TAKE CONTROL IN BAGHDAD; BUSH ELATED; SOME
RESISTANCE REMAINS.

An analysis of the difference between how the *Times* related this news versus how many of their counterparts in other American newsrooms reported the story is detailed in Chapter Twelve, regarding how the *Times* covered the war with Iraq.

WHEN THE HEADLINE DOESN'T REFLECT THE STORY

The headline doesn't always have to reflect what is reported in the article; it can ignore the facts and directly reflect the editor's desired effect on public opinion. For example, the *Times* is convinced that a reduction in the capital gains tax benefits the wealthy and no one else, so it is always eager to use its influence to persuade "working families" to oppose any capital gains tax cut. So, when the chairman of the Federal Reserve Board expressed reservations about using a cut in the capital gains tax as a short-term measure to boost the economy, the *Times* took out its megaphone and printed the following front-page headline:

STRONG OPPOSITION: FED CHAIRMAN IS AMONG THOSE WARNING ABOUT CAPITAL GAINS CUTS

The second sentence of the article (September 26, 2001) read:

> Alan Greenspan, the Federal Reserve chairman, and Robert E. Rubin, the former treasury secretary, advised Congress against cutting the capital gains tax, the favored approach of many Republicans on Capitol Hill, or reducing corporate income taxes, the idea mentioned by the Bush administration.

Whatever may be the views of Robert E. Rubin, the former treasury secretary *under President Clinton*, the lead was a complete distortion of the views of Chairman Greenspan on the subject of the capital gains tax, and the headline exaggerated that distortion.

As the article stated, a few inches above its final paragraph in the interior of the paper:

> Mr. Greenspan restated his support for reducing or eliminating the capital gains tax in the long run, but he said it was not the best way to deal with the economy's short-term problems.

Another newspaper might have run the headline:

FED CHAIRMAN ADVOCATES ELIMINATION OF CAPITAL GAINS TAX FOR LONG TERM; NOT AS SHORT-TERM FIX FOR ECONOMY

Perhaps as a result of being confronted with the blatant distortion, the *Times* changed the headline in its Late Edition to "CONGRESS GETS PLEA TO DROP TAX BENEFITS FOR INVESTORS AND WIDEN ECONOMIC RELIEF." While it corrected a direct falsification, the replacement headline still distorted the story. No one that day suggested to Congress that it "drop tax benefits for investors," only that reducing the capital gains tax would not provide enough immediate stimulus to the economy under the circumstances (i.e., the aftermath of the September 11 attacks).

Nor did anyone advise that "economic relief be widened," which suggests that cutting the capital gains tax would not have provided economic relief to a wide enough number of people. The reduction in the capital gains tax benefits everyone; it just would not be big enough or take effect soon enough to stimulate the economy in the short run. What Congress was advised was that any stimulus package had to be sizable and immediate to be effective.

The *Times* seems perfectly willing to write headlines that scoff at practically any effort by the Bush administration to do its job, regardless of how serious the matter or how earnest the effort. For example, shortly after the federal government put the nation on "high" terror alert, the Bush administration provided some guidelines on how the public might prepare for a possible terrorist attack. As reported on page 12 in the *Times*, in "ADMINISTRATION GIVES ADVICE ON PREPARING FOR TERRORIST ATTACK" (February 11, 2003), the Bush administration urged that families prepare a "disaster supply kit" that included a battery-powered radio, a change of clothes, an extra set of car keys, cash, and a three-day supply of food and water. Characterizing these measures as "mostly-common sense," the *Times* then foreshadowed its coming mini-crusade against the administration's homeland security efforts. When the administration advised that "people keep a supply of duct tape and plastic sheeting in their homes," the *Times* couldn't see the common sense in that and injected its opinion that this recommendation was "not so obvious."

The next day, op-ed columnist Maureen Dowd, in a piece entitled "PASS THE DUCT TAPE" (February 12, 2003), accused the Bush administration of doing nothing, "other than plastic and duct tape," to protect the public from a potential Al Qaeda attack. The following day, in "DUCT TAPE AND PLASTIC SHEETING PROVIDE SOLACE, IF NOT SECURITY" (February 13, 2003), the *Times* found an "expert" to help them belittle the recommendation that families maintain a supply of duct tape and plastic sheeting, even though the American Red Cross has recommended for more than a decade that families do so.

Television news reports immediately started showing people stocking up on bottles of water and duct tape, but when one news program televised a woman applying plastic sheeting to her windows, the appearance of misunderstanding, if not panic, was something Homeland Security Secretary Tom Ridge decided to address in a speech the following day. Providing clarification on the question of duct tape and plastic sheeting, he stated emphatically, "We don't want folks sealing up their doors or sealing up their windows." This time, the *Times* reported the story on its front page, but under a headline that seemed calculated to ridicule more than to inform: "TERROR ADVICE FROM WASHINGTON: DO NOT SEAL DOORS AND WINDOWS" (February 15, 2003). Terror advice?

After mocking Secretary Ridge with that front-page headline, the *Times'* headline writers went further and actually mischaracterized Ridge's action that day. The original advice, as reported in the *Times*, was that "people keep a supply of duct tape and plastic sheeting," not actually apply them immediately. At his press conference, Secretary Ridge reconfirmed that advice, as the *Times* even reported in the article:

> Mr. Ridge said he wanted to remind the public that the emergency supplies should be kept available—but not used.

Yet, the jump headline above the continuation of the article on page 11 declared, "RIDGE CHANGES ADVICE TO NOT SEAL DOORS AND WINDOWS." In fact, the administration's advice had not changed—neither Secretary Ridge nor anyone else in the administration ever suggested that doors and windows be sealed at this time. Nor did the article itself, other than the headline, report a change in advice by Ridge or the administration.

At the end of the day, the series of headlines effectively gave an impression of the news that the *Times* seemed to want to convey: that the advice provided by the Bush administration on homeland security had been ineffective and inconsistent.

COMPARING HEADLINES WITH THOSE OF OTHER PAPERS

As we have seen, one way to determine how a newspaper slants its headlines is to compare the headlines written by other news organizations when covering the same story. But a comparison of headlines written by the *Times* against those by other newspapers will not always result in a fair assessment. Such an analysis tends to underestimate the influence the *Times* has on the editorial decisions of other papers. Because nearly all major metropolitan newspapers subscribe to the Times News Service, a headline in another newspaper may have been derived from the headlines and lead sentences slanted by the *Times*.

Once in a while, however, such a comparison reveals the *Times'* unmistakable bias against its political opponents. Columnist Andrew Sullivan discovered the following instance where three news organizations covered the same simple story arising from standard economic statistics released by the Commerce Department on October 31, 2002, just a week prior to the midterm 2002 elections:

ECONOMY RACES AHEAD AT 3.1 ANNUAL RATE IN SUMMER
—*Associated Press*

ECONOMY GROWS AT 3.1 PERCENT PACE
—*Washington Post*

ECONOMY GREW AT 3.1% IN 3RD QUARTER, SLOWER THAN EXPECTED
—*New York Times*

CRUSADING WITH HEADLINES

The editors at the *Times* have been adept at "flooding the zone" with articles to support ideological crusades aimed at weakening a Republican's standing in the polls. A series of negative headlines will take its toll on any politician, including the president of the United States.

Not long after he took office, President Bush became the victim of a series of front-page headlines in the *New York Times* apparently aimed at weakening the president's public approval ratings. A front-page *Times* article trumpeting a drop in Bush's popularity, according to a *New York Times*/CBS News poll, was sure to follow.

In an opinionated front-page article, under the headline "PRICE OF GASOLINE MAY POSE PROBLEM FOR WHITE HOUSE" (May 10, 2001), the *Times* reported:

> Republicans in the White House and around the country are increasingly nervous that surging gas prices and rolling blackouts will pose a colossal political problem for President Bush because they are matters that he has limited control over but that touch people in their daily lives.

In other words, the *Times* noticed that gasoline prices were rising, and rolling blackouts created by liberal environmentalists were startling Californians.

Seizing an opportunity to pressure the Bush administration, the *Times* cobbled together a prediction—that the circumstances "may" cause "colossal political problems" for the president—and then reported it in the form of a "straight" news story. At the same time, the *Times* knew that it was in the process of taking a public opinion poll ("POLL: ENERGY BUSH'S TOP TASK," *New York Times*/CBS News, May 14, 2001) asking whether the public believes the president was indebted to the oil industry. So the second sentence of the article drove home the desired point:

> For Mr. Bush, the issue is particularly perilous. He is trying to defuse a political time bomb while not threatening the oil industry, which once employed both him and his vice president and was a huge source of donations to his campaign.

Notice how that last clause strongly suggests the president and vice president of the United States were beholden to the oil industry, purely for "special interest" purposes—that is, the *Times* suggested that Bush and Cheney had been politically corrupted by the oil industry. The reverse spin, of course, would have been to support the credibility of Bush and Cheney's views on energy policy by emphasizing their hands-on energy industry experience and pointing out how that gives them an understanding of energy policy greater than that of most Democrats in power and even the editors of the *New York Times*.

That spin, however, would not have been as effective in supporting the credibility of the sentence that followed it:

> Even as the president scrambled to blame the Clinton administration for the energy woes, House Democrats held a news conference today to upbraid Mr. Bush as having a "do-nothing response" because he is captive to the industry.

The next day, the *Times* slapped President Bush with another negative headline: "BUSH NAMES A DRUG CZAR AND ADDRESSES CRITICISM" (May 10, 2001). The article began:

WASHINGTON, May 10—President Bush today nominated as his drug czar John P. Walters, who has long argued for jail time over voluntary treatment for drug offenders, calling him the man to battle illegal drugs that rob people "of innocence and ambition and hope."

Mr. Bush's choice of the conservative Mr. Walters to head the White House Office of National Drug Control Policy was criticized by groups that want to emphasize curing drug addiction rather than punishing drug offenders or cutting off the supply of narcotics.

Labeling the appointee as a "conservative" is automatic, but so was the kicker in the headline: ". . . AND ADDRESSES CRITICISM." No matter what kind of person the president appointed, the headline was sure to say ". . . AND ADDRESSES CRITICISM."

In the article itself, the *Times* could not take the president at his word when he stated the administration would emphasize drug treatment. Here's the *Times* spin on the statement:

> As he introduced Mr. Walters, who served as the deputy drug director under his father, Mr. Bush tried to defuse criticism of his choice by declaring that the administration would emphasize treatment, including through religious organizations. He also said, however, that Mr. Walters would lead "an all-out effort to reduce illegal drug use."

Bush was declaring a policy favoring treatment, but the *Times* spun this as the president merely trying to "defuse criticism," suggesting that Bush was not serious about drug treatment.

More to the point, if the president had chosen a drug czar who emphasized curing drug addiction over drug enforcement measures, the reporter could easily have found quotes from those critical of the president's weakness on drug enforcement. Hence, the headline would remain: ". . . AND ADDRESSES CRITICISM."

At a gathering at the White House to celebrate the first anniversary of the "No Child Left Behind Act," at which President Bush announced that federal spending on elementary and secondary education had increased by an astounding 49 percent over the previous two years, the *Times* reported (January 9, 2003):

AMID CRITICISM, BUSH PROMISES TO PRODUCE EDUCATION GAINS

With a headline like that, it really didn't matter what else the *Times* said about the president's speech that morning. Since only a small percentage of those who read the headline actually read the rest of the story, the *Times*' swipe at the president would be what a vast majority of people who picked up the paper that day would gain from Bush's progress on education.

In a later chapter, we will see a more powerful example of how the *Times* used a series of headlines to crusade against President Bush's policies on Iraq and how the Bush administration conducted the war.

The power of influencing the public by slanted headlines is enormous. Bush cannot raise enough money in his next election to overcome the soft-money resources being deployed against his candidacy by the headline writers at the *New York Times*. Campaign spending by the Republican party is now limited by law—a law that the *Times* has itself expended considerable resources to see enacted. Campaign spending by the *Times* and its news divisions, however, is limited only by its revenues, about $3 billion next year (plus what it can borrow or raise in equity)—that's $3 billion that Bush's Democratic opponents can consider as part of their own coffers without being in violation of campaign finance laws.

We have thus explored how the *Times* distorts its lead sentences and its headlines. In the next chapter, we explore how the *Times* distorts the rest of the story.

FIVE

Distorting the Facts

He fabricated statements. He concocted scenes.
He stole material from other newspapers and
wire services. He selected details from photographs
to create the impression he had been somewhere
or seen someone, when he had not.

—regarding Times' *disgraced reporter Jayson Blair from
the front page of the* New York Times *(May 11, 2003)*

lanting the facts is the most basic tool in an editor's stock of techniques to bias a story in favor of the publisher's editorial point of view. Facts may be slanted in four basic ways:

1. Omission

2. Distortion

3. Falsification

4. Emphasis

This chapter will consider how each of these techniques is used to bias a story.

OMITTING KEY FACTS

The omission of key facts is a form of slant that is nearly impossible to detect and one that will always provide the editors with plausible deniability. Should a reporter ever be caught doing it, a paper can always claim ignorance or contend that the omission was inadvertent.

A newspaper can slant by omission to either harm its opponents or help its allies. Here is a front-page example of how the *Times* omitted a key fact to the detriment of one its political opponents (July 9, 2002):

> WASHINGTON, July 8—President Bush defended himself today against a barrage of questions about his own dealings even as he vowed to take a tougher line in a speech in New York on Tuesday against corrupt corporate executives.
>
> As pressures mounted today from Democrats in Congress, Mr. Bush repeatedly dismissed criticism that he had failed to disclose a 1990 stock sale as nothing more than a political attack, although he acknowledged he still did not know why the sale had not been disclosed as promptly as required by law.

As suggested in the previous chapter, you can always put a Republican on the defensive by emphasizing that he is "responding to criticism." Here, in a variation of that theme, Bush "defended himself"—a political observation that is given emphasis by placement at the beginning of the lead sentence. The actual *What* of the story—that the president gave a speech in which he took a tough line against corporate corruption—was given secondary treatment in the lead.

Later in the same "news" article the *Times* stated or, should we say, opined:

> It was unclear whether Mr. Bush's news conference would put the questions behind him, particularly because he offered less of an explanation today than he and his advisors have in the past for why he was eight months late disclosing his 1990 sale of Harkin stock on a document called a Form 4.

Perhaps the *Times* would have looked foolish publishing that opinion had they not omitted a critical fact about the president's Harkin stock sale: the fact that it *was* properly disclosed. The specific information the *Times* apparently chose to suppress was that several days before Bush sold his Harkin stock he properly disclosed the sale to the SEC on what is called a Form 144. By properly filing the Form 144 *before* he sold the stock, the late filing of the Form 4, due only after the sale, was insignificant. The Form 144 effectively put the public on notice that he was going to sell his shares.

It is not as though the *Times* reporter could have missed this fact. When asked at his press conference why he was late in filing a stock *sale* report (i.e., the Form 4), the president answered, "When I made the decision to sell, I filed a Form 144. I think you all have copies of the Form 144. It's an intention to sell. And I did sell."

A few minutes later, Bush was asked the same question, and he answered it with the same information, "You know, the important document was the 144, the intention to sell. That was the important document. I think you've got a copy of it. If you don't, I'll be glad to get you one. That showed the intention to sell. As to why the Form 4 was late, I still haven't figured that out completely."

Again, the Form 4 is the form you file with the SEC *after* you sell your shares. This was the one that was filed late and referred to in the *Times* article. The article entirely omitted any reference to the more important form, Form 144, which Bush filed properly and on time.

As the president said repeatedly, Form 144 was the important document. Because Form 144 was filed properly before he sold the stock, there could be no harm done to the public by the late filing of the Form 4 *after* he sold the stock, which would essentially add no new material information.

The omission, however, of the fact about the properly filed Form 144 allowed the *Times* to position the entire article around the Harkin "stock sale," rather than the efforts the president was making to strengthen the rules on the scandalous activities that were making news—activities that basically arose out of ethics lapses that took place during the tenure of the Clinton administration, also a fact not mentioned in the *Times* article.

Nevertheless, the tactical omission enabled the *Times* to undermine the president's efforts against corporate fraud with the following headline in the most influential newspaper in the country:

BUSH DEFENDS SALE OF STOCK AND VOWS TO ENHANCE S.E.C.

Bush had not defended his stock sale; he provided details about how it was publicly disclosed. As if this were not enough, the story was accompanied by an editorial "News Analysis," also appearing on the front page under the headline "OLD BUSINESS IN NEW LIGHT, '90 STOCK SALE BY BUSH SHADOWS ETHICS DRIVE."

This "News Analysis," which also omitted the key fact about the properly filed Form 144, actually suggested that the failure to file the meaningless Form 4 on time was analogous to the Clinton Whitewater scandal.

In a front-page article in the *Times* under the headline "QUESTIONS ON HALLIBURTON DEAL UNDER CHENEY" (August 1, 2002), the *Times* successfully created, by this same technique of factual omission, the impression that Vice President Cheney had an illegal financial motive for selling his Halliburton stock.

The article began with the following lead:

WASHINGTON, July 31—With Washington focused on corporate responsibility, Vice President Dick Cheney's tenure is under scrutiny from government investigators and his political opponents.

The article, however, fails to identify a single government agency or investigator who the reporters allege to be investigating "the deal" referred to in the headline. Nor do they quote or even allude to a single "political opponent" of the vice president.

It seems, rather, that the allegations of scrutiny of "the deal"—Halliburton's acquisition of a company who later disclosed, previously unbeknownst to Halliburton, the existence of asbestos liability—were raised entirely by the *Times* (i.e., presumably, the political opponents to whom the article's lead alluded).

Moreover, the paper cleverly employed the technique of factual omission. After the so-called scrutiny of Cheney's involvement in a deal that turned out financially disappointing, the paper stated:

Halliburton's stock has fallen sharply as the extent of the asbestos problem has become clear since Mr. Cheney left the company to join the Republican presidential ticket in August 2000.

Thus, the paper suggested that the fallen stock price was caused by the asbestos problem, a supposition for which there was neither factual support nor even a reasonable basis, especially given the precipitous decline in the stock market during that period. But the glaring omission comes with the next sentence of the article:

> Mr. Cheney sold nearly $40 million in Halliburton stock around the time he left the company at prices above $50 a share. The stock closed yesterday at $13.20.

The clear implication is that Cheney may have known about the asbestos problem—that it would cause the stock to drop—and he sold the stock with this in mind.

Omitted from the article, however, were the circumstances of the sale which had previously been reported—that is, the fact that Cheney sold the stock at great reluctance shortly after he became Bush's vice presidential nominee. He made the sales only after having been hounded by reporters on the issue, culminating in an editorial in the *Washington Post* that demanded that he divest his stock to eliminate any potential conflict of interest.

Had the reporters included this background, readers (including other journalists) could come to an informed opinion as to what might have been Cheney's real motives with respect to his sales of Halliburton stock.

To illustrate the power the *New York Times* has on setting the agenda at other news organizations, consider what happened on the very morning the *Times* ran this fabricated story on the scrutiny of Cheney's "Halliburton deal."

On the CBS morning newscast "The Early Show," CBS News reporter Jane Clayson had the opportunity to interview Paul O'Neill, the secretary of the treasury at that time. Rather than begin the interview with questions about the economy, Clayson took a different tack. Echoing the distortion the *Times* article sought to achieve, she opened her interview of Secretary O'Neill with the following question:

> Let me ask you first about this story on the front page of the *New York Times* this morning that suggests that Vice President Dick Cheney is under scrutiny by government investigators for what he did as CEO of Halliburton. How much trouble is the vice president in here?

In other words, how often does the vice president beat his wife? O'Neill was being asked a question containing the unwarranted premise that the vice president had done something wrong to begin with.

Secretary O'Neill replied, "I think none at all." Then Clayson followed up with the howler:

> The vice president sold, as you know, nearly $40 million worth of stock in Halliburton two years ago when it was about $50 a share. As you know, now it's about $13 a share. Did the vice president do what we're hearing so many CEO's have been doing recently?

It is not likely Clayson would have asked such a stupid question if the *Times* article had included the key information about the circumstances surrounding Cheney's stock sale. A television news organization can protect itself from such mishaps by encouraging its reporters to take a more skeptical approach when using the *Times* as a source of news or as a basis for topical discussion.

The technique of omitting key facts may also be employed to protect your allies. In an article entitled "WITH EYE TO 2002, DEMOCRATIC PARTY CHIEF REPROACHES BUSH" (August 11, 2002), Terry McAuliffe, the chairman of the Democratic National Committee, berated the qualifications of President Bush for cracking down on questionable corporate business practices:

> In his speech today, Mr. McAuliffe argued that Mr. Bush was not in a position to crack down on questionable corporate practices because of his own business background. He again raised questions about financial dealings at the Harkin Energy Corporation when Mr. Bush was on its board.

While allowing McAuliffe to use the *Times* as a platform to attack President Bush on the very corporate ethics issue previously fabricated by the *Times*, the article conveniently omitted important facts surrounding McAuliffe's own business practices, practices previously reported by the *Times* that arguably make him uniquely unqualified to credibly criticize anyone on corporate ethics.

In an article entitled "CLINTON'S TOP FUND-RAISER MADE LOTS FOR HIMSELF, TOO" (December 12, 1999), the *Times* reported the following colorful but non-accusatory story about Terry McAuliffe:

His political contacts are myriad and beneficial.

One, a union executive, helped arrange more than $50 million in union pension fund loans to Mr. McAuliffe's real estate ventures. One loan, for $6 million in 1992, helped Mr. McAuliffe clear up his entanglements with a failed savings and loan, court records show. This year the Labor Department sued the union executive, calling the $6 million loan imprudent.

Mr. McAuliffe's connections also led to his being retained in 1997 by Gary Winnick, a Los Angeles multibillionaire, who in turn provided the opportunity for Mr. McAuliffe to turn a $100,000 investment into an almost $20 million windfall, Mr. McAuliffe said. This year Mr. McAuliffe said he arranged a golf game for Mr. Winnick with Mr. Clinton, during which Mr. Winnick pledged $1 million for the Clinton presidential library, which is to be built in Little Rock, Ark.

Gary Winnick later made the front page of the *Times* by virtue of his being the famed chairman of Global Crossing, a Bermuda corporation whose bankruptcy devolved into one of the greatest financial debacles of the decade. It's now clear that McAuliffe sold $20 million worth of Global Crossing stock, shares that now lay worthless in the brokerage accounts and 401(k) plans of thousands of defrauded shareholders. If the questions of "What did he know? When did he know it?" were ever asked of McAuliffe by a *Times* news reporter, the answers were never reported.

As if to rub salt in the wound, the *Times* actually used the Global Crossing scandal to smear former President George H. W. Bush. The article that blew open the Global Crossing scandal appeared on the front page of the *Times* under the headline "S.E.C. SCRUTINIZING ANOTHER COMPANY" (February 9, 2002). The *Times* reported that that Global Crossing had come under investigation by both the SEC and the FBI for illegal accounting practices and other fraudulent conduct. With characteristic flair, the *Times* employed the guilt-by-association technique with the following:

> Among the shareholders of Global Crossing at one point was former President Bush, who took an $80,000 speaking fee in stock that at the peak was worth $14 million. It is not known when, or if, he sold his position.

If one didn't read this carefully, one might think that the current President Bush, not his father, received the speaking fee. Nevertheless, while connecting former President Bush with Global Crossing, whose bankruptcy was the largest ever by a telecommunications company and is now a poster child for securities fraud, the *Times* conveniently omitted Terry McAuliffe's close political ties to the failed company and the $20 million windfall it afforded him.

The McAuliffe-Global Crossing connection was omitted from several subsequent articles on the scandal, including two articles published in the weeks leading up to the 2002 midterm elections. No mention of McAuliffe was made in an article under the headline "MEMO INDICATES GLOBAL CROSSING CHIEF KNEW OF TROUBLES" (October 1, 2002) or in the following day's article under the headline "GLOBAL CROSSING HEAD OFFERS WORKERS $25 MILLION" (October 2, 2002), in which a lawmaker made the following comment:

> The committee's chairman, Billy Tauzin, Republican of Louisiana, said: "I wonder who has the billions for the investors who lost big in the telecommunications crisis?"

The *Times* failed to volunteer that $20 million of it went into the pockets of the chairman of the Democratic National Committee, Terry McAuliffe.

A few months later, in "ADDING TO CLAIMS AGAINST GLOBAL CROSSING" (January 30, 2003), the *Times* reported that executives at Global Crossing may have begun disguising the company's financial difficulties earlier than previously disclosed. According to new allegations, the deception may have begun prior to the time Terry McAuliffe dumped his shares, but the *Times* again omitted the McAuliffe connection.

It is ironic that a basic tenet of the law of securities fraud is that you cannot only be found guilty of fraud by making a false statement of fact but also by making truthful statements if at the same time you omit material facts which by their omission makes the truthful statements misleading. Fortunately for the *New York Times*, journalists are not held to the same high standards demanded by the law of corporate executives like Cheney. In the *Times'* newsroom, Clinton supporters, like McAuliffe, are not held to any such standards.

Another example of omitting a key fact to aid your friends occurred when President Bush was invited to speak at a spring commencement ceremony at Yale. The *Times* reported, under the headline "BUSH RETURNS TO YALE, BUT WELCOME IS NOT ALL WARM" (May 22, 2001):

NEW HAVEN, May 21—President Bush returned to Yale University today and warmly reached out to an alma mater he had spent much of his political life pushing away, but the embrace was not entirely mutual.

The *Times* described the "catcalls" and "boos" President Bush received from the students. It then reported that on the previous day Senator Hillary Rodham Clinton delivered to the graduating class the "Class Day" speech and observed:

> She did not draw the kind of negative reaction that Mr. Bush did on the decidedly liberal campus, where not only Al Gore but also Ralph Nader beat Mr. Bush in the 2000 election.

The *Times* declined to report, in this article or in any story during the weeks leading up to the Yale commencement, the controversy that had been fomenting at Yale over the invitation extended to Clinton. A band of conservative students had publicly protested the selection of Clinton and had considered various means of expressing their displeasure during her presentation.

However, in a syndicated column by Yale graduate William F. Buckley Jr., the conservative columnist urged the students of his alma mater to not only welcome Clinton as a speaker but also be civil to her. The fact that she did not receive catcalls and boos during her speech was no evidence of a lack of controversy over her presence, a tempest which had even been reported in the *Yale Daily News*, but rather a tribute to the civility of the conservative students, especially in comparison with the conduct of their liberal classmates on the day Bush addressed the students.

Let these examples of omission stand as a powerful illustration of the influence a newspaper can have on public opinion by simply omitting key facts—facts that would weaken its editorial support of liberal causes or its assault on conservative causes. And remember, slanting by omission is by its nature very difficult, if not impossible, for the average reader to detect.

DISTORTING KEY FACTS

The distortion of facts is riskier than bias by omission, but it seems that as long as the distortion supports the *Times*' political ends, the means are justified.

The worst case will be a correction published days or weeks later in a section of the paper few will read.

Recall our earlier reference to the crusade the *Times* waged against President Bush's approach to the war on terrorism with a relentless series of editorials and slanted news articles throughout 2002. The crusade included a front-page article that seized on opinion articles written by prominent Republicans offering their thoughts on the best way to proceed against Iraq ("TOP REPUBLICANS BREAK WITH BUSH ON IRAQ STRATEGY," August 16, 2002):

> WASHINGTON, Aug. 15—Leading Republicans from Congress, the State Department and past administrations have begun to break ranks with President Bush over his administration's high-profile planning for war with Iraq, saying the administration has neither adequately prepared for military action nor made the case that it is needed.
>
> These senior Republicans include former Secretary of State Henry A. Kissinger and Brent Scowcroft, the first President Bush's national security advisor.

To support its conclusion that Kissinger broke ranks with the president on his Iraq policy, the *Times* published abbreviated quotes from a Kissinger op-ed piece:

> In an opinion article published on Monday in The Washington Post, Mr. Kissinger made a long and complex argument about the international complications of any military campaign, writing that American policy "will be judged by how the aftermath of the military operation is handled politically," a statement that seems to play well with the State Department's strategy. "Military intervention should be attempted only if we are willing to sustain such an effort for however long it is needed," he added.

There was nothing in these quotes that even suggests a divergence between Kissinger's view and that of the administration on either the goal or the means of a preemptive move against Iraq. On the contrary, Kissinger, in his op-ed piece, called preemptive action "imperative," stating:

> The imminence of proliferation of weapons of mass destruction, the huge danger it involves, the rejection of a viable inspection system and the demon-

strated hostility of Hussein combine to produce an imperative for preemptive action.

Not only was preemptive action "imperative" in Kissinger's view, such action should be taken soon. "Waiting will only magnify possibilities for blackmail," he said. Nevertheless, none of these statements were quoted or even considered by the *Times* before it declared that Kissinger broke ranks with the president's policies on Iraq.

Brent Scowcroft did write an op-ed piece expressing his reservations about the U.S. taking on Iraq without international support, but Scowcroft also supported the president's objective of disarming Iraq. Nevertheless, Scowcroft, who hadn't seen the light of day since the first Bush administration, could hardly be considered a "top Republican." Moreover, without Kissinger, the mere views of Brent Scowcroft would hardly have justified a front-page article, which continued on page 9 under the headline "REPUBLICANS BREAK WITH BUSH ON IRAQ ATTACK."

While the *Times*' news division was printing its distortion of Kissinger's op-ed piece, the *Times*' editorial page editors seemed to betray a different reading of Kissinger's views. On the same day the *Times* declared on its front page that Kissinger broke ranks with Bush, a *Times* editorial entitled "WARNING SHOTS ON IRAQ" celebrated Scowcroft as a "cautious, deliberate man" and praised Scowcroft's criticism of the Bush administration's approach on Iraq. However, the editorial made no mention of Dr. Kissinger or his views on Iraq.

Could the *Times*' editors have actually read the Kissinger op-ed piece and said, "Oops," but found it too late to change the front page? Not likely. It seems that, contrary to the news editors, the *Times*' editorial writers did not view Kissinger's comments as inconsistent with the Bush administration's policies. Yet the next day, the paper repeated the distortion in the lead story on its front page (August 17, 2002), calling it a "growing chorus of concern from Republicans, which now includes former Secretary of State Henry A. Kissinger and Brent Scowcroft." Given the circumstances, it appears the news division hadn't read its own editorial page, or its distortion was quite deliberate.

Only after the *Times* was heavily criticized from many quarters, perhaps by Henry Kissinger himself, and over three weeks after they made the "mistake," did the news editors finally concede to print a clarification. In a half-hearted

"Editor's Note" printed on page 2 of the *Times* (September 4, 2002), underneath the table of contents, the *Times* stated:

> A front-page article on Aug. 16 and one on Aug. 17 reported on divisions among Republicans over President Bush's high-profile planning for a possible war with Iraq. The articles cited comments by former Secretary of State Henry A. Kissinger and by Brent Scowcroft, the first president Bush's national security advisor, among others.
>
> The Aug. 16 article described Mr. Kissinger's expressed concerns about the need for building an international coalition before waging war and his doubts about the Bush administration's plan to make "regime change" the center pole of its policy. But it should have made a clearer distinction between his views and those of Mr. Scowcroft and other Republicans with more categorical objections to a military attack. The second article listed Mr. Kissinger incorrectly among Republicans who were warning outright against a war.

The grudging "Editor's Note," in its final flourish, went on to mischaracterize both Bush's policy on Iraq and Mr. Kissinger's statement about it:

> Most centrally, Mr. Kissinger said that removing Mr. Hussein from power—Mr. Bush's justification for war—was not an appropriate goal. He said an attack on Iraq should be directed toward a more limited aim, eradicating weapons of mass destruction.

This last statement makes one truly wonder whether the *Times* had followed any of the president's speeches or actually read Kissinger's article. Eliminating Iraq's weapons of mass destruction—because of their potential use against the United States by either the madman himself, by a madman who might replace him, or by fanatics who the madman might supply for that purpose—has always been the foundation of President Bush's policy on Iraq.

Kissinger did not say that removing Hussein from power was not an appropriate goal. He said that a goal of regime change "should be *subordinated* in American declaratory policy to the need to eliminate weapons of mass destruction" (emphasis added). Once Saddam's weapons of mass destruction are destroyed, regime change, which was never an end in itself, becomes an insurance policy against recidivism.

Readers must be asking themselves: is the *Times* harboring such a blind, unmitigated hatred toward the Bush administration that its news editors would mindlessly attack positions coined by its own imagination? What could explain a news reporting policy that appears to support lying about the facts, owning up to those lies only reluctantly, and, in a feeble defense, compounding the lie with another?

An explanation might be found in remarks made by *Times* executive editor Joseph Lelyveld (Raines' predecessor and, after the latter's resignation, also his interim replacement) to an internal gathering of more than eighty *Times* editors at Tarrytown, New York, in September 2000:

> Within a week or so, we'll be announcing some refinements on our corrections policy, designed to make our contract with our readers more enforceable. We're going to start doing a better job of telling them how to get in touch with us. We're going to start tracking their complaints to make sure they get a timely response. And we're going to commit ourselves to go beyond corrections—to write full stories in all cases where the mistakes were so serious that the headlines and leads of the originals can no longer be said to have stood up.

It seems that the *Times* went to great lengths in its "Editor's Note" to satisfy itself that the headlines and leads about the Kissinger affair still "stood up." Had it not done so, then, under its own new "contract" with its readers, the *Times* would have had to write a full story to correct its mistake. Alternatively, perhaps Howell Raines simply scrapped his predecessor's commitment "to write full stories where the mistakes were so serious that the headlines and leads of the originals can no longer be said to have stood up." (Judging from Raines' handling of the Blair fiasco, this seems to be the better explanation.) Either way, it seems the *Times* editors could not find it in themselves to write a mea culpa involving a distorted attack on the Bush administration, especially during the days leading up to the 2002 midterm election.

Whether they eventually chose to publish an honest retraction or not, the distortion had its effect. The front-page article falsely declaring "TOP REPUBLICANS BREAK WITH BUSH ON IRAQ" caused a firestorm in the broadcast media during the latter half of August 2002, creating public doubts about the

Bush administration's policy on Iraq that immediately began to be reflected in opinion polls. The *Times* inflicted its damage, and when it was over, its disingenuous "Editor's Note" was published in a little-read section with no public apology made either to Bush or to Kissinger, the person whose views it distorted for its own editorial purposes.

Another kind of factual distortion takes the form of a creative interpretation of the law. When the law does not support the outcome you want, don't just report what the law says and let the reader decide; get an expert to say the law is unconstitutional or that it otherwise doesn't apply to the facts. In the absence of an expert, just provide your own interpretation. The easiest way to attack the law's credibility is simply to say, it's "unclear."

In a front-page lead article on the withdrawal of Senator Torricelli from his re-election bid just 36 days prior to the election, under the headline "CAMPAIGN IN PERIL, TORRICELLI LEAVES NEW JERSEY RACE" (October 31, 2002), the *Times* opined:

> New Jersey election law allows political parties to change candidates 51 days or more before the election, but the law is unclear about making a switch after that point.

In this "objective" news story, the *Times* cited no one to support its legal opinion that "the law is unclear about making a switch" after the 51-day deadline. In fact, the law is quite clear: a candidate may be replaced in the event of a "vacancy, howsoever caused, among candidates nominated at primaries, which vacancy shall occur not later than the 51st day before the general election." If a law that states you must be at least eighteen years old to purchase a cigarette, the law is clear that if you are younger than eighteen, you may not purchase a cigarette. The law does not need also state the reverse: that anyone under eighteen may not purchase a cigarette. It is sufficient to say that you must be at least eighteen. If every statute were required to state its rule in the negative, our law books would be needlessly redundant.

The New Jersey election statute could not have been more perspicuous (and clear): a party may replace a candidate nominated in a primary in the event of a vacancy only if the vacancy occurred 51 days or more before the election. If this did not implicitly mean that a party may not change candidates 50 days or less before the election, the statute would have no meaning whatsoever.

Resigning for the purposes of switching candidates 36 days before the election (15 days after the deadline) was too late. Knowing, however, that the New Jersey Supreme Court is packed with liberals who would be willing to apply the "Florida Rule" of statutory interpretation (i.e., statutes can be ignored to help Democrats get elected), the *Times* editors presciently opined, in an "objective" news story, its opinion that the law was "unclear."

Furthermore, the same day, in an editorial entitled "SENATOR TORRICELLI BOWS OUT" (October 1, 2002), the *Times* downplayed the legal obstacle facing the Democrats and actually encouraged the court to ignore the statute:

> The Democrats, led by Gov. James McGreevy, must move quickly to find a credible replacement. The courts must then expeditiously approve the ballot substitution, which in turn will clear the way for an energetic one-month campaign that, with Mr. Torricelli out of the picture, can now focus tightly on loftier issues than his seamy behavior.

It did not seem to matter whether it was the right thing for the courts to do, as long as they acted "expeditiously."

The following day, in one of two front-page news articles about the Torricelli matter, under the headline "DEMOCRATS SELECT EX-SENATOR TO RUN IN TORRICELLI SPOT" (October 2, 2002), the *Times* repeated the distortion but backed off its original legal interpretation:

> New Jersey election law allows parties to change candidates up to 51 days of the election, but it is unclear whether the courts will allow a candidate substitution after that date.

Apparently, after a day to think about it, the law became a little clearer to the *Times*. (Before, the law itself was unclear; the next day, it was unclear what the courts would say about the law.) However, the *Times* apparently remained confident that the New Jersey Supreme Court would follow in the footsteps of the Florida Supreme Court. With its strong editorial and its front-page legal analysis, the *Times* seemed to be sending a clear message to the New Jersey Supreme Court: an expeditious ruling favorable to the Democrats, regardless of its basis, would be hailed in the *New York Times* as a sensible means of promoting an "energetic" campaign.

This is precisely what happened. As reported the next day in the *Times* under the headline "NEW JERSEY SUPREME COURT ALLOWS SUBSTITUTE ON SENATE BALLOT" (October 3, 2002), the Supreme Court discarded the statute and invoked its "equitable powers in favor of a full and fair ballot choice for the voters of New Jersey." The next day, the *Times* published an editorial stating, "New Jersey's Supreme Court made the right call yesterday."

FALSIFYING KEY FACTS

Apparently, when a journalist has nothing to omit or distort, he will not hesitate to engage in the outright falsification of facts to please his boss and advance his paper's political agenda. Never has this been more forcefully and convincingly demonstrated than by the actions of disgraced *New York Times* reporter Jayson Blair. A full account of his widespread acts of factual falsification and plagiarism, needless to repeat here, was detailed in the *Times*' investigative report "TIMES REPORTER WHO RESIGNED LEAVES LONG TRAIL OF DECEPTION" (May 11, 2003), briefly discussed in Chapter One. One poignant example should suffice.

In the fall of 2002, Howell Raines sent Jayson Blair to Washington, D.C. to cover the Washington-area sniper shootings occurring at that time. Shortly after arriving in Washington, Blair wrote a front-page story, "U.S. SNIPER CASE SEEN AS A BARRIER TO A CONFESSION" (October 30, 2002) that virtually accused the U.S. attorney's office of botching the prosecution of sniper suspect John Muhammad. On the basis of several unnamed sources, Blair wrote:

> ROCKVILLE, Md., Oct. 29—State and federal investigators said today that John Muhammad had been talking to them for more than an hour on the day of his arrest in the sniper shootings, explaining the roots of his anger, when the United States attorney for Maryland told them to deliver him to Baltimore to face federal weapons charges and forcing them to end their interrogation. . . .
>
> "It did not look like the juvenile was going to talk," a local law enforcement official said. "But it looked like Muhammad was ready to share everything, and these guys were going to get a confession."

The article drew fire from the U.S. attorney's office and the FBI, both of which issued statements denying the central point of the article—that federal officials had cut short an interrogation by local law enforcement officials just as the suspect was about to confess. Concerns about the truth of the story were also raised with senior editors, before the article was published, by several veteran reporters in the *Times'* Washington bureau.

Six months later, in its investigative report of the Blair scandal, the *Times* admitted to Blair's falsification of facts and reflected upon its cause. When assigning Blair to the sniper story, Raines failed to tell Blair's supervising editors of the young reporter's history of shoddy work, saying he didn't want to "stigmatize" Blair. Jim Roberts, the *Times'* national editor, and Nick Fox, the editor who supervised much of Blair's coverage of the sniper story, told the *Times* that Blair's reporting would have raised far more serious concerns in their minds had they been aware of the reporter's history of inaccuracy.

"I can't imagine accepting unnamed sources from him as the basis of a story had we known what was going on," Fox said. "If somebody had said, 'Watch out for this guy,' I would have questioned everything that he did. I can't even imagine being comfortable with the story at all, if I had known that the metro editors flat out didn't trust him." Raines and Boyd, who knew more of Blair's history, also did not ask him to identify his sources.

Nevertheless, that front-page story in the *Times*, the bell cow of American journalism, set off a firestorm of criticism in the media over the handling of the case by federal prosecutors, causing a huge (and undeserved) embarrassment for Attorney General John Ashcroft and the justice department. On December 22, 2002, another article about the sniper case by Blair appeared on the front page. Citing unnamed law enforcement officials once again, Blair's article explained why "all the evidence" pointed to Muhammad's teenage accomplice, Lee Malvo, as the triggerman. And once again his reporting drew strong criticism, this time from a prosecutor who called a news conference to denounce it.

At his televised press conference (December 22, 2002), a visibly angry Virginia prosecutor Robert Horan vented his outrage at the *New York Times* in these terms:

> I am not going to get in the business of telling you pre-trial what the facts are, but I am going to tell you that whoever put that stuff out is putting out

information that is simply not true, and I want the media to know that, particularly the media that follows like lemmings behind the New York Times, and says whatever the New York Times said as if it were the gospel. They've been wrong before, and they are wrong on this one.

What was Raines' reaction? Blindly trusting his young protégé and turning a deaf ear to the impassioned complaints of a veteran prosecutor, Raines sent a note to Blair praising his "great shoe-leather reporting." After all, his rising star just made a fool out of John Ashcroft. Raines further rewarded Blair by turning over to him responsibility for *leading* the coverage of the sniper case, what the *Times* called "a plum assignment."

Even after the *Times* exposed the stories' factual flaws and Raines' complicity in their cause, Raines stubbornly rejected criticism of his handling of the matter saying, rather mechanically, "I'm confident we went through the proper journalistic steps." Proper journalistic steps? The *Times* prides itself on having the most experienced and able editors in world. Considering the circumstances, would not a competent editor have asked himself how a rookie reporter with a history of sloppy reporting could be dropped in the midst of an unfamiliar beat to cover a multi-faceted murder investigation and suddenly find himself bathing in a pool of five unnamed law enforcement sources, a scoop that eluded all the other D.C. area reporters covering the same story? Didn't this all sound too good to be true? Would Raines have responded differently had the story not been a potential embarrassment to the Bush administration but rather a setback to one of his favorite crusades?

Under normal circumstances, at times other than when the Blair scandal is casting a spotlight on the subject (down to the expense accounts of roving correspondents), the chances of a reporter getting caught falsifying a fact, a source, or a quote are slim. When the mistake is discovered, it can be corrected in a section of the paper that nobody reads.

In what was more likely a case of selective listening or erroneous note-taking by a *Times* reporter or editor, rather than an intentional fabrication, the following example is instructive. As part of a series of "straight" news articles attacking the Bush administration's policies on Iraq, a *Times* reporter wrote the following, which appeared under the headline "BRITISH AIDE SAYS TOPPLING HUSSEIN IS NOT A GOAL FOR LONDON" (August 23, 2002):

LONDON, Aug 22—Reinstating United Nations weapons inspectors—not the removal of Saddam Hussein—is the centerpiece of Britain's policy toward Iraq, Foreign Secretary Jack Straw said today.

The apparent, sudden change in British policy reported here was so striking one would think the *Times* editors would double check the accuracy of the report prior to its publication; but since the report provided another opportunity to undermine the case for a war against Iraq, why bother? The *Times* was soon forced to print the following retraction, buried in its "corrections" page (August 27, 2002):

The assessment that removing Saddam Hussein is "not an object of British foreign policy" was made by a BBC interviewer, not by Mr. Straw.

Recall, however, that only a year before Raines assumed control of the news division, his predecessor promised "to write full stories in all cases where the mistakes were so serious that the headlines and leads of the originals can no longer be said to have stood up." Having been deemed by the *Times* to be completely erroneous, the August 23 story would seem to be a perfect candidate for the publication of a "full story" correction.

Whether intentional or not, the error, and the political blinders which caused the *Times* editors to miss the error, was the basis of an entire article that succeeded in fabricating for millions of American readers the non-existent differences between the U.S. and Britain on the subject of Iraq. More important, according to a columnist for the *Washington Post*, the *Times* article created what the British embassy called a "bloody mess."

Had the *Times*' correction policy been completely discarded by the paper's new executive editor, or could the *Times* just not bring itself to correct a story that served so well in its crusade? Or both?

A more direct example of false facts appeared in an article entitled "IN TWIN SPEECHES, BUSH AND CHENEY VOW TO FIGHT FRAUD" (August 8, 2002), which began:

SAN FRANCISCO, Aug. 7—In a rare public appearance, Vice President Dick Cheney today defended the administration's stewardship of the faltering economy and vowed to punish corporate misconduct.

Recall that when Republicans espouse their views, the *Times* freely portray them as "defending" their position or record on the issue, as it did in the foregoing lead. The article continued:

> The vice president's speech, billed as a talk on the economy and national security, sounded at times like an address a chief executive might give to shareholders.

We have seen this useful technique before—using what a speech was "billed as" (e.g., a "policy" speech) to compare it to what, in the paper's opinion, it really was (e.g., a talk "laden with politics"). Here, the *Times* injected its opinion in the middle of a straight news story to disparage the vice president's policy speech on the economy and national security. Liking Cheney to a "CEO" addressing "shareholders," during the time when several prominent CEOs have been under investigation, could only serve to undermine the substance of what the vice president had come to say about the economy and national security.

But the reporter went beyond injecting her opinion in the article by not only responding to the vice president's statements on her own accord but also getting the facts wrong when doing so:

> On the economy, he said that it was now "clear from the data" that "the nation had slid into a full blown recession" by the time he and President Bush took office, "with the economy contracting throughout the first, second and third quarters of 2001." He credited the administration's tax cuts with helping the country to "climb out of the recession and to weather the terrible financial effects of Sept. 11," although the recession has not abated and the stock market today continued its decline.

Both parts of that final statement injected by the reporter—"although the recession has not abated and the stock market today continued its decline"—were so wrong that it had to be officially corrected a week later by the *Times* (August 15, 2002):

> An article on Aug. 8 about speeches by President Bush and Vice President Cheney defending the administration's stewardship of the economy referred

incorrectly to the 2001 recession and to the direction of the stock market on Aug. 7. Economists agree that the recession has ended, not continued. The Dow Jones Industrial average rose the day of the speeches, by 182 points; it did not decline.

Again, the correction appeared on the "corrections" page, a part of the paper that virtually no one reads.

EMPHASIZING THE INSIGNIFICANT

Sometimes a paper can attack the credibility of its opponents, not just by omitting, distorting, or fabricating a key fact but also by emphasizing an otherwise insignificant fact in the context of a story.

In August 2002, the Bush administration announced it would hold a forum on the economy at which the president, vice president, and at least seven members of the Bush cabinet would be joined by over 200 economists, government officials, small investors, teachers, workers, corporate executives, small-business leaders, and professors.

The well-oiled political wheels at the *Times* must have immediately begun to spin a variety of ideas on how to discredit the event. After the White House first announced who would be speaking at the event, the *Times* editors outdid themselves. Recall that the *Times* has lead a ten-year, multi-billion dollar crusade to convince the public that campaign contributions were the cause of government corruption. Since virtually every prominent business leader who would likely be asked to speak at the forum—or just about any conference like this—would have made a campaign contribution, what better way to discredit the forum than to suggest that some of its prominent participants were campaign donors? Since the nation's privacy laws don't protect information about one's use of money for political causes, the details of the participants' political contributions are a matter of public record, easily accessible using online databases.

Thus, in a *Times* article covering the announcement of the economic forum (August 8, 2002), the unimpeachable business reputations of Charles Schwab, CEO of the stock brokerage bearing his name, John Chambers, CEO of Cisco

Systems, and Glen Barten, CEO of Caterpillar, were impugned with a single headline:

BUSH'S FORUM ON ECONOMY IS TO FEATURE G.O.P. DONORS

In a rare moment of candor, the *Times* did confess in the article that John Chambers had donated over $250,000 to Democrats and that other speakers included Charles Vest of The Massachusetts Institute of Technology, who made political contributions to liberal Senator Edward Kennedy (D-Massachusettes) and speaker Tom Donohue, president of the U.S. Chamber of Commerce, a Republican who donated to the campaign of liberal Senator Robert Torricelli (D-New Jersey). Given those facts, how could the *Times*' copy editor have possibly come up with the headline "BUSH'S FORUM ON ECONOMY TO FEATURE G.O.P. DONORS"?

If the *Times* published a balanced headline, "BUSH'S FORUM ON ECONOMY TO FEATURE DEMOCRATIC AND G.O.P. DONORS," what could possibly have been the newsworthy point of the article? There hasn't been an event held by any president of United States in the past 100 years that didn't feature someone who has made a campaign donation to one or the other party.

The answer is that, other than the mere announcement of the event itself, there was no newsworthy point to the article. Its purpose was simply to ridicule the event. Of course, that could have been accomplished by an op-ed piece or *Times*' editorial, but that would not be nearly as effective as disguising the editors' ridicule in the form of an "objective" news story.

When the *Times* found some college professor willing to opine on the record that the event was "purely P.R.," the discrediting frenzy took on a life of its own. With a "straight" *New York Times* article in hand suggesting the event was purely a "public relations" event, other news organizations, in their usual lock-step, began dismissing the event as a non-substantive P.R. stunt to be attended by mere campaign donors. Of course, there was no shortage of Democrats who fed the necessary sound bites supporting the view that the *Times* had initiated.

The next day, the *Times* ran an editorial (August 12, 2002) expressing an opinion based on the "straight" news it read in its own newspaper:

Now, the question is whether tomorrow's forum, which is reportedly going to include Republican donors and exclude administration critics, will do anything to resolve the administration's failure to speak with one reassuring voice on the economy.

In truth, the forum, according to the original article itself, was going to include both Republican *and* Democratic donors; and, in regards to the accusation that the forum would "exclude administration critics," the invitation list hadn't even been completed. If, however, as the *Times* suggested, only GOP donors and administration supporters would be attending, wouldn't that have completely rectified what the *Times* deemed in the same sentence as "the administration's failure to speak with one reassuring voice on the economy"?

In any case, on the eve of the event, the Bush administration released a more complete list of those who confirmed they would attend the forum, a list that included a number of "administration critics."

The *Times* responded by writing a front-page story that repeated the accusation that the event was a mere "public relations" vehicle and assigning a motive to the Bush administration's release of the final list of participants: "to counter criticism"—criticism which, of course, was initiated by the *Times* itself.

The article entitled "BUSH'S FORUM ON ECONOMY: MORE THAN THE USUAL CROWD" (August 13, 2002) began:

> WACO, Tex., Aug. 12—The White House moved today to counter criticism that President Bush's economic forum here on Tuesday was a public relations vehicle by releasing a list of participants that included a sprinkling of prominent Democrats and some influential corporate leaders not usually associated with politics.

Recall from Chapter Three that when you want to emphasize something, put it at the beginning of the lead. Here, the reporter successfully emphasized "criticism" and "public relations vehicle" over the real story—the "list of participants." In addition, the use of the word "sprinkling" conveyed the *Times'* opinion that the participant list was not really diverse but was populated with a few partisans from the other side (avoiding the word "token" for racial reasons) for the sake of appearances and "to counter criticism."

As a final slap at the president, the *Times* suggested that the White House not only released the list of attendees to respond to criticism but also actually withheld the list until it was too late for reporters to be able to obtain quotes from attendees prior to the event:

> The White House did not release the list of invitees until midafternoon when most of those named on it were out of reach traveling to Waco.

The *Times* was obviously upset about being denied the pleasure of getting participants to speculate "on-the-record" in advance of the forum. The lesson here is: don't be shy about attacking your opponents for making your job of discrediting them more difficult.

This second article, of course, reiterated the campaign donations made by some of the better-known attendees. The article was also accompanied by a "News Analysis," the purpose of which was to place another cloud over the event; it bore the headline "FED DEBATE AND CORPORATE ACCOUNTING MAY OVERSHADOW BUSINESS CONFERENCE."

Beleaguered before it even began, the event finally opened and, not surprisingly, the next morning the *Times* continued its relentless attack on the forum and its participants in a third article. This mere "public relations" event was again heralded with front-page fanfare (August 14, 2002):

> WACO, Tex., Aug. 13—President Bush said today that he was optimistic about the long-term health of the beleaguered American economy as he heard from a selection of 240 carefully chosen guests who praised his policies at an economic forum created to showcase his concerns.

A high school journalism student could have written a more professional lead for this front-page story about a forum chaired by the president of the United States, but the lead was only a harbinger for the spin that was to follow. Further down on the front page, the reporter continued with an assault that contradicted itself:

> The president offered no new programs or ideas to repair the economy, although he did choose the literal center stage of the forum to announce that

he would not release $5.1 billion in emergency spending requested by Congress to fight terrorism, saying he wanted to move toward a balanced budget as soon as possible.

The *Times* reporters did not believe, apparently, that the announcement, a signal that the Bush administration was moving to crack down on government spending, was an idea to "repair" the economy. If they had any doubt, they should have read the lead of an article that appeared in the same issue of the *Times* under the headline "CITING ECONOMY, BUSH WON'T SPEND $5.1 BILLION APPROVED FOR SECURITY AND OTHER USES" (August 14, 2002):

WASHINGTON, Aug. 13—President Bush said today that he would not spend $5.1 billion approved by Congress last month for domestic security, the military and a variety of other initiatives, saying reduced spending would help stabilize the economy.

Moreover, the single biggest idea the Bush administration had been espousing to invigorate the economy—before, during, and after the forum—was to accelerate the implementation of the temporary tax cuts passed in 2001 and make them permanent. In fact, according to the article, speaker after speaker offered suggestions for invigorating the economy, and there was a general agreement among the participants to make permanent the temporary tax cuts passed in 2001. Nevertheless, being that this was not a "new" idea, it apparently seemed best, in the *Times*' view, to leave the reader with the impression that no ideas worth reporting had been proposed at the forum.

If the speeches of an admittedly diverse group, including, according to the *Times*, "executives, economists, students, union leaders, professors, owners of small businesses and a sprinkling of Democrats" from nearly forty states, echoed that of the president, including general agreement on making the tax cuts permanent, then perhaps the conclusions reached by the participants should be taken more seriously. (If anything, the *Times* could have at least acknowledged the Bush administration was "speaking with one reassuring voice" on the issue of tax cuts to aid the sluggish economy.)

Instead, the front-page article in the *Times* that day made a mockery of the event. The reporter even suggested that "talking points" were provided to participants by the administration without apparently bothering to ask the participants if they had actually received any.

In the same issue, the *Times'* lead editorial—one that actually appeared on its editorial page—began:

> President Bush's stage-managed economic forum in Texas yesterday was billed as a chance for average Americans to express their views on the economy.

Here, by the way, we see the familiar technique of declaring how an event was "billed" followed by an opinion of what the *Times* really thought of it, a technique usually reserved for "straight" news stories. About the only thing that was stage-managed was the calculated campaign by the *Times*, beginning weeks before the forum began and in the form of a series of "straight" news stories reinforced by the *Times'* editorial page, to discredit the forum as a "public relations" event.

Yet, the story didn't end there. We said earlier that slanting a story by omitting key facts is one of the most difficult means of bias to detect. It has been said, however, that "truth, like the sun, submits to be obscured; but, like the sun, only for a time." Sooner or later, the truth comes out.

Directly contradicting the *Times'* assertion that "the president offered no new programs or ideas to repair the economy," the *Times* reported, three months after the forum, the following, under the headline "TALK IN CAPITAL OF EASING TAXES ON DIVIDENDS" (November 20, 2002):

> This year, though, there has been a flurry of interest in the subject because of comments made by President Bush in Waco, Tex., in August after hearing Charles Schwab, founder of the discount brokerage firm, push for the change. "That makes a lot of sense," the president said.

It's important to understand why the reporting of any substantive ideas arising from Bush's economic forum would have to wait at least ninety days before the *Times* could report it. After the *Times* successfully billed the forum, before it started, as a mere "public relations" event, the *Times* would have lost credibility by reporting any substantive idea arising from the forum, at least during the period immediately following the event when the *Times'* characterization of the event was still fresh in the readers' minds.

To see how much the *New York Times*' bias against Bush blinded the paper to the newsworthiness of the president's economic forum, you only have to turn to the front page of the *Times*, which later declared, "BUSH BUDGET PLAN WOULD ELIMINATE TAX ON DIVIDENDS" (January 6, 2003). As you would expect, the article failed to mention that the idea for eliminating the double taxation of dividends surfaced prominently at the Bush economic forum.

It was not until the next day, in a *Times* editorial entitled "CHARLES SCHWAB TAX CUT" (January 7, 2003), that the *Times*' editorial page editors wiped the proverbial egg off Howell Raines' face when it acknowledged that "mega-broker Charles Schwab" made a pitch for the dividend-tax cut idea "at the economic summit meeting at Waco last summer." The *Times* editors even had something good to say about the "dividend-tax cut," suggesting that it would reverse some of the "perverse incentives" that the tax code provides to companies (though the *Times* found it "hard to believe that that's the problem this administration had in mind" in proposing the change). The editorial page editors failed to mention that in 1977 President Carter had formally proposed the elimination of the double-taxation of dividends, a move that the *New York Times* supported.

Contrast the *Times*' treatment of President Bush with its treatment of Howell Raines' favorite son, Bill Clinton. When President-elect Clinton announced a similar economic forum in 1992, the *Times* refrained from any fanfare disparaging the credibility of the participants, the intentions of the organizers, or the ideas it may have been expected to produce. The Clinton economic forum was to be held during the president-elect's interregnum, and the *New York Times* reported its official announcement as though it were serving as Clinton's personal public relations firm, conveying messages exactly as they were handed down from Clinton's political advisors.

The article entitled "CLINTON TO USE ECONOMIC CONFERENCE TO BUILD SUPPORT" (November 25, 1992) began as follows:

LITTLE ROCK, Ark., Nov. 24—Advisors to President-elect Bill Clinton said today that a meeting on the economy scheduled here next month, originally described as an important policy conference, would be a televised discussion aimed at building support for his economic proposals.

The conference will be held Dec. 14 and 15 in Little Rock, probably at the State House, Clinton aides announced at a news conference. It will resemble Mr. Clinton's highly successful town meetings during the campaign; he will preside over the conference and ask questions at the sessions, whose participants include what Clinton aides called "real Americans."

Thus, the *Times* not only reported the facts just as they had learned them but also injected its own opinion that the event would be "highly successful." Moreover, even though the "discussion" was to be "aimed at building support for [Clinton's] economic proposals," the *Times* didn't consider that aim to be a "public relations" activity. Rather than calling the forum what it was—a "P.R. event"—they conveyed to the public the precise positioning that Clinton's political advisors wanted the press to use:

They also called the conference a "retreat," not the graver sounding "summit" that Clinton advisors had originally described. And they said the meeting would break into sub-sessions on four or five economic topics but that the conference would not conclude with any report or policy pronouncements.

While the *Times* maligned President Bush's forum as "stage-managed," they simply reported the following about Bill Clinton's "important policy conference":

Clinton aides are said to be using extreme caution in choosing participants because some fear that the event could backfire, with attendees using the forum to make highly visible and embarrassing attacks on the incoming Administration.

While the guest list was still being put together today, people involved in the process, speaking on the condition of anonymity, said participants were certain to include John Scully, chairman of Apple Computer; John A. Young, president of Hewlett-Packard; Paul A. Allaire, chairman of Xerox; Roger W. Johnson, chairman of Western Digital; Robert M. Solow, a Nobel laureate in economics at the Massachusetts Institute of Technology; and John H. Bryan, chairman of Sara Lee.

The *Times* apparently wasn't sure whether these were donors to Clinton's presidential campaign, so they didn't report it.

Now, we have seen how a newspaper can bias a story in favor of its editorial views by omitting, distorting, and falsifying key facts and also by emphasizing the insignificant. In the next chapter, we explore how newspaper editors and reporters can slant a story with their own opinion or those of others who agree with them.

Distorting with Opinion

The feeble tremble before opinion, the foolish
defy it, the wise judge it, the skillful direct it.

*—Madame Jeanne-Marie Roland, who died
by guillotine, November 8, 1793*

istorting a story with opinion—by including someone else's speculation or directly injecting one's own view into a story—is another
basic technique of disguising a newspaper's political viewpoint in the
form of a straight news story.

Opinions may be employed for influencing public opinion in the following
basic ways:

1. Quoting someone who agrees with you

2. Directly injecting your opinion

3. Omitting the opposing opinion

4. Faking fairness and balance

We will review these one at a time.

QUOTE SOMEONE WHO AGREES WITH YOU

Readers of Bernard Goldberg's *Bias* may recall an excellent account of how reporters use the opinions of experts as a means of conveying the views of the reporter. A news organization may insert into a story its own editorial views by actively seeking and then reporting the opinion of someone who agrees with the editors. Coulter accurately called this the "Quote-Someone-Who-Agrees-With-Us" technique.

Good reporters develop a reservoir of people in politics, business, education, and other circles that they can count on for a quote reflecting their newspaper's opinion on any subject. The kind of people who a reporter can draw upon for just the right quote include (a) partisan politicians, (b) political pundits and other experts, and (c) common people.

Quoting Partisan Politicians

A reporter rarely has trouble finding a partisan politician ready to serve up a lively quote that is consistent with the *Times'* opinion about a person or subject. In "DEMOCRATS SEEK A STRONGER FOCUS, AND MONEY (May 26, 2003), the front page of the *Times* carried a colorful quote by the vice chairwoman of the Colorado Democratic party. She called President Bush "the village idiot from Texas."

Early in the 2000 presidential race, Al Gore gave a cue to the left-wing of his party that he was going to connect Bush with racism and bigotry ("IN DUELING SPEECHES, GORE AND BRADLEY TRY TO COURT PROMINENT DEMOCRATS," September 26, 1999):

> Both men saved their sharpest criticism for the Republican front-runner, Gov. George W. Bush of Texas, and his reluctance to expand his state's hate-crimes law.
>
> "I'm for affirmative action because it's still needed," Mr. Gore said. "And I am also for the passage of a hate-crimes law. When James Byrd is dragged from the back of a pickup truck because of his race. When Matthew Shepard is crucified on a split-rail fence by bigots, how can any political leader in either party say that there is not a difference between hate crimes and other crimes?"

The article read like a press release for the Democratic contenders, with Gore's statement going unchallenged by any Republican or independent free speech advocate—hate crime laws would increase penalties if the accused uttered any racial, bigoted, sexist, or similarly non-politically correct statement during the commission of a crime. Later during the campaign, Gore supporters ran a highly publicized advertisement that featured a graphic reminder of Byrd's murder in which his surviving daughter associated the crime with Bush's stance on hate crime laws. The Gore campaign disavowed any association with the ad.

As we will explore in the next chapter, when quoting a politician, a paper will try to manipulate the credibility of the speaker by the use of creative labeling. For example, a Republican might be labeled a "staunch conservative," "ultraconservative," or "far right-wing conservative." Liberal Republicans and most Democrats are labeled "moderates" and "centrists."

Quoting Experts

There is no shortage of "experts" on a variety of political specialties from economics to foreign policy who would be delighted to be quoted in the *New York Times*. Good reporters have a pool of political pundits working for liberal "think tanks," or just about anyone who has recently written a book on political affairs, at their disposal to support a story.

College professors are an easily accessible source of liberal opinion. The overwhelming majority of professors at universities like Harvard, Yale, and Georgetown are left-leaning, and their association with the Ivy League provides instant credibility for just about any editorial slant the *Times* chooses to place on a story. By contrast, left-wing economists and businessmen are very rare; but they do exist and, when one is willing to be quoted, the liberal news reporter should, as Polonius in *Hamlet* put it, "grapple them to thy soul with hoops of steel."

The *New York Times* is notorious for having its reporters gin up feature stories that further the paper's ongoing promotion of one liberal cause or another. These articles often find themselves on the front page, and more often than not, their sole basis consists of quotes from one or two experts who agree with the *Times*' view of the matter.

For example, the *Times* is well known for its vigorous and persistent opposition to the death penalty, publishing over twenty editorials on the subject during just the first three years of the new millennium. But despite the *Times'* spirited editorial diatribe against it, capital punishment continues to enjoy overwhelming public support. Accordingly, the *Times* turned to a more effective means of influencing public opinion on the subject.

In a front-page news article under the headline "DEATH ROW NUMBERS DECLINE AS CHALLENGES TO SYSTEM RISE" (January 11, 2003), the *Times* stated:

> For the first time in a generation, the number of inmates on death row has dropped. And the number of new death row inmates in 2001, the most recent year for which comprehensive data is available, was the lowest since 1973.
>
> Despite enduring and strong public support for the death penalty, these numbers suggest that those directly involved in the justice system have serious concerns about the way capital punishment is carried out.

With the premise of the story being there are "serious concerns" about and "challenges" to the death penalty, you would think there might be a quote or two in the article supporting that premise. But you won't find any. The article does quote a political science professor from Amherst College (not exactly your hotbed of conservative wisdom), who has written a book that appears to be aligned with the *Times'* view of the subject:

> "We're in a period of national reconsideration," said Austin D. Sarat, a professor of political science and law at Amherst College and the author of "When the State Kills: Capital Punishment and the American Condition" (Princeton University Press, 2001).
>
> "People are asking if the death penalty is compatible with values which in the American mainstream are taken seriously: equal protection, due process, protection of the innocent," Professor Sarat said.

While supporting the *Times'* unpopular editorial position against the death penalty, the professor's quote in no way supports the premise of the article. Also, it is hard to determine which "people" the professor is talking about— public opinion shows that over 70 percent of the public continue to support the death penalty.

More remarkably, the premise that there are serious concerns about how capital punishment is carried out is specifically refuted in the article's next two quotes, both of which attribute the decline in the number of people sentenced to death to refinements in the justice system.

> "The trend has more to do with practical problems than bedrock beliefs," said Richard C. Dieter, executive director of the Death Penalty Information Center, which opposes capital punishment.

Could not the drop in death row inmates be explained by the sharp reduction in violent crime since 1973? Might not that drop be explained, at least in part, by the increasing willingness by juries to apply the death sentence? The answer to both questions is yes, and the reporter quotes another expert—on page 13 where the article continues—to that effect:

> "The fact that the murder rate is down accounts for some of the softening," said Kent Scheidegger, the legal director of the Criminal Justice Legal Foundation. "To some extent it's paradoxical: the death penalty brings down the crime rate and that lessens the need to impose the death penalty."

So how does the *Times* justify the conclusion trumpeted in its front-page headline that the drop in the number of death sentences suggests serious concerns about the way capital punishment is carried out? It doesn't. That was simply the opinion that the *Times* chose to paste on its front page in the form of a "news" story.

As we shall see, an alternative strategy is to quote only those who agree with the views of the paper. The result is referred to as the "one-sided story." Because the bias of the one-sided story is a little too obvious, prudence will dictate that the reporter find someone who will support the other side of the issue. But even here the paper can manipulate the credibility of the opposition by finding an extremist to express the opposing point or by simply using the weakest argument or most lackluster quote that the opposing expert uttered during the interview. The credibility of experts may also be manipulated with labels—a subject which is explored at length in the next chapter.

Quoting Common People

There are literally millions of welfare mothers, union workers, soccer moms, and others who can easily be manipulated to provide the right quote for a slanted article. Brownie points seem to be awarded to those reporters who can wrestle a quote from a Republican that is critical of a Republican or conservative policy positions. For example, get a Bush supporter to say he disagrees with the president on an issue. If there's a hidden reason for the criticism (e.g., the supporter lost a son in a prior war), that fact can be omitted.

When President Bush announced his economic stimulus package in early 2003, the *Times* embarked on a crusade against it, distorting the effects of the proposed tax cuts by quoting common people in two articles appearing within just a few days of each other. In "PLAN GIVES MOST BENEFITS TO WEALTHY AND FAMILIES" (January 7, 2003), the *Times* rolled out some common people to attack it:

> For Robert and Bee Moorhead of Austin, Tex., who together earn about $88,000, the Bush plan is not impressive.

A few days later, an editorial critical of this classic *Times* distortion was published in the *Washington Times*. Entitled "MEET THE MOORHEADS" (January 10, 2003), the *Washington Times* reported what the *New York Times* left out of its article:

> As it happens, the *Times'* poster family would make a killing under the Bush plan. Effective immediately. No, sooner than that. Effective Jan. 1. No fewer than four separate tax cuts would shave more than 30 percent off the Moorheads' federal income-tax bill. Assuming the Moorheads take the standard deduction (in terms of absolute tax relief, the calculations make little difference if they itemize their deductions), the Editorial Page of *The Washington Times* has prepared 1040s for the Moorheads under current law and under the Bush plan. Their federal income taxes would plunge nearly $3,000, falling from about $9,600 to about $6,600.

A few days later, in "JUDGING THE TAX PLAN: FOUR FAMILIES SHRUG" (January 13, 2003), the *New York Times* reached a conclusion completely at odds with its own research. Here is the conclusion, as reported in the lead sentence of the article:

> WASHINGTON, Jan. 12—How has a new round of proposed federal tax cuts stirred the emotions and economic aspirations of American families? The answer from four of them seems to be: not very much.

The actual research was reported in the body of the article. Accountants at Deloitte & Touche calculated that the Bush tax cuts would annually save the four families featured in the article at least the following amounts: $4,500, $2,300, $100, and $1,000, respectively. The woman who would only gain $100 from Bush's proposal, it turned out, does not pay *any* federal income taxes; in fact, she is eligible for the earned income tax credit, which yields her about $2,300 per year in payments from the federal government. As to the others, the article does not say what percentage these tax reductions represent to their total tax bill, and the article says nothing of the potential income increases or improved job security the families might experience as a result of a stimulated economy.

When the *Times* used its news division to campaign against the use of military force to depose Saddam Hussein, it sent one reporter into Republican territory to find some Bush supporters who agree with the *Times*. The article was run under the headline "BACKING BUSH ALL THE WAY, UP TO BUT NOT INTO IRAQ" (August 3, 2002) and featured fresh quotes from ordinary Americans—a jewelry store manager, a Vietnam veteran, a shoe store manager, and a high school teacher, all of whom backed Bush, but not his policy on Iraq.

As common people may be employed to oppose Republican policies, they may also be employed to defend Democrats in trouble, as when President Clinton was facing impeachment proceedings. In a front-page "news" article run under the headline "AN AMERICAN PLACE: TWO YEARS LATER; BELLWETHER'S RANK AND FILE STRONGLY SUPPORT CLINTON" (September 30, 1998), the *Times* visited Stark County, Ohio:

> This is a political bellwether, a place that votes as America does for President, that swung to the Republican Presidents during the 1980's and to

Mr. Clinton in the 1990's, and from extensive interviewing here it is clear that people still strongly support the President. Even right after the Starr report was issued, when the sentiment against Mr. Clinton was most heated, calls to the newspaper's telephone response line favored the President's remaining in office; that first weekend, 56 percent of the 674 callers opposed impeachment.

Fifty-six percent is hardly a large percentage in this context. If 44 percent of a given population actually supported the constitutional impeachment of a United States president, what objective news organization could possibly conclude that these people "strongly support" the president?

> It is the ordinary people of Stark County, not the political elite, who are behind the groundswell for the President.

Groundswell for Clinton? Forty-four percent of them wanted him impeached! And what scientific basis did the *Times* use to support that conclusion?

> Although there has been no scientific polling done in Stark recently (it is too expensive for the local paper to undertake), from six dozen interviews conducted here at supermarkets, factories, a bar, a book shop and a hair salon, as well as with community leaders like Representative Ralph Regula, the Republican Congressman here, and Jim Repace, president of the union at the Hoover vacuum cleaner factory, it appears that Mr. Clinton's support is still strong.

The *Times* had no trouble finding the common people it needed to support its blatantly political opposition to the impeachment of Clinton. The article concluded with a quote from a steelworker who said that, for the first time in years, "I'm just voting straight Democrat."

Sometimes the opportunity to bash a Republican by the use of like-minded common folks just falls right into the reporter's lap. For example, in an article about Kevin F. Gill, the man in charge of school lunches in New York public schools, under the headline "FOOD CHIEF DEFENDS THE $2.18 LUNCH" (September 20, 2000), the *Times* quoted Mr. Gill as follows:

"It's very easy to take a free kick against school lunch," Gill said Monday. "It's just about the easiest kick you can make. Except maybe George Bush."

If the last two words of the quote were "Bill Clinton," it would have been easy to boot them out of the story.

In an article under the headline "2 LONG RUNNING INTERNET MAGAZINES SHUT DOWN" (June 11, 2001), the *New York Times* actually drew on an anonymous comment from an Internet "chat room" for what it termed the "best explanation" of the Internet "dot-com" failures:

This has got to be some type of conservative plot out to restrict free-thinking attitudes.

Thus, when an opportunity presents itself to publish a cheap shot by a common man, even an anonymous quote from a "respected" source, such as an Internet chat room, is fair game.

DIRECTLY INJECT YOUR OWN OPINION

Politicians, experts, and common people are not the only sources of opinion a reporter can drop into a story to slant the news. There is a fourth source of expert opinion: the reporter himself, where the reporter directly injects his own opinion, or that of his editors, into the story.

A reporter can cleanly inject his own opinion into a news story—in a way that is virtually unnoticeable—by simply calling upon fictional people to present their views. Examples include:

• Experts feel . . .

• Critics believe . . .

• It is widely thought . . .

• Observers say . . .

• European leaders feel . . .

- Americans believe . . .

- History suggests . . .

- Most economists believe . . .

Using fictitious persons to advance an editorial opinion is so common that not only would it be impractical to list all the recent examples here, it would be unnecessary, as you merely need to pick up a copy of today's *New York Times* to find this technique employed by one reporter or another. The practice is so frequently employed that, occasionally, you find the technique used not only multiple times in the same story, but more than once in the same paragraph.

In an article under the headline "BUSH WANTS TAX CUT SOONER TO AID ECONOMY THIS YEAR" (February 5, 2001), the *Times* demonstrated how far it is willing to go to oppose tax cuts proposed by the Bush administration. The *Times* had just published a flurry of editorials opposing Bush's tax cut plans: "INTERPRETING MR. GREENSPAN" (January 25, 2001), "MEDICINE FOR THE ECONOMY" (February 1, 2001), and "ESTATE TAX FOLLY" (February 3, 2001).

However, as the *Times* was well aware, a more effective way to influence the public to oppose the Bush tax cuts would be to make the editorial case against it in the form of a straight news article. Rather than suggest that tax relief would not improve the economy, the *Times* believed that it would simply come too late to help the economy. So, the *Times* printed the following unsupported statement:

> Many economists doubt that the tax relief can be enacted quickly enough
> to make much difference in the economy this year.

Needless to say, none of the "many economists" were quoted in the article. Considering, for a moment, the substance of this line of thought, what difference would it make if tax relief couldn't have an effect before the end of the year? If the tax relief could improve the economy by early the following year, would not "many economists" support it? And why would an economist be considered an expert on the length of time it would take Congress to enact the legislation?

As to the timing of the legislation, the article referred to another anonymous group, "Republican leaders":

Republican leaders in Congress say they probably cannot send a tax bill to Mr. Bush this summer, suggesting that any changes in withholdings would take effect in late summer or early fall.

We know today that Congress passed the tax relief bill on May 11, 2001, over a month *before* the start of summer. Either the Republican leaders were wrong or the *Times* was wrong, but we won't know because the *Times* didn't quote any of these "Republican leaders" to support the statement attributed to them in the article.

Rounding out the *Times'* thesis that tax relief was unneeded, the article employed the classic "history suggests" trick to inject the paper's opinion and concluded:

> History suggests that the economy is likely to be recovering by then, especially since the Federal Reserve is already cutting interest rates and is considered likely to continue doing so in coming months.

Since the economy will recover before tax relief would be effective, it shouldn't be enacted to begin with, according to the *New York Times*. Of course, we know the tax relief was enacted, the recession soon ended, but the economy remained sluggish for some time, suggesting that the administration's desire to accelerate the original timetable of the tax relief was probably the correct course of action.

The lesson is not that the *Times'* judgment on economic policy is questionable but that, without having to quote any experts, a newspaper can inject an entire argument against a proposal in what readers would otherwise be led to believe is an objective news story.

Sometimes, the *Times* doesn't even need to conjure up a fictional character—like "many economists" or "history suggests"—to inject an opinion into a story. Occasionally, the opinion is simply inserted without guise of any kind. In an article under the headline "G.O.P. AIDES CONSIDERING CAPITAL-GAINS TAX RATE CUT" (April 21, 2001), a policy which the *Times* has obstinately opposed, the paper included its view of a capital gains tax cut:

> A capital-gains tax cut would mostly benefit the well-to-do and would offer relatively little directly to typical taxpayers.

No expert is quoted to support that view. Advancing the perception that cutting the capital gains tax would only help the wealthy is a primary political objective of the *Times*. That objective would not be served by bringing to the reader's attention the 50 million Americans who own stocks and bonds by virtue of their 401k accounts, mutual funds, and IRAs. Nevertheless, either the *Times* couldn't find an "expert" or fictional person (e.g., "economists agree . . .") to state the opinion, or the *Times*' own parochial *opinion* of the capital gains tax is so ingrained that it has been transformed in its editors' minds into an objective *fact*.

OMIT THE OPPOSING OPINION

Otherwise known as writing the "one-sided" story, omitting the opposing opinion can become a most powerful means of bias. A paper may report a story by merely quoting people whose opinion agrees with its editors and completely ignoring the other side. The best examples of this technique appear in articles about a liberal issue the *Times* editors are especially eager to champion.

An article under the headline "PANEL CALLS FOR HIGHER MILEAGE STANDARDS" (July 13, 2001)—the "panel" might well have been the editorial staff of the *New York Times*—reported that a subcommittee of the House of Representatives voted to require carmakers to raise the fuel economy of sport-utility vehicles and minivans. The article quoted a spokesman for the Sierra Club, a liberal environmental organization, but no one from the automobile industry, which opposed the measure, was mentioned.

The headline "STATE'S POOREST FACING LOSS OF U.S. AID" (February 10, 2001) should make any decent person shudder, but you have to read halfway through the article to learn about the "Safety Net" in place that betrays the alarmist headline. Of course, the article quotes and paraphrases a "poor people's advocacy group" and a "liberal-leaning group" but no one who might be said to favor welfare reform. Why bother?

A lead front-page article—referred to previously, "BUSH SLASHING AID FOR E.P.A. CLEANUP AT TOXIC SITES" (July 1, 2002), the facts of which we said actually supported a headline such as "E.P.A.: TOXIC CLEANUP FUNDING INCREASE STILL NOT ENOUGH"—quoted spokesmen from two environmental groups, the Edison Wetlands Association and the League of Conservation

Voters. No one from the EPA was quoted, nor anyone else who might have supported the Bush administration's management of the cleanup of toxic waste sites.

In "DRUG COMPANIES INCREASE SPENDING ON EFFORTS TO LOBBY CONGRESS AND GOVERNMENTS" (June 1, 2003), the *Times* wrote about the industry's lobbying plans for the coming year by disclosing portions of what it identified as "confidential budget documents" from the leading drug industry trade association. While printing numerous excerpts from the internal documents, the *Times* quoted no one from the trade association in the article. Steve Brill, a media critic writing at media website Poynter.org (June 2, 2003), observed:

> What's missing should be clear to anyone who's ever taken a high school journalism class—no effort to get the lobby group itself to comment. . . [I]f the explanation is that someone at the *Times* thinks quoting from the internal memos is allowing the group to speak for itself, that is not only absurd but also dangerous in the sense that nowhere in the story are we even told that [the reporter] confirmed with the group that the internal documents are real—i.e., that they aren't fake or aren't superceded by later drafts.

FAKING FAIRNESS AND BALANCE

The problem with the one-sided story technique is that it is the one means of bias that is most readily understood as bias by the average reader. Being that it is the prototypical form of bias, the *Times* uses the technique sparingly. There is, however, a clever alternative: the one-sided story that fakes a balance.

Faking the balance—reporting only one side while making it appear you are reporting both—was employed to perfection by the *Times* in a lead story on the front page under the headline "PARTIES JOUSTING OVER WRONGDOING BY U.S. BUSINESSES" (July 8, 2002). The hard news was a report that President Bush was planning to announce, during a trip to New York City, the administration's response to the corporate accounting scandals that had plagued the stock markets earlier in the year. The *Times* didn't appear to have any further information on what the president was going to say, and without that information, there wasn't much of a story, especially not one warranting front-page coverage.

Yet, remember, the *Times* is not about reporting the news as much as it is about influencing public opinion. Given that the president was going to give a speech the next day, in the *Times'* own backyard, the paper was not shy about taking the initiative to advance their opposition to Bush. The result was the following lead that appeared on the front page of the *Times* on the day of Bush's speech:

> WASHINGTON, July 7—The two political parties opened a critical week of jousting today over how to respond to corporate wrongdoing with Democrats seeking to exploit what they see as President Bush's vulnerability on the issue and business executives pressing for action to restore confidence in the financial markets.

Thus, when the president's entourage arrived in New York that morning for the speech, they found that, before Bush uttered a single word, the front page of the *Times* had already transformed what was to be a policy speech by the president of the United States into what the newspaper now defined as a mere thrust in a "political joust."

More important, in a lead that begins "two political parties," note how only the position of the Democratic party is mentioned. It was important to get across the notion that the Democrats see the corporate scandal as "President Bush's vulnerability."

It was equally important that the *Times* bury—actually omit—what the Republicans are charging: that the accounting scandals, particularly the earnings announcements upon which they were based, all took place during the eight-year watch of the Clinton administration, a point not mentioned at all in the article. That the revelations, investigations, prosecutions, and plans for reform were all occurring during the Bush administration was something that must be suppressed at all costs.

But, like the tango, it takes two to joust. Where is the other side of the story? To avoid reporting the Republican side of the joust, the *Times* came up with, as an apparent counterpoint to the Democrats' attack, "business executives pressing for action." Thus, the jousting, a game usually played by two opponents, was spun to be (a) Democrats exploiting Bush's vulnerability, on the one side, and (b) business executives pressing Bush for action, on the other.

As for the news, it finally arrived in the next paragraph but was prefaced brilliantly by a gratuitous slam at Bush using two of our old friends, the anonymous "on the defensive" and "criticism":

> After being put on the defensive by questions about his role in a stock sale a dozen years ago and criticism of his administration as having failed to act aggressively enough against fraud and mismanagement, Mr. Bush will set out his latest plan in a speech in New York on Tuesday.

Thus, before the *Times* revealed the news, it first highlighted, without any source or attribution, (1) the president's alleged vulnerability on the issue, (2) his purported roll in a stock sale a dozen years ago, and (3) criticism of his administration for failing to act.

Using the terminology of lead writing, the *Who* is Mr. Bush, the *Where* is New York, the *When* is Tuesday, and the *What* is the president's proposals. None of these *W*s were included in the lead, but when they finally got around to reporting the news, the treatment was classic: by calling the *What* Bush's "latest" plan, the *Times* falsely alluded to a previous string of failed plans.

If this were a report on a Clinton speech, the *Times* would no doubt have written the lead in the following way:

> WASHINGTON, July XX — In the wake of the recent accounting scandals on Wall Street that have devastated investor confidence, President Clinton will fly to New York on Tuesday to detail reforms aimed at restoring confidence to the financial markets.

To have written such a lead for President Bush would have been unthinkable. Reporting only one side while making it appear you are reporting both sides is very difficult to pull off, but this example should demonstrate the lengths to which the *Times* is willing to use its front page to crusade against the policies and initiatives of the Bush administration.

We have explored how both facts and opinion may be omitted, distorted, and falsified to slant a seemingly objective news story to reflect the editorial views of a newspaper. In the next chapter, we will explore how a story may be slanted by the use of "labels"—really just another means of injecting editorial opinion into what the paper purports to be an objective news article.

SEVEN

Distorting with Labels

It will be my earnest aim that The New-York Times
give the news, all the news, in concise and attractive form,
in language that is parliamentary in good society.

—*Adolph S. Ochs, publisher of the* New York Times, *1896-1935*

L abels are the subject of a carefully documented book by Ann Coulter, who applies a more graphic term to the technique: *Slander.* Coulter makes the case that the liberal media acts like a classic propagandist, using name-calling to advance their political agenda. "Progress cannot be made on serious issues," she says, "because one side is making arguments and the other side is throwing eggs."

In *Slander*, she supports her case by citing a long list of editorials, op-ed pieces, and television commentary that persistently demonize Republicans and conservatives by blatant name-calling. Just to cite a few examples, the editors of the *New York Times* continually turn their back on their founder's aim of using "language that is parliamentary in good society":

- "CLUELESS ON GLOBAL WARMING" (July 19, 2001), an editorial in which the *Times* takes issue with Bush's opposition to the Kyoto treaty without accounting for the president's reasons for his opposition.

- "HALF A COMMANDER-IN-CHIEF" (November 5, 2001), a *Times* editorial accusing President Bush of ignoring economic policy.

- "MR. NADER'S ELECTORIAL MISCHIEF" (October 26, 2000), in which the *Times* opined that Ralph Nader's presidential election campaign was a "disservice to the electorate" and dubbed Nader's actions "willful prankishness."

- "KEN STARR'S MEDDLING" (February 2, 1999), wherein the *Times* calls the special prosecutor a "narcissistic legal crank" who has "an obsessive personality," excoriates him with charges of "legal mischief," "meddling," "customary blundering," and says he is in need of a "slap" by the U.S. Senate.

In addition, the *Times* has allowed its op-ed pages to be graced with even finer language that is less than "parliamentary in good society":

- "BEHIND THE SMILE" by Bob Herbert (November 11, 2002), in which the *Times* columnist calls the Republican party "slick," "sly," "slippery," "wily," "cunning," "insidious," and "dangerous."

- "AMERICA'S MOST WANTING" by Bill Keller (November 2, 2002), in which the United States Congress is called "a collection of the spineless led by the cynical, constantly lap-dancing for special-interest cash."

- "THE PITT PRINCIPLE" by Paul Krugman (November 1, 2002), in which the *Times* columnist declared that Attorney General John Ashcroft, a former U.S. Senator and attorney general for the state of Missouri, "doesn't have much respect for the law or for the Constitution—particularly silly stuff about due process, separation of church and state, and all that."

- "RUMMY RUNS RAMPANT" by Maureen Dowd (October 30, 2002), portraying the war-time secretary of defense, Donald Rumsfeld, as being a drunkenly out of control "empire builder."

- "DEAD PARROT SOCIETY" by Paul Krugman (October 25, 2002), accusing the president of the United States of being "slippery and evasive" and of running an administration that "lies a lot."

- "Springtime for Hitler" by Paul Krugman (October 18, 2002), suggesting the strategy used to sell President Bush's tax cut plan was not unlike Hitler's strategy of repeating the lie often enough.

- "All the President's Enrons" by Frank Rich (July 6, 2002), accusing the Bush administration, with overtones of Nixon's wrongdoings, of doing little to bring Enron executives, Andersen accountants, and other corporate wrong-doers to justice.

- "High and Low" by Maureen Dowd (December 3, 2000), in which the Pulitzer Prize-winning columnist likens the U.S. Supreme Court to mafia hit men working for the Bush family: "For the Kennebunkport Corleones, the Supreme Court deliberation serves the same function as the dazzling cross-cut scene in 'The Godfather,' when Michael attends his godchild's christening while his capos fan out to ice his rivals."

- "Mistrust in the Trust" (November 15, 2000) and "What He's Thinking" (November 19, 2000) both by Maureen Dowd, in which the columnist twice, within the course of a week, suggested that George W. Bush "was already think-ing about how he could repay" then-Florida Secretary of State Katherine Harris with a quid pro quo, such as a "cushy job as an ambassador," for "how she brazenly tried to grab the election and declare the winner."

- "May the Best Man Lose" (November 18, 2000), in which columnist Frank Rich called Katherine Harris "the Sunshine State Evita."

Coulter's indictment of the *Times'* op-ed page editors as disgraceful name-callers is irrefutable, but the question remains whether the *Times'* publisher is a propagandist. "The essence of propaganda," wrote Joseph Goebbels, Hitler's chief propagandist, "is not in variety, rather the forcefulness and persistence with which one selects ideas from the larger pool and hammers them into the masses using the most varied methods."

Whether the *Times* owes its methodology to Joseph Goebbels' playbook would seem to depend on how "varied" and "persistent" its methods are.

Certainly, the *Times* has been persistent, but does it limit the forceful expression of its views and its abusive name-calling to its editorial and op-ed pages? Or has it used more "varied" methods, such as using purportedly objective front-page articles and headlines to persistently hammer its views and invectives into the minds of the masses? It would seem, from what we have documented thus far, the answer is obvious.

The *Times* is both open about and adept at "throwing eggs" at its opponents from its editorials and op-ed pages. Its reporters are adept at, but not open about, doing the same from its straight news stories. While writers of op-ed pieces are given an open season to assail Republicans and conservatives with abusive language, reporters who seek to pass off editorial opinion in the form of objective news stories must be more subtle. To preserve the credibility that editorial opinion gains from being wrapped inside objective news, such opinion must be cleverly disguised.

Editors and reporters skilled in the art of propaganda, however, have no difficulty camouflaging their eggs in straight news stories. The means of lacing objective news with propaganda should be familiar: (1) quote the name-callers, or (2) draw upon the vocabulary established by them.

QUOTE THE NAME-CALLERS

A newspaper can effectively disparage those who oppose its political views by lacing its news stories with eggs thrown by others. This is just a variation of the Quote-Someone-Who-Agrees-With-Us technique.

Democrats and liberals often accuse Republicans and conservatives of being "racist," "sexist," "bigoted," "homophobic," or "anti-Semitic." When they use words like "obscene" to describe Republican economic policies, Democrats are called "strident." When Republicans accuse Democrats of being "big-spenders" and "tax-increasers," they are called "mean-spirited."

When the left does a particularly good job of smearing a Republican, the *Times* is sure to write a story to amplify and legitimize the slander in the "newspaper of record." For example, after Al Gore's 2000 election defeat, his campaign press secretary called then Florida Secretary of State Katherine Harris a "hack" and "Commissar Harris." Then, others on the left piled on with even worse epithets.

Not surprisingly, the *Times'* op-ed columnists joined the act, calling her the "Sunshine State Evita" and suggesting that Harris' decisions were based on the prospect of a "cushy job" in a future Bush administration. Finally, the *Times* ran a summary of this travesty in an article entitled "A HUMAN LIGHTNING ROD IN A VOTE COUNTING STORM" (November 20, 2000). The article opened:

> They just can't stop talking about her. Her integrity, her ignorance. Her lashes, her lipstick.
>
> She, of course, is Katherine Harris—Florida's secretary of state, co-chair-woman of Gov. George W. Bush's campaign here and scion of a citrus aristocracy who eight years ago was playing a Vanna White-like character in a Sarasota nightclub act.

The *Times* article then proceeded to provide a forum for the free-wheeling name-calling from the left, in case you hadn't heard it elsewhere:

> Alan M. Dershowitz, the liberal Harvard law professor who was among the legions of lawyers who arrived here last week, has called Ms. Harris "a crook." A Gore campaign aide, Paul Begala, likened her to Cruella De Vil, the lithe and mean villain of "101 Dalmatians" fame. (He apologized a few days later, though it stuck in the national discourse.) The Washington Post yesterday devoted an entire, entirely snarky piece to her makeup. Those were surely falsies, the article concluded of her eyelashes—"cartoon lashes," the Post article declared.

As we explored in the previous chapter, to cast aspersions against Republicans and conservatives, a reporter doesn't even have to quote anyone. The concept of the "undisclosed source" gained instant credibility during the Watergate era with the infamous Deep Throat, the secret informant of two young *Washington Post* reporters who were out to take down President Nixon. Today, undisclosed sources usually take the form of "Bush administration advisors," "senior administration officials," or "sources close to the president." But because the Bush administration has carefully controlled its communications with the press corps, expressions like "critics suggest," "experts feel," and "it is widely thought" have become increasingly common.

The beauty of these anonymous allusions is (1) the reputation of the *Times* is being used to lend credibility to the attack and (2) no one can check the source out for themselves. So common is the use of anonymous references in the *Times* to ridicule Republicans that it would be impossible to list a fair sampling of them here. Suffice it for us to print just one story in its entirety in which the *Times* flouts all notions of journalistic propriety.

In an article entitled "OUT OF WASHINGTON" (August 12, 2001), the *Times* repeatedly slandered President Bush with anonymous references. Here is the text of the entire article:

> President Bush began a 31-day vacation, which only added to the image among some critics that "W" is a loafer. Not so, the president protested from his 1,600-acre ranch in Crawford, Texas. To underscore that actual work is going on, the break has been dubbed "Home to the Heartland," Mr. Bush has made field trips—like one to hammer a few nails for Habitat for Humanity—and his aides have created a new cardboard seal, hung on the blue curtain at the press center in Crawford, proclaiming a "Western White House." Critics, of course, never cease, with some suggesting that Mr. Bush speeded up his decision to allow federal funding for limited stem-cell research in part to divert the public's attention from his lengthy summer break.

According to the most recent edition of *The New York Times Manual of Style and Usage* (Three Rivers Press, 1999), "Anonymity should not become a cloak for attacks on people, institutions or policies." A more honest, updated version might add, "unless the attacks are against President Bush, his administration, and those who support his policies."

DRAW UPON ESTABLISHED VOCABULARY

Calling the president of the United States a "loafer" in a news story is one way to ridicule him, but there is a subtler way to affect public opinion about a person—by using the right label. Labels can be used to manipulate the credibility of the people about whom and the ideas about which you are reporting. When you apply a label to someone, or to an idea, you link that person or idea to a positive or negative symbol. This is a classic technique of propaganda. The propagandist hopes the reader's receptivity to the substance of the issue will be tainted by the negative label or aided by the positive label.

Of course, while newspapers can freely quote the name-callers who continually disparage Republicans with invective, it would be unseemly for even the *Times* to constantly engage in their egg-throwing in front-page stories.

For this reason, the *Times* turns to a more subtle form of name-calling: the use of words or phrases that are selected for their positive or negative emotional charge. For example, one might characterize a fiscal conservative as "stingy" rather than "thrifty." Both words refer to the same behavior, but they carry entirely different connotations. By the same token, a Republican is more likely to be "mean-spirited," a Democrat, just "spirited."

We can thus sort labels into two basic kinds: (1) *euphemisms* (i.e., labels that have a positive charge) and (2) *pejoratives* (i.e., labels that have a negative charge). With that in mind, we can formulate the following basic *New York Times* two-pronged rule of labeling:

- Use euphemisms to make the paper's political allies seem more reasonable or sympathetic and avoid euphemisms that would make political opponents seem more reasonable or sympathetic.

- Use pejoratives to make the paper's political opponents seem less reasonable or sympathetic and avoid pejoratives that would make political allies seem less reasonable or sympathetic.

With this rule in hand, we only need to determine which terms are the euphemisms and which are the pejoratives. Of course, the degree to which a particular label carries a positive or negative charge changes over time. Nevertheless, we can safely consider several established examples.

"Liberal" v. "Conservative" v. "Moderate"

It is generally agreed that the words "liberal" and "conservative" have each become pejorative terms in today's political vocabulary. By contrast, the terms "moderate" and "centrist" have become euphemisms. Thus, you will find the *Times* liberally using the term "conservative" to label its opponents but avoiding the use of "liberal" to label its supporters. Instead, to lend credibility to liberals, they will label them as "moderates" wherever possible.

A straightforward application of this technique appeared in the first three words of the lead sentence of a front-page story on homeland security in the *Times* under the headline "BUSH IS THWARTED ON WORKERS RIGHTS" (September 24, 2002):

> WASHINGTON, Sept. 24—A moderate Republican senator gave the Democrats the votes they needed today to keep President Bush from firing workers in a new Homeland Security Department, setting up a veto battle with an administration determined to transform federal work rules in the name of national security.

The "moderate Republican" referred to in the lead was none other than Lincoln D. Chaffee (R-Rhode Island), who by nobody's standard could be considered a "moderate." Senator Chafee voted against the president's 2001 tax cut legislation and is pro-choice. If Chafee is a "moderate Republican," then there's no such thing as a "liberal Republican."

Of course, there is no news in a "liberal Republican" voting against the president on homeland security. But, if a Republican is going to vote against the president, then by labeling the liberal senator as a "moderate Republican," the *Times* is doing two things: (1) making the Republican who voted with the Democrats look reasonable, and (2) making the president look extreme (i.e., "conservative," or at least not a "moderate").

In an article run under the headline "CENTRIST SENATOR FOUND MIDDLE GROUND" (April 7, 2001), the *Times* turned a Republican political triumph— passage of a $1.2 trillion tax cut—on its ear, actually calling it a "political blow" to President Bush. In doing so, the *Times* awarded credit for passage of the bill to Senator Breaux of Louisiana, whom they labeled a "centrist":

> Making good on the hope of centrists that the 50-50 split in the Senate could work to their advantage, Mr. Breaux pulled together enough moderate Republicans and conservative Democrats to force a budget compromise through the Senate.

Ann Coulter, in her book, marveled at the use of the terms "moderate Republican" and "conservative Democrats," asking rhetorically, why not "liberal Republicans" and "moderate Democrats"? "'Moderate Republican' is simply how the blabocracy flatters Republicans who vote with the Democrats," quipped Coulter. "If it weren't so conspicuous, the *New York Times* would start referring to 'nice Republicans' and 'mean Republicans.'" The *Times* hasn't gone that far, but neither has it abandoned its favorite propaganda technique.

"Ultraconservative"

Most people perceive any extreme as inherently unnatural—anathema to the golden mean. Accordingly, the use of labels associated with extreme views will immediately assail the credibility of the person or idea to whom or which it is applied. Thus, when referring to conservatives, reporters will liberally use the terms "ultraconservative," "staunch conservative," "stalwart conservative," "social conservative," "religious conservative," "Christian conservative," "ardent conservative," and "far right wing."

In a straight news article regarding the announcement of the retirement of Senator Jesse Helms, the *Times* (August 22, 2001) opined:

> Mr. Helms often offended many liberals and moderates with his ultraconservative views on race and homosexuality, making him an enduring bogeyman to the American left.

If the senator were truly "ultraconservative," wouldn't he have offended ordinary "conservatives," too? Moreover, using the term "ultraconservative" in this context could mislead the reader into believing that Helms favors segregation for blacks and homosexuals, which is not the case. Why not avoid ambiguity by stating Senator Helms' views on race and homosexuality?

Here's the text of a *Times* news summary, "POLITICS; HELMS ON AIDS" (March 31, 2002):

> Senator Jesse Helms, below, North Carolina's conservative icon, called for $500 million to fight the global AIDS pandemic. He wrote in The Washington Post, "I know of no more heart-breaking tragedy in the world today." Mr. Helms,

80 and retiring soon, said he was shifting his view with the view that his conscience was "answerable to God." But as for the U.S., he still believes AIDS is caused by "the homosexual lifestyle."

Most people would agree with Senator Helms that the spread of AIDS in the United States was largely due to homosexual practices, but that does not make people who hold that belief "ultraconservative." Likewise, a large segment of the population finds homosexuality offensive to their religious beliefs, and a vast majority of the population would find entering into a homosexual relationship as personally abhorrent, but that does not make a vast majority of the population "ultraconservative."

The *Times* employs these extreme labels persistently and tends to apply them more on the right than on the left. According to Coulter, "In the entire *New York Times* archives on LexisNexis, there are 109 items using the phrase 'far right wing,' but only 18 items that use 'far left wing.' There are 149 uses of 'ultraconservative,' but only 59 uses of 'ultraliberal.'"

The word "staunch" means "faithful" but in ordinary usage connotes a blind faith that would not always be open to reason. Naturally, you would never use the term "staunch liberal." So, in a news profile (January 3, 2001) about President Bush's first choice for secretary of labor, the *Times* kicked off a negative campaign that succeeded in derailing the nomination with the following use of the label:

> Once a liberal Democrat who worked for the American Federation of Teachers, Linda Chavez, President-elect George W. Bush's pick as labor secretary, is now a staunch conservative who supports school vouchers.

The application of the label here did more to ridicule school vouchers than Chavez. If supporting school vouchers makes one a staunch conservative, then a majority of inner-city black parents, not to mention Senator Joseph Lieberman (D-Connecticut), would be surprised to read of their new political affiliation in the *New York Times*.

In the same article, the *Times* also declared:

> Though she is intensely political, Ms. Chavez has never been elected to public office.

No one was quoted to explain what the *Times* meant by "intensely political." Nor did the *Times* explain why it would be unusual for a cabinet member to have "never been elected to public office." Colin Powell, Condolezza Rice, and Donald Evans, all members of Bush's cabinet, have never been elected to public office.

In a front-page article about a "private dinner" in a "dark-paneled room" at the Metropolitan Club in New York— "BUSH'S AIDES SEEK TO FOCUS EFFORTS ON THE ECONOMY" (September 9, 2001)—the *Times* was sure to label the attendees:

> At the dinner on Tuesday—attended by conservative stalwarts including David Keene, Haley Barbour, Kenneth D. Duberstein, Vin Weber, Charles Black, Linda DiVall, Bill Paxon, and Ed Gillespie—several participants said they pressed Mr. Rove to get the president to act assertively.

Several of these "conservative stalwarts" had previously been labeled "moderate" by the newspaper. Later in the article, the American public was then informed with the following "objective" news:

> But in his public discourse about the economy, Mr. Bush sometimes sounds disjointed; he has trouble moving beyond a few set sentences about the relationship between free trade and the creation (not to mention the loss) of jobs in the United States. And so far, he has not developed many skills in talking to players in the financial markets, something Mr. Clinton learned from his treasury secretary, Robert E. Rubin. (Mr. Bush's treasury secretary, Paul H. O'Neill, is also viewed widely in the administration and Congress as a poor communicator of economic strategy.)

That paragraph reads more like a *Times* editorial than what one would expect from a factual news story. In what was billed, in the headline, as a report on the administration's attempts to focus on the economy, this front-page article turned out merely to be an editorial critical of President Bush's leadership and communications skills—something better suited for the paper's editorial or op-ed pages, whether you agree with it or not.

The balance of the article was laced with similar opinions, though cleverly crafted to make it appear they came from "White House officials," "other advisors," and "even some Republicans." Yet none of these officials, advisors, or Republicans were quoted in the article supporting the negative assessments expressed by the *Times*—on the contrary, those officials who were quoted all complimented the president's skills and supported his positions on the issues. Can we really ever trust the *Times*' use of "unnamed sources" after the Jayson Blair scandal?

Knowing that it had a pure op-ed piece on its hands, the *Times* had only one way to justify the story's appearance as an objective front-page news story—by giving it a serious, albeit misleading, headline: "BUSH'S AIDES SEEK TO FOCUS EFFORTS ON THE ECONOMY." But that headline is an inaccurate summary of both the lead and the body of the article. The lead sentence of the article was:

> WASHINGTON, Sept. 8—As White House officials move to refocus President Bush's energies on the precarious economy, they are working to present him as a more commanding leader in what may be the most treacherous stretch of his first year in the White House.

An accurate headline derived from such a lead would be "AIDES WORK TO PRESENT BUSH AS MORE COMMANDING LEADER." A truthful headline, however, would have openly betrayed the opinionated nature of the article, and its placement on the front page would have become problematic (assuming there is anyone left at the *Times* who is serious about guarding the paper's integrity).

"Ideological"

At one level, the word *ideological* simply means "having to do with an ideology," a particular way of thinking about a problem and its solutions. Yet, because the word also connotes a point of view that is idealistic, abstract, or impractical, it carries a negative charge. For this reason, the *Times* finds the word "ideological" a useful term to apply to policies supported by Republicans and conservatives.

For example, in a front page news story in the *Times* entitled "EMBATTLED, SCRUTINIZED, POWELL SOLDIERS ON" (July 25, 2002), the *Times* expressed its approval of Secretary of State Colin Powell in these terms:

Mr. Powell's approach to almost all issues—foreign or domestic—is pragmatic and nonideological. He is internationalist, multilateralist and moderate. He has supported abortion rights and affirmative action and is a Republican, many supporters say, in no small measure because Republican officials mentored and promoted him for years.

Thus, according to the *New York Times*, it is "nonideological" to support abortion rights and affirmative action. Those are the views of a "pragmatic" person. Those who oppose abortion and affirmative action are "ideological."

"Pragmatic"

As the above article suggested, the opposite of the "ideological" person is the "pragmatic" person. A "pragmatic" person is one who agrees with the *New York Times*.

In an article entitled "MAN IN THE NEWS; A PRAGMATIST AT TREASURY" (December 10, 2002), the *Times* wrote the following lead:

> John W. Snow, the railroad executive President Bush has chosen to be his next secretary of the Treasury, is a pragmatic business executive who once campaigned vociferously to place top priority on balancing the budget rather than on cutting taxes.

Thus, if you oppose tax cuts, you are "pragmatic." If you believe tax cuts will improve the economy, you are "ideological" and impractical. The article continues:

> In picking Mr. Snow as his chief salesman on economic policy, Mr. Bush settled on a middle-of-the-road Republican whose greatest strengths are not his ideological fervor but rather his skills as a manager and a communicator, his credibility in the business world and his familiarity with Washington.

By the way, research does not turn up the belittling term "chief salesman" as ever having been used in a news article to label President Clinton's secretary of the treasury.

"Embattled"

Embattled is a code word for someone who the *New York Times* would like to see defeated. For example, the *Times* had often expressed its displeasure with Israel's conservative government, and it was only a matter of time before the conservative leader would find himself "embattled," according to the *New York Times*. In an article under the headline "SHARON SAYS ARAFAT'S TRUCE CALL AIMS AT INFLUENCING ISRAELI VOTERS" (January 13, 2002), the *Times* declared:

> JERUSALEM, Jan. 12—Israel's embattled prime minister, Ariel Sharon, spoke dismissively today about Yasir Arafat's appeal for a pre-election halt to attacks on Israeli civilians, clearly implying that the Palestinian leader was trying to help his dovish opponent.

Though, in the article "EMBATTLED, SCRUTINIZED, POWELL SOLDIERS ON" (July 25, 2002), the *Times* spoke in endearing terms about the "nonideological" secretary of state, you can be sure the *Times* would like nothing more than to report Colin Powell's political defeat or, better yet, his joining the Democratic party. After all, if a future president of the United States is to be black, it won't count if he's a Republican.

Harvey L. Pitt, the former chairman of the Security Exchange Commission, must have had a target painted across his chest. It seemed the *Times* had identified him early on as someone to be taken down at all costs, and a front-page crusade against the SEC chairman had begun soon after he was nominated to that position.

By the summer of 2002, owing to the crusade the *Times* launched against him, Chairman Pitt became irrecoverably "embattled." A *Times* news summary regarding Chairman Pitt's rejection of calls for his resignation was run under the headline "EMBATTLED, BUT STAYING" (July 15, 2002).

Several days later, in "S.E.C. CHIEF SET TO PURSUE FORMER CLIENTS" (July 18, 2002), the *Times* employed the "embattled" label again:

> WASHINGTON, July 17—Harvey L. Pitt, the embattled head of the Securities and Exchange Commission, said today that with the expiration of ethics restrictions that have bound him during his first year in office, he would

play a direct role in enforcement cases involving companies and accounting firms that were once his law clients.

Once Pitt was labeled as "embattled," he should have braced himself for the firestorm to come. As soon as Congress passed legislation to create an accounting oversight board, the *New York Times* was determined to have an anti-business crusader head the board. Pitt soon discovered that when the $3 billion *Times* soft-money machine wants something, either you give it to them, or watch out.

Shortly after Pitt pushed for the appointment of William H. Webster to lead the oversight board, rather than the *Times'* preferred candidate, the *Times* unleashed its fury. Harvey Pitt is a man of principle—what the *Times* would call an ideologue, not a pragmatist—and he didn't care what the newspapers would write about the nominee. But what Pitt did not understand, or did not expect, was how powerful the front page of the *Times* can be as a means of influence.

A week before the midterm 2002 elections, the "newspaper of record" dropped an atomic bomb on the "embattled" Harvey L. Pitt. The front page of the *New York Times* announced, "OVERSIGHT CHIEF TOLD PITT OF JOB AND A RED FLAG" (October 31, 2002):

> WASHINGTON, Oct. 30—Shortly before William H. Webster was appointed to head a new board overseeing the accounting profession by the Securities and Exchange Commission last Friday, he told the commission's chairman, Harvey L. Pitt, that he had until recently headed the auditing committee of a company that was facing fraud accusations, Mr. Webster recounted today.
>
> Mr. Pitt chose not to tell the other four commissioners who voted on Mr. Webster's nomination that day, according to S.E.C. officials. White House officials said they, too, were not informed about the details of Mr. Webster's work for the company.

The news that Pitt not only knew of Webster's problems but also failed to tell his fellow commissioners prior to their vote on Webster's appointment set off a firestorm of criticism from not just Democrats but the Bush administration as well—all of whom, apparently, believed what they read on the front page of the *New York Times*.

If what had been said on the front page of the *Times* had been true, you could hardly fault the criticism—the *Times* made Pitt look pretty stupid.

Naturally, the White House was furious, and the Democrats not only called for Pitt's immediate resignation but also launched several investigations into the matter, as the *Times* reported the next day in "3 INQUIRIES BEGUN INTO S.E.C.'S CHOICE OF AUDIT OVERSEER" (November 1, 2002).

The same day, the *Times* enhanced the "facts" that were reported on its front page in an editorial entitled "THE MESS AT THE S.E.C." (November 1, 2002), suggesting that Pitt actively concealed the facts from his fellow commissioners:

> That "Pitt knew of Webster's role and hid that fact from fellow commissioners makes matters worse."

In the *Times*' classic one-two punch style, the editorial was coupled with a scorch-the-earth op-ed piece entitled "THE PITT PRINCIPAL," in which the *Times* columnist repeats the accusation as fact:

> So Harvey Pitt decided not to tell other members of the Securities and Exchange Commission a small detail about the man he had chosen to head a crucial new accounting oversight board, after turning his back on a far more qualified candidate.

When you read a fact on the front page of the *New York Times*, you expect it to be the truth. Even Republican senators sometimes believe what they read in the *Times*, and after reading the latest story about the chairman, *they* became the fuel for another front-page story that appeared the next day under the headline "SENIOR REPUBLICAN JOINS IN CRITICISM OF S.E.C. CHAIRMAN" (November 2, 2002):

> WASHINGTON, Nov. 1—The political troubles of the chairman of the Securities and Exchange Commission deepened today when the senator who will become the senior Republican on the banking committee supported calls by Democrats for hearings into the selection of an overseer of the accounting profession.

The senator, Richard C. Shelby, Republican of Alabama, criticized the judgment of the S.E.C. chairman, Harvey L. Pitt. He cited Mr. Pitt's failure to tell other commissioners that William H. Webster, the man picked to head the accounting oversight board, had headed the audit committee of a company accused of fraud.

Within a week after the story first broke, on the night of the midterm election, the "embattled" Harvey Pitt finally resigned, as the *Times* gleefully reported on its front page in "S.E.C.'s Embattled Chief Resigns in Wake of Latest Political Storm" (November 7, 2002). In that front-page story, the *Times* echoed the context two more times:

> His hold over the agency cracked last Thursday with the disclosure that he had *failed to tell* either the White House or the four other commissioners at the S.E.C. that he had known that William H. Webster, the new accounting board chairman, had headed the audit committee of a company accused of fraud. Mr. Webster, who was recruited for the post by the White House, was approved by the commission 10 days ago in a bitterly divided vote in which two of the five commissioners said he was unqualified for the job.
>
> The disclosure that Mr. Pitt *withheld information* about Mr. Webster's ties to the ailing company, U.S. Technologies, led to the immediate start of three investigations into Mr. Pitt's handling of the selection of the new board, including a Congressional inquiry that was preparing for three days of Senate hearings this month. (emphasis added)

Soon the *Times* printed a follow-up article, "Praise to Scorn: Mercurial Ride of S.E.C. Chief" (November 10, 2002), which included a photo of Pitt and a timeline of his short chairmanship. The caption read, "An embattled 14 months."

But wait. Remember those investigations instigated by the Democrats ("3 Inquiries Begun into S.E.C.'s Choice of Audit Overseer," November 1, 2002)? The results of those investigations were reported a few weeks later in the following article published not by the *New York Times* but by the *Associated Press* (December 19, 2002):

PITT UNAWARE OF PROBLEMS WITH NOMINEE

WASHINGTON (AP) — A congressional investigation found no evidence that Harvey Pitt, the former Securities and Exchange Commission chairman, knew in advance about problems with the first nominee approved to lead a new accounting oversight board.

In other words, unlike Howell Raines, who knew about Jayson Blair's history of shoddy reporting but did not pass the information on to Blair's supervising editors, Pitt never knew of Webster's problems and therefore could not have withheld the information from his fellow commissioners as the *Times* charged.

"We found no evidence that the SEC chairman was informed of any other information about the company's history and Judge Webster's role prior to the Oct. 25 vote," the report said.

If they believed their own October 31 story, the editors of the *Times* must have been stunned by this news. The headline and the lead of their front-page October 31 article no longer held up. Any civilized journalist would have expressed remorse over an error so egregious it cost a person his high placed government position and tarnished his personal reputation. But apparently, civility is not a core principal of journalism, at least not at the *New York Times*. Perhaps another news organization would have published a correction, an editor's note, or a full story rectifying the error on its front page, which is the *Times'* policy in such instances. Perhaps a private note of apology to Pitt was in order, too. On the contrary, for the *Times* the situation clearly called for a cover up.

What it chose to do was spin the GAO report in a way that buried its guilt and poured salt on the wounds of the "embattled" Pitt. According to the *Associated Press* wire story:

The report released Thursday by the General Accounting Office, the investigative arm of Congress, was critical of the SEC's selection and vetting process, saying it "was neither consistent nor effective and changed and evolved over time."

The *Times* read into the report something that just wasn't there—that the entire SEC was "chaotic"—and it made that charge on its front page (December 20, 2002):

GOVERNMENT REPORT DETAILS A CHAOTIC S.E.C. UNDER PITT

WASHINGTON, Dec. 19—The Securities and Exchange Commission under Harvey L. Pitt was described today as dysfunctional by a government report examining the agency's selection of a new accounting oversight board.

The General Accounting Office report did nothing of the kind; it reported no general "dysfunction" of the SEC but merely, just as the *Associated Press* reported, expressed its criticism of the SEC's process for selecting the head of the accounting oversight board.

If you weren't aware of the fact that the *Times* had the story completely wrong in its critical October 31 article—the one that "cracked" Pitt's hold over the SEC—you would hardly know it from reading this article. The headline of the *AP* story—that Pitt was unaware of Webster's problems prior to the SEC's vote on his appointment—didn't appear on the front page of the *Times*. The *Times* buried that aspect of the story—which was the real news—in the tenth paragraph of its December 20 article, a paragraph that did not even appear in the same section of the paper but was virtually hidden on page 4 of the *Times'* Business section.

Moreover, it was reported in the following convoluted way:

On that morning, according to the report, Mr. Herdman learned that Mr. Webster had dismissed the outside auditors of U.S. Technologies after the auditors complained of significant financial problems. But Mr. Herdman, a long-time friend and close adviser to Mr. Pitt, decided that the information was not significant and did not need to be shared with the commissioners.

Last month, Mr. Webster, Mr. Pitt and Mr. Herdman announced their resignations.

In other words, it was Herdman who withheld the information from the SEC commissioners, including Chairman Pitt. Since Pitt was not aware of

Webster's troubles, he could not have withheld the information as the *Times* previously reported, and reported, and reported.

It appeared from the article that the *Times* was concerned that it may have opened itself to a defamation lawsuit. The *Times* seemed to go out of its way, in the following paragraphs, to detail the basis of its original October 31 front-page story:

> In an interview on October 30, Mr. Webster said that before his selection he had told Mr. Pitt and Mr. Herdman that the company had been accused of fraud.

But this is not a quote from Webster, only the word of the reporter. If there had been a quote in the reporter's notes directly stating what Webster said he told Pitt, you can be sure the *Times* would have printed it. But the *Times* apparently couldn't come up with it and published only the following quote, which is substantially ambiguous about what Webster said and whom he said it to:

> "I told them that people are making accusations," Mr. Webster said of his conversation with Mr. Pitt and Mr. Herdman.

The word "them" suggests that Webster may have told any number of people at the SEC, not necessarily Pitt. In fact, in a sign that the *Times* may have been admitting some uncertainty about its original story, the above version indicates that Webster's conversation was with both Pitt *and* Herdman. Here's how the sentence read in the original October 31 article:

> "I told them that people are making accusations," Mr. Webster said of his conversation with *Mr. Pitt,* before he was appointed last Friday. (emphasis added)

The December 20 article offered no explanation for the mysterious addition of Herdman's name to the new version of this paragraph. Recall, the October 31 article also charged:

> Mr. Pitt chose not to tell the other four commissioners who voted on Mr. Webster's nomination that day, according to S.E.C. officials.

The "S.E.C. officials," to whom that information was attributed, were never quoted nor even identified. If they existed at all, they would have to have been very close to Pitt to have known what information the chairman knew and what he chose to do (or not do) with it. Apparently, they were not close enough to know the truth.

In fact, there is some indication that the editors of the *Times* may have been uncertain about the truth of its story even on the day they originally printed it. The morning of October 31, the article originally ran in the *Times'* national edition under the headline "OVERSIGHT CHIEF TOLD PITT OF JOB AND A RED FLAG." Mysteriously, later editions of the *Times* that day ran the article under the revised headline "AUDIT OVERSEER CITED PROBLEMS WITH PREVIOUS POST"—the editors eliminated the reference to Pitt and were no longer specific about the identity of the person to whom Webster allegedly raised his "Red Flag," now called "problems."

Could the *Times* have known on October 31, and throughout the political firestorm that ensued during the week before the 2002 midterm election and Pitt's resignation, that he was unaware of the potential problems with Webster's appointment? It certainly looks that way.

The GAO's finding that there was "no evidence that the SEC chairman was informed of any other information about the company's history and Judge Webster's role prior to the Oct. 25 vote" was directly contrary to what was not only reported but also crusaded in the *New York Times*—in its news pages, editorial pages, and op-ed pages. The *Times'* accusation that Pitt "hid" information from his fellow commissioners was palpably wrong.

Given the *Times'* defensive reaction to the truth during the day the *Times* originally reported the story and in the aftermath of the GAO's report, it would seem that an investigation of the affair is in order—the question being, "What did the *Times* know, and when did it know it?"

It is not clear, however, who, if anyone, conducts independent investigations of egregious errors by leading newspapers. Do we allow the *Times* to conduct another Blair-style mea culpa on the front page and then move on? One thing is certain: such an investigation is not likely to take the form of a lawsuit against the *Times*. For Pitt to prevail in an action against the *Times* for defamation of character, he, being a public figure, would have to show that the *Times* acted in "reckless disregard of the truth." That is a difficult standard to meet—with the facts centering on Webster's word against that of the *Times'* reporter.

Nevertheless, there may come a day when a public official who is treated by the *Times* the way Pitt was treated might just take the paper to court. Perhaps the Blair scandal will provide the impetus needed for a lawsuit. Such a lawsuit could expose reporters and editors to legal depositions that could lead to some enlightening revelations about the *Times'* editorial decision process.

"Unrepentant"

The term "unrepentant" is reserved for those who either refuse to conform to the worldview of the *New York Times* or who simply make life difficult for political candidates the *Times* supports.

In the months leading up to the 2000 presidential election, the *New York Times,* fearing that Ralph Nader might cost Al Gore the election, openly pleaded with Nader to drop out of the race. Nader, whose Green party attracted votes that otherwise might have been cast for Gore, was later blamed for Gore's defeat.

In an editorial entitled "MR. NADER'S MISGUIDED CRUSADE" (July 30, 2000), the *Times* accused Ralph Nader of running as a "spoiler" and engaging in a "self-indulgent exercise that will distract voters from a clear-cut choice" represented by the major party candidates. Just a few days before the 2000 presidential election, in an editorial entitled "MR. NADER'S ELECTORIAL MISCHIEF" (October 26, 2000), the *Times* lashed out at Nader's refusal to withdraw from the campaign, stating that Nader's "willful prankishness" was a disservice to the electorate and that the country deserved "a clear up-or-down vote" between George W. Bush and Al Gore.

The *Times* ignored comparisons to the 1992 election when presidential candidate Ross Perot garnered over 10 percent of the popular vote, most of which was at the expense of President Bush; Clinton won the 1992 election with only 43 percent of the popular vote, robbing the electorate of a "clear-cut" choice.

After the 2000 election, Nader not only refused to express remorse for his role in the election but also continued to travel the country to raise money for the Green party. His attitude and actions, both before and after the election, had, it seemed, more than irritated the editors of the *Times*.

In retaliation, the *Times* has since punished Nader with the label "unrepentant" expressed right in the headlines (April 23, 2001):

AN UNREPENTANT NADER SEES A POSITIVE SIDE OF BUSH POLICY

And, later that year (August 6, 2001):

AN UNREPENTANT NADER UNVEILS A NEW GRASS-ROOTS PROJECT

Nader, the "unrepentant," is in good company. The *Times* has also applied the label to Slobodan Milosevic in an extensive profile of the alleged war criminal in a *Times Magazine* article entitled simply "THE UNREPENTANT."

Congressman James Traficant Jr. was convicted on corruption charges and expelled from the House of Representatives. His crime, in the eyes of the *Times*, was voting once too often with the Republicans, earning him the label "unrepentant," as in this *Times* piece (July 31, 2002):

> Expelled from Congress a week ago, an unrepentant James A. Traficant Jr. was sentenced today to eight years in jail for corruption, and he made it clear that he expected to win re-election from his prison cell.

The article failed to mention that the convicted congressman was a Democrat.

"Millionaire"

In an article on the election of James K. Hahn as mayor of Los Angeles, who succeeded Republican mayor Richard Riordan, the *Times* (December 5, 2001) reported:

> Mr. Hahn, a Democrat like Mr. Villaraigosa, will succeed Mayor Richard J. Riordan, the millionaire Republican businessman who has led the city since 1993 but was barred from seeking a third term and is, in fact, considering seeking the Republican nomination to challenge Gov. Gray Davis, a Democrat, next year.

The *Times* continued its infatuation with Riordan's "millionaire's life," publishing a story later that month entitled "TWO CENTS FROM A RICH EX-MAYOR; LOS ANGELES' RIORDAN GIVES BLOOMBERG A FEW TIPS" (December 17, 2001).

Research does not turn up a single instance of the *Times* using the label "millionaire Democrat" in that way—such as "Senator Ted Kennedy, millionaire Democrat from Massachusetts," or "Senator Don Corzine, millionaire Democrat from New Jersey."

"Public Interest Group"

Organizations serving the "public interest" sound bi-partisan and moderate. Thus, when referring to a think tank or issue-advocacy group that is liberal or left-leaning, the *Times* will often identify it as a "public interest group." By contrast, conservative think tanks and advocacy organizations are typically labeled "conservative."

For example, in an article entitled "ENRON'S COLLAPSE: CAMPAIGN FINANCE" (January 25, 2002) about campaign contributions made by Enron and Arthur Andersen to congressmen serving on House committees charged with investigating wrongdoing at those companies, the *Times* called TomPaine.com "a public interest group." By most standards, TomPaine.com is an extremist, left-wing organization that has run ads with the following headlines:

CAN LIBERALS SAVE CAPITALISM AGAIN? LAISSEZ-FAIRE ITSELF IS THE ULTIMATE CORPORATE FRAUD

GEORGE BUSH CHANNELS GEORGE ORWELL: CAN A SITTING PRESIDENT BE CHARGED WITH PLAGIARISM

GOP CROSS DRESSING ON SOCIAL SECURITY

According to TomPaine.com's own website, "Our principal funding comes from the Florence and John Schumann Foundation, a major supporter of other independent media efforts, including National Public Radio, the *Columbia Journalism Review*, public TV's "Frontline" and "POV" documentary series, and *The American Prospect* magazine." These hardly count as middle-of-the-road media outfits.

In an article on the economy run in the *Times* under the headline "AS FISCAL ENGINE STALLS, THE MECHANICS LINE UP" (November 24, 2001), a Cato Institute economist who was promoting across-the-board tax cuts, a position angrily opposed by the *Times*, was labeled a "conservative." By contrast, the economist from the liberal Center on Budget and Policy Priorities, who was advocating a six-month spending stimulus, was unlabeled.

A front-page article under the headline "MANY STATES CEDING REGULATIONS TO CHURCH GROUPS" (July 27, 2001) was an editorial disguised as an objective news story supporting the *Times'* opposition to President Bush's "faith-based" initiatives. The article quoted a policy director for Citizens for Missouri's Children, which the *Times* labeled a "public interest group." A review of the website for Citizens for Missouri's Children reveals that the group opposes any legislation that calls for a reduction in taxes.

"Apolitical"

Another word for "public interest" is "apolitical." In a story run under the headline "CONSUMER PRODUCT SAFETY CHIEF SETS DEADLINE TO RESIGN" (August 9, 2001), the *Times* used the euphemism "apolitical" to support the credibility of Senator Hillary Clinton, who led the charge to oppose the nomination of Mary Sheila Gall as chairman of the Consumer Product Safety Commission. The *Times* reported:

> Senator Clinton said the fact that Consumers Union, the typically apolitical organization that publishes Consumer Reports, opposed Miss Gall's nomination figured in her opposition to the nomination.

Consumers Union could hardly be considered "apolitical," as a simple check of its website would reveal. Employing the technique of slanting by omission of key facts, the article merely alluded to the fact that Mary Sheila Gall was a sitting member of the commission. Had it made that point clear, it could not have avoided a fact that might have undermined the assertions made against Gall by Senator Clinton: Gall was appointed to the commission by President Bill Clinton.

"Nonprofit"

Profits are bad. So "nonprofit" must be good, or at least neutral, moderate, centrist, or "in the public interest." As we know, the labels "liberal" and "conservative" are pejorative. Thus, a newspaper can support the credibility of

159

a liberal group by labeling it with the euphemism "nonprofit." A conservative organization, even if it is "nonprofit," would be labeled "conservative."

Predictably, the *Times* did just that in an article run under the headline "SIGNALING CHANGE, BUSH PICKS 3 EXECUTIVES FOR PENTAGON JOBS" (April 25, 2001):

> "I'm troubled that we're setting the stage for promoting the interests of the military-industrial complex," said Eugene Carroll, a retired admiral who is vice president of the Center for Defense Information, a nonprofit policy group. "I see no inclination on the part of the Bush team to rein in our military programs."
>
> But other military analysts said that corporate executives could bring the kinds of business skills needed to shake up a stodgy and inefficient bureaucracy.
>
> "Who better to know how the business runs than those who have run the business?" said Jack Spencer of the Heritage Foundation, a conservative policy organization.

Thus, while labeling the Heritage Foundation as "a conservative policy organization," the *Times* calls the Center for Defense Information "a nonprofit policy group." The Center for Defense has been highly critical of President Bush's defense proposals, calling, for example, recent attempts to build a missile defense system "a sham."

"Extreme"

Conservatives are extremists and amateurs, especially when it comes to serious questions of freedom, individual rights, and the U.S. Constitution. In an article appearing in its Sports section, the *Times* profiled a little town located in the state of Utah, the home of the 2002 Winter Olympics. The headline was simply "EXTREME SPORTSMAN" (February 11, 2002), and it featured the 57-year-old mayor of La Verkin, Utah, Jay Lee:

> "Around here we don't have much use for the outside opinion," he said. "We're conservative people and we look after ourselves."

Noting that the town passed an ordinance requiring all town residences to "maintain arms," the *Times* then injected this comment on the residents of half the state of Utah:

> Lee's attitude and his unique approach to defense of the American way won him admirers all across the southern tier of Utah, a stretch of country peppered with survivalists, militiamen and amateur experts of the Constitution and the Second Amendment.

The "professional" experts on the Constitution and the Second Amendment, it seems, all live in New York.

"Republican-backed"

When something goes wrong, blame it on Republicans—that seems to be the motto of the *Times*. So, in "WHEN ASYLUM REQUESTS ARE OVERLOOKED" (August 15, 2001), an article on the struggle of an illegal immigrant from Colombia—a potential Democrat voter—to obtain asylum in the United States, it honed in on the culprit: a "Republican-backed" law that was intended to attack illegal immigration and streamline the review of illegal immigration cases.

> Before passage of a Republican-backed law five years ago, only an immigration judge could order the deportation of someone who arrived without valid travel documents. Now, an immigration officer can exercise that power, called expedited removal, on the spot, a move intended to cut down on fraud.

The *Times* failed to mention that the bill was also "Democrat-backed," having passed the House on a 370-37 votes, and was signed into law by President Clinton, who "got everything he wanted on immigration," according to *USA Today* ("GOP RETREATS ON A COMPROMISE IMMIGRATION BILL," September 30, 1996).

Note that within a month after the *Times* article appeared, nineteen "immigrants" crashed commercial airliners into the World Trade Center and the Pentagon. After September 11, giving credit to Republicans for strengthening the immigration laws became something to be avoided.

Cluster-Bombing with Labels

An effective way for a newspaper to brand its ideological opponents is to write an article that is completely plastered with the appropriate pejorative labels. By cluster-bombing the victim with negatively charged labels, you cannot fail to influence readers into forever associating the person with the pejorative branding.

A front-page *Times* article entitled "RELIGIOUS RIGHT MADE BIG PUSH TO PUT ASHCROFT IN JUSTICE DEPT" (January 7, 2001) is a prime example of cluster-bombing with labels. The article, published shortly after President Bush nominated John Ashcroft for the position of attorney general, began as follows:

> WASHINGTON, Jan. 6—Within days of Senator John Ashcroft of Missouri's narrow re-election defeat by a candidate who died three weeks before Election Day, religious and conservative leaders began promoting him for a major position in a Bush administration.

Within the four corners of just this one article, the following labels were dropped on Senator Ashcroft and those who supported him (with the numbers on the left indicating how many times that label appeared in the article):

6   religious conservatives

2   conservative leaders

2   religious groups

2   Christian conservatives

2   Christian right

2   conservatives

1   religious and conservative leaders

1   religious conservative

1   religious right

1   religious organizations

1   religious fundamentalism

1   conservative religious leaders

1   conservative religious school

1   conservative wing

1   conservative donors

1   socially conservative positions

1   modern Christian political movement

1   conservative Christian movement

1   organizations with a religious orientation

1   fundamentalist Christian values

1   prominent Christian philanthropist

The only non-conservative/religious labels used in the article were single uses of the terms "abortion rights groups" and "abortion rights advocates." This front-page "news" story lent important credibility for liberal groups who subsequently waged a pitched battle to oppose Ashcroft's nomination on the basis that the senator's "conservative religious" beliefs and associations made him ineligible for the position of attorney general.

Not surprisingly, shortly after the above article appeared, John Ashcroft became, in the *Times'* view, "Mr. Bush's embattled attorney general choice" (in "INTERIOR CHOICE FACES SHARP QUESTIONING," January 19, 2001) and "the embattled nominee for attorney general" (in "DEMOCRATIC LEADER ASSURES BUSH ON ASHCROFT NOMINATION," January 25, 2001).

DISCREDIT COUNTER-LABELING BY OPPONENTS

When the opposition tries to create their own label for political advantage, a newspaper can seek ways to belittle the attempt.

For example, anticipating that the press would brand him with the politically charged label "conservative," George W. Bush conceived the idea of identifying himself with a set of values he dubbed "compassionate conservatism." It was a label that was intended to attract conservatives while also conveying a message of moderation, and perhaps a touch of liberalism, to appeal to those in the center of the political spectrum.

To prevent a politician from advancing their cause with this form of self-styled label, the simplest thing a paper can do is put the label in quotes—as in "compassionate conservative," which the *Times* did in its editorial "THE NATION, THE PRESIDENT, THE WAR" (January 29, 2003). In that way, the paper is communicating that the label is contrived and does not warrant official entry into the nation's political vocabulary (unlike "staunch conservative," "stalwart conservative," and "ultraconservative").

Alternatively, a newspaper can use a more direct means of attack. For example, in a front-page *Times* article run under the headline "BUSH PUSHES ROLE OF PRIVATE SECTOR IN AIDING THE POOR" (May 21, 2001), the *Times* took the following swipe at Bush's self-styled label:

> Mr. Bush was trying to lend definition to his stated philosophy of compassionate conservativism, a slogan that remains fuzzy in the minds of some voters and empty in the minds of others.

Though the reporter seemed well acquainted with them, none of the "voters" or "others" whose minds were "fuzzy" or "empty" on the concept of "compassionate conservatism" were quoted to support the above statement. Yet, it seems the reporter was unacquainted with anyone who had a clear understanding of the term. Branding the term a "slogan," the reporter simply injected his own opinion as to how voters have come to understand compassionate conservatism.

RE-LABEL WHEN CONVENIENCE DICTATES

You can't always brand a person with a label that doesn't quite fit his or her objective description. Sometimes, to maintain some measure of journalistic credibility, a little honesty is called for. And there are times when being honest won't hurt the cause—such as when you know you can't win anyway.

After President Bush was elected in 2000, his party maintained control of the U.S. Senate, and with that control, just about any of Bush's judicial nominees would be guaranteed at least a floor vote, where enough moderate and conservative Democrats would not oppose a qualified appointee.

So, when Bush announced his initial eleven nominees to the federal judiciary, the *Times*, in an editorial entitled "A BATTLE FOR THE COURTS" (May 11, 2001), used the following language to "label" the president's nominees:

> President Bush's initial batch of nominations for the nation's Circuit Courts of Appeal has turned out to be more eclectic and conciliatory than most people expected. It contains fewer hard-right legal activists than expected and also includes a number of mainstream conservatives who will be acceptable to Senate Democrats.

In other words, Bush's judicial nominees were not as controversial as the *Times* or anyone else expected. In fact, two of the eleven were African-American who had been originally nominated by President Clinton. As the *Times* knew, with an apparently "moderate" group of nominees and a Republican-controlled Senate, the confirmation of these nominees was sure to occur without much controversy.

Suddenly, a funny thing happened on the way to the Capitol: Senator Jim Jeffords deserted the Republican party, and the Democrats took control of the Senate.

The *Times* immediately recognized that since a Democrat-controlled Senate judiciary committee would now be in a position to block the president's judicial nominees and use the opportunity to paste the White House with charges of packing the court with right-wing hardliners, it was time for the *Times* to take a different tack on Bush's nominees,

In a "straight" news article under the headline "ROAD TO FEDERAL BENCH GETS BUMPIER IN SENATE" (June 26, 2001), the *Times* wrote that when Bush submitted his original nominations,

> the Democrats, then in the minority, seemed inclined to go along even though many of the 11 nominees were strong conservatives and seemed to confirm that Mr. Bush was determined to reinforce a rightward tilt in the nation's courts.

What was only a month before an "eclectic" group of "conciliatory" judicial nominees, including a number of "mainstream conservatives who will be acceptable to Senate Democrats" were now re-labeled as "strong conservatives" that "seemed to [in the opinion of the *Times*] reinforce a rightward tilt in the nation's courts."

The lesson is: how strongly a newspaper plays the label card may depend upon how useful it will be to its political allies. The *Times* is, after all, a "pragmatic" organization, not "ideological."

Thus, a classic technique of propaganda is to link a person or idea to a positive or negative symbol. The propagandist hopes the reader's receptivity to the substance of the issue will be tainted by the negative label or aided by the positive label. A modern application of this propaganda technique is the journalistic practice of labeling the people or organizations who are the subject of a story or who contribute quotes or information to it. Labeling is a subtle way of slanting the story to reflect the editorial views of a newspaper.

Other subtle techniques of bias also involve the use of language, such as grammatical construction or selective diction, to slant a story. Those techniques will be explored in the next chapter.

EIGHT

Distorting with Loaded Language

More matter with less art.

—*Gertrude to Polonius in Shakespeare's* Hamlet

---

he concept of *spin*—literally, the turning of a story to favorably reflect upon one view or another—could be applied to virtually all of the techniques discussed in this book: slanting the *Who*, omitting or falsifying the facts, "quoting-someone-who-agrees-with-us," labeling to manipulate credibility, and the like. A more subtle form of spin, however, deserves its own attention: a kind we call spinning with diction and grammar, or *loaded language*.

Spinning with loaded language is simply the use of selective diction and grammatical construction to reflect the news organization's bias on a story. Editors and reporters are discovering new forms of loaded language all the time. The best way to identify the better known forms is to list them by key watchwords.

"Even"

When a reporter uses the word "even" as an adverb, it is used for emphasis, often to carry the meaning "went so far as," "though it may seem improbable," or "can you believe that?"

In a story run under the headline "BUSH AND GORE STEADFAST IN BELIEF IN OWN VICTORY" (November 22, 2000) about the Florida Supreme Court's decision to permit the recount Al Gore requested in the 2000 presidential election, the *Times* stated:

> Some Bush advisors said they were surprised by the decision tonight—and even suggested that it was tainted because the court was dominated by Democrats.

By inserting the word "even," the reporter conveyed this slant: "Though you are not going to believe this, the Republicans actually suggested the decision was tainted just because Democrats dominated the court." The sentence could be rendered unbiased by simply removing the word "even":

> Some Bush advisors said they were surprised by the decision tonight and suggested that it was tainted because the court was dominated by Democrats.

"Costly"

Military programs, especially those that the *Times* opposes, are "costly." But it is not terribly helpful to characterize as "costly" social programs that the *Times* supports, such as Social Security, Medicare, welfare, school lunch programs, and the like. In an article under the headline "ANTIMISSILE DEFENSE HITS TARGET TEST, PENTAGON SAYS," the *Times* reported (December 4, 2001):

> A prototype antimissile weapon demolished a mock warhead tonight high above the Pacific Ocean in the second consecutive success for the Pentagon's costly missile defense program, military officials said.

Does anyone really think the military officials "said" their antimissile weapon system was a "costly" one? Whether the program is "costly" is purely a matter of opinion, and this is just another means by which the *Times* laces its opinions into seemingly objective news stories.

"RESPONDING TO CRITICISM"

Before reporting the actual news, the *Times* will frequently announce its editorial spin on the *Why* of the story in an introductory clause or phrase of the lead sentence. In this way, the reader's subsequent reception of the facts will be pre-tainted by the paper's editorial views on the subject.

One excellent example was how the *Times* pre-spun the circumstances of a potential presidential assassination to politically embarrass the president of the United States. In an article run under the headline "AIDES SAY BUSH WAS ONE TARGET OF HIJACKED JET" (September 13, 2001), concerning the circuitous route President Bush was advised to take on return to Washington the day of the September 11 attacks, the *Times* employed the pre-spin technique to report a political fall out. Unable to quote a single person who was critical of the president's actions on the day of attacks, the *Times* nevertheless lead the front-page article as follows:

> WASHINGTON, Sept. 13—Stung by suggestions that President Bush had hurt himself politically by delaying his return to Washington on Tuesday, the White House asserted today that Mr. Bush had done so because of hard evidence that he was a target of the terrorists who hijacked airliners and slammed them into the World Trade Center and the Pentagon.

Who made the suggestion referred to in the introductory phrase of this lead? The charge is given emphatic placement in the first few words of the first sentence of a front-page article, yet the article doesn't say who made the suggestions. If the suggestion that President Bush hurt himself politically by delaying his return was pronounced enough to have "stung" the White House, why was the *Times* unable to quote a single person who made that suggestion? If major politicians or even other members of the media made these suggestions, then it would have been easy to track the quotes. It appears the only source of the suggestion that President Bush hurt himself politically was the *New York Times* itself.

We've seen earlier another example of the pre-spin technique ("BUSH, AS TERROR INQUIRY SWIRLS, SEEKS CABINET POST ON SECURITY," Friday, June 7, 2002):

> WASHINGTON, June 6—Responding to widespread criticism of the government's handling of terrorist threats, President Bush called tonight for the creation of a new Cabinet department for domestic defense that would combine 22 federal agencies into a single one aimed at preventing future attacks against the United States.

Again, notice the opening participial phrase announcing the *Times'* editorial opinion on the *Why* before the reader is presented with the news.

We have also seen the *Times* spin its editorial view before reporting the news in "BUSH SIGNS BILL AIMED AT FRAUD IN CORPORATIONS" (July 31, 2002):

> WASHINGTON, July 30—In a sign of how profoundly the nation's business scandals and volatile stock market have rocked his administration, President Bush signed a sweeping corporate-fraud bill today with central provisions that he opposed just three weeks ago.

Thus, the lead begins by suggesting the president was somehow at fault for the scandals and ends by suggesting that not only does the president deserve no credit for signing a bill to prevent future business scandals, but also he is signing the legislation reluctantly. All of this could have been expressed on the *Times'* editorial page, but with much less influential force than being laced into the lead sentence of a "straight" news article appearing as the lead story on the front page.

The editorial pre-spinning of a story with the loaded introductory phrase is a relatively new phenomenon of *New York Times* journalism. A few examples from the past will illustrate.

When President Nixon accepted the resignations of three members of the White House staff in connection with the Watergate break-in, the four-line, eight-column headline was "NIXON ACCEPTS ONUS FOR WATERGATE; BUT SAYS

HE DIDN'T KNOW ABOUT PLOT; HALDEMAN, EHRLICHMAN, DEAN RESIGN; RICHARDSON PUT IN KLEINDIENST POST" (May 1, 1973). Nixon was not someone who the editors of the *Times* warmly embraced, but the lead was reported without any *Times* pre-spin:

> WASHINGTON, April 30—President Nixon told the nation tonight that he accepted the responsibility for what happened in the Watergate case even though he had had no knowledge of political espionage or attempts to cover it up.

You would think this action would have "stunned" or "rocked" the Nixon administration. Certainly, at the very least, Nixon was "responding to widespread criticism." What restrained the reporters and news editors of that time—who well knew the liberal editorial views of their publisher—from pre-spinning the news with the *Times'* editorial abhorrence of President Nixon?

Another favorite of the *Times* was Spiro T. Agnew. Here's how the *Times* reported Agnew's resignation under an eight-column, three-line headline of "AGNEW QUITS VICE PRESIDENCY AND ADMITS TAX EVASION IN '67; NIXON CONSULTS ON SUCCESSOR" (October 11, 1973):

> WASHINGTON, Oct. 10—Spiro T. Agnew resigned as Vice President of the United States today under an agreement with the Department of Justice to admit evasion of Federal income taxes and avoid imprisonment.

Another straightforward lead without the pre-spin. A few months later, the following headline appeared across the top of the *New York Times*: "FEDERAL GRAND JURY INDICTS 7 NIXON AIDES ON CHARGES OF CONSPIRACY ON WATERGATE; HALDEMAN, EHRLICHMAN, MITCHELL ON LIST" (March 2, 1974):

> WASHINGTON, March 1—A federal grand jury today indicted seven men, all former officials of President Nixon's Administration or of his 1972 re-election campaign, on charges of covering up the Watergate scandal.

Apparently, the Nixon administration, unlike George W. Bush's administration, was still not "rocked" or "stunned" by events on the front page of the *Times*.

Finally, under the headline "NIXON RESIGNS: HE URGES A TIME OF 'HEALING'; FORD WILL TAKE OFFICE TODAY" (August 9, 1974), the *Times* reported:

> WASHINGTON, Aug. 8—Richard Milhous Nixon, the 37th President of the United States, announced tonight that he had given up his long and arduous fight to remain in office and would resign, effective at noon tomorrow.

Comparing the leads written in the *New York Times* over twenty-five years ago with those published today makes one wonder whether the current publisher and managing editor of the *Times* ever really understood or appreciated the newspaper that Arthur S. Ochs and his family had developed through the mid-20th century.

"HEAD OFF CRITICISM"

The *Times* seems to know when the Bush administration will be criticized before anyone has a chance to criticize it, and the *Times'* prescience, and nothing else, often becomes front-page news. A front-page story entitled "WHITE HOUSE AIDES LAUNCH A DEFENSE OF BUSH TAX PLAN" (January 7, 2003) was published a day before President Bush announced an economic stimulus plan and opened with the following lead:

> WASHINGTON, Jan. 6—White House officials rolled out statistics and new details of President Bush's sweeping tax plan today in an effort to head off criticism that it favors only the rich.

Naturally, the article did not list a single one of those "statistics" supposedly "rolled out" by the administration but stated as fact, above-the-fold on its front page, exactly the Democrat's class warfare slant on the Bush plan:

> But in focusing on the dividend plan, which could cost the federal treasury $300 billion over 10 years, Mr. Bush also selected the one proposal that most emphatically benefits a sliver of the nation's richest households.

Now, Bush's tax cut proposal not only benefits just the wealthy, according to the *Times*; it "most emphatically" benefits them. The *Times* neglected to mention that over 50 percent of the benefits of the dividend proposal will benefit senior citizens. Moreover, the *Times*' opinion of the elimination of the "double taxation of dividends"—which is what the proposal has been called over the past thirty years of academic debate—failed to take into account the vast structural benefits that proponents of the plan have been writing about for years. Finally, the article went out of its way to quote like-minded economists who expressed doubt about how the Bush plan—which had not even been announced yet in full form—would stimulate the economy.

So much for the negative spin of the Bush economic stimulus plan. The same issue of the *Times* contained a story on a competing stimulus package announced by the Democrats, which had been announced in full form. The *Times*' coverage of that plan received an entirely different slant. In "DEMOCRATS IN HOUSE PROPOSE A PACKAGE RIVALING BUSH'S" (January 7, 2003), the *Times* reported:

> Democrats also said that while their package called for spending $136 billion, the net cost to the Treasury over 10 years would be only $100 billion, in part because of the added economic activity that they said would be generated by the plan.

Wouldn't the same analysis be true of the Bush plan? The article contained no quotes from economists or other "experts" critical of the Democrat plan.

"WAS CRITICIZED"

The use of passive voice is a classic means of spinning a story with the views or speculations of a reporter or editor. Recall from your basic grammar classes that a sentence is considered using the *passive voice* when the subject is the receiver of the action. It is the reverse of the *active voice*, where the subject is the performer of the action indicated by the verb. For example:

Active voice: The cat ate the canary.
Passive voice: The canary was eaten by the cat.

Use of the active voice is generally considered preferable, but the passive voice can be acceptable where the doer is obvious or routine (e.g., "John was elected president"). The passive voice can also be quite useful where the doer of the action is unknown (e.g., "The entrance was hidden cleverly"). Thus, in news reporting, the passive voice can be used where the doer is unknown and the reporter wishes to inject his opinion on the doer's identity. It can also be used to conceal the doer's identity.

When the *Times* is critical of a Republican but doesn't have a like-minded source to quote, it will simply employ the passive voice construction "was criticized" to stand in the place of a quote from the *Times*' editorial staff.

In an article we reviewed earlier in this chapter ("AIDES SAY BUSH WAS ONE TARGET OF HIJACKED JET," September 13, 2001), the *Times* first reported a political fallout with no factual or expert support. The *Times* then took the next step and actually criticized the president's action itself. The paper employed the passive voice (i.e., "was criticized") and, like before, included no factual or expert support for the criticism (except for one anonymous comment that suggested that the president might have overruled the Secret Service):

> "We are talking about specific and credible intelligence," Mr. Rove said, "not vague suspicions." But neither Mr. Rove nor other officials explained why this information was not made public on Tuesday. Partly because it was not, Mr. Bush was criticized for spending the day traveling a zigzag route.

You just can't tell from this article the identity of any of the people who either criticized the president or suggested he might be hurt politically by his actions. And that's the beauty of the passive construction: you can directly attack the president of the United States in a "straight" news story and you don't have to report any fact, or even the opinions of others, to back it up.

"SEEMED TO" AND "APPEARED TO"

A variation on the previous technique is when a paper spins a fact with its own opinion by adding what "seemed" or "appeared" to be the case. With this technique, it is not necessary to disclose *to whom* it "seemed" or "appeared"— using the passive voice will eliminate the need to report the doer.

In a *Times* article run under the headline "REPUBLICANS, IN NEW TACTIC, OFFER INCREASE IN TAX BREAKS" (March 15, 2001), reporting on tax cuts proposed by House Republicans, the paper used the "seemed" technique to speculate on what was going on in the *minds* of Republicans:

> The Republicans' motives seemed to include giving some fresh meat to their conservative supporters, putting pressure on the Senate not to cave in to pressure from moderates, forcing Democrats into casting difficult votes and maybe even allowing President Bush to appear to be taking a middle ground.

The article quoted no person and cited no authority to support its speculations about the motives—what was going on in the minds—of the Republicans. Nevertheless, this provided the cover needed for the *Times* to label the Republican proposal a "new tactic." Also, notice the use of the word "even" to express the paper's incredulity: "Can you believe these guys are trying to make President Bush's position on tax cuts look moderate?"

Lightning rarely strikes twice in the same place, but it did in this article. Later, the paper stated:

> The Republican leaders estimated that their plan would cost $2.2 trillion over 10 years, well above the $1.6 trillion that Mr. Bush has said was his maximum, and the leaders' projection seemed to be on the low side.

Again, no quote or authority provided here for the opinion that the projection "seemed to be on the low side."

"PARLIAMENTARY TRICKS"

When Republicans use "parliamentary tricks" to affect the fate of legislation, they are being "thuggish." When Democrats use the same "parliamentary tricks," they "accomplish" their political goals and, with the help of the *Times*, their public relations goals.

In a front-page article on an agreement by then Majority Leader Trent Lott to bring the McCain-Feingold Campaign Finance Reform Bill to the Senate floor, run under the headline "LOTT IS ASSURING SENATE DEBATE ON FINANCE BILL" (January 27, 2001), the *Times* stated:

> Mr. Lott's commitment to a debate was significant because Republican leaders have previously used parliamentary tricks and filibusters to stop the bill from ever coming to final vote.

One of the "parliamentary tricks" to which the *Times* referred became the subject of a *Times* editorial entitled "MR. HASTERT'S DEBACLE" (July 13, 2001), in which the editors accused the Speaker of the House of using "thuggish tactics":

> After hours of bluster and threats, the House speaker, Dennis Hastert, resorted yesterday to the old-fashioned way of trying to kill campaign finance reform. . . . Mr. Hastert's parliamentary maneuvering may well backfire, and deserves to. Republicans have been hoping to minimize public attention for campaign finance reform, arguing that Americans do not care about it. But by using parliamentary tricks to try to defeat campaign reform, Republicans will now draw attention to themselves.

When Democrats use "parliamentary tricks," it is often presented as the use of a time-honored procedure to achieve a noble political goal. In a news article run under the headline "SENATE DEMOCRATS REBUFFED ON A DRUG BILL" (June 23, 2000), the *Times* played its usual role of the "PR" firm of the Democrat party by writing precisely the story Senate Democrats would have expected about their use of a "parliamentary trick":

> At a time when public opinion polls show the rising prices for prescription drugs as a priority among voters, Senate Democrats seized on a parliamentary trick today to force a vote on their bill. In so doing, they accomplished two political goals: They got the chance to talk about their plan

for making prescription drugs more affordable to senior citizens and they forced Republicans to cast a difficult vote, perhaps the only one of the year, on the issue.

In other words, the Democrats' use of "parliamentary tricks" drew favorable attention, at least from the *New York Times*.

"ONLY"

When there is a vote on legislation, the *Times* will often characterize the size of the vote in a way that best reflects upon the paper's own editorial views on the subject.

For example, the *Times* had just published an editorial entitled "TAX CUT FEVER IN THE HOUSE" (March 8, 2001), which expressed the paper's opposition to a Bush administration tax cut proposal. The next day, in an article run under the headline "CENTRAL ELEMENT OF BUSH TAX PLAN PASSES THE HOUSE" (March 9, 2001), regarding a vote of the House of Representatives on the tax cut proposal, the *Times* reported:

> In the end, no Republicans voted against the bill, and only 10 Democrats broke ranks and voted for it.

By using the word "only" here, the *Times* characterized as minimal the number of Democrats who broke ranks. The same news could have been written as follows:

> In the end, no Republicans voted against the bill, and 10 Democrats broke ranks and voted for it.

Or:

> In the end, House Republicans voted unanimously for the bill, and all but 10 Democrats voted against it.

Which of the three versions is closest to the truth? Given the context, it is clear that the version chosen by the *Times* was the furthest from the truth. The context was reported in an article appearing in the prior day's issue of the *Times* ("PLAN TO TIE TAX CUT TO SURPLUS GAINS; G.O.P TRIES TO STOP IT," March 8, 2001):

> The best estimate, party leaders said, was that all Republicans would vote for the measure and that they would be joined by a half-dozen or so Democrats.

Since the number of Democrats who voted with the Republicans was nearly twice as many as party leaders expected, an unbiased story should have reflected that fact. The "only 10 Democrats" slant neglected the context and conveyed the opposite impression.

Note further how a paper can take a swipe at those Democrats who turn their back on the liberal line. For example, rather than characterizing the Democrats as "supporting the president," the paper could disparage the Democrats by saying they "broke ranks"—disloyalty is not a virtue admired by most Americans.

To illustrate the power of this form of spin, consider another version of the story that would better have reflected the truth in the context of the previous report in the *Times*:

> In the end, House Republicans voted unanimously for the bill, and 10 Democrats, more than had been expected by party leaders, voted with the Republicans to support the president's tax cut proposal.

"SURE TO"

The *Times* habitually speculates on reactions by politicians and ignores public reactions where they may prove embarrassing to Democrats. This technique tends to give further credence to the stereotypes the paper creates with effective labeling.

For example, in an article under the headline "DEMOCRATS PROPOSE BLEND OF MAKING AND SAVING ENERGY" (March 23, 2001), the *Times* reported:

The proposal, which creates an array of tax incentives, pointedly leaves out a Republican plan to open the Arctic National Wildlife Refuge in Alaska for oil exploration, an initiative fiercely opposed by most Democrats and some Republicans.

To make this story fair, the *Times* would have had to have mentioned that the initiative to open the Arctic National Wildlife Refuge to oil drilling was "fiercely supported by most Republicans and virtually all unions."

The legislation, in an approach sure to rankle Republicans, calls for limits by 2008 on the amount of fuel that light trucks and sport utility vehicles, which consume more gas than cars, can use.

If the approach "pointedly leaves out a Republican plan" and was "sure to rankle Republicans," why wasn't this labeled a "new tactic" or a "partisan ploy"? And wouldn't the approach be even more "sure to rankle" union workers, both those in the auto industry who oppose limits on fuel consumption and those who support the drilling of oil in the Arctic National Wildlife Refuge, the fact of which the Democrat legislation "pointedly leaves out"?

The only thing that is certain is that this approach is "sure to" save the *Times* the trouble of actually seeking the views of the union officials who would surely "rankle" Democrats with critical quotes.

"ENGINEERED"

Republican victories at the polls are not earned but "engineered," usually by corporate lobbyists and executives. The *Times* appears to take every opportunity to spin the Republican party as the party of, by, and for the wealthy and corporate interests. In addition, since the *Times* supports strict limitations on campaign contributions, fund raising, particularly by the Republican party, is typically reported as a means of corrupting public officials.

The *Times* accomplished this goal in a front-page article in the *Times* under the headline "BUSH GALA EXPECTED TO NET $15 MILLION" (May 20, 2001). The lead read as follows:

WASHINGTON, May 19—Organizers of a multimillion-dollar Republican dinner that will be President Bush's debut as fund-raiser in chief include dozens of corporate lobbyists and executives who helped engineer his election and whose industries stand to benefit from his energy plan, his tax cuts and his other early moves in the White House.

The *New York Times* and virtually all of its shareholders, employees, and readers also stand to benefit from the president's energy plan, tax cuts, and other early moves in the White House (whatever they are), despite the fact that the *New York Times* did everything it could to "engineer" the election of Al Gore.

Interestingly, the *Times* also used the occasion to ridicule the Republicans by reporting on a fund-raising practice that has been employed by both parties since the beginning of time:

> Two members of the organizing committee for the dinner, speaking on condition of anonymity, said that donors who wanted to be seated next to a particular cabinet member or other Republican official were directed to make the request to the committee and that the decision would be made partly on the basis of how much they had contributed to the party.

Then the *Times* flexed its muscles by taunting Bush cabinet officials who would dare to meet with any businessman who has made a campaign donation to the Republican party:

> Originally, the National Republican Senatorial Committee had planned to invite donors who were coming to Washington for the dinner to special briefings with cabinet members.
>
> But at least two of them, Education Secretary Rod Paige and Energy Secretary Spencer Abraham, said through spokesmen today they had declined the invitations because of schedule conflicts. Tommy G. Thompson, the secretary of health and human services, was criticized for meeting with Republican donors in his office after the meeting was disclosed last month in The New York Times.

Paradoxically, the *Times* must have been pleased with its apparent influence over the meeting schedules of Bush cabinet members, yet frustrated that no embarrassing meetings took place. Nevertheless, this did not stop the *Times* from attempting to terrorize Bush's cabinet officers when, a full two days later, the *Times* published another front-page story under the headline "3 BUSH CABINET MEMBERS DROP MEETINGS WITH G.O.P. DONORS":

> WASHINGTON, May 22—While President Bush greeted Republican donors at a $23.9 million fund-raising dinner tonight, at least three members of his cabinet backed out of private meetings that had been set up with some of the donors for later this week.

In other words, the *Times* took the opportunity to bash the Bush administration for conducting themselves exactly as the *Times* wanted them to! Recall, this very same "news" had already been reported in the *Times* three days before. So why the front-page placement? Perhaps for the opportunity to include a few more digs—such as applying the Quote-Someone-Who-Agrees-With-Us technique for some egg-throwing by the political opposition:

> "Rather than the Lincoln Bedroom, it's now the Cheney Bedroom," the House minority leader, Representative Richard A. Gephardt of Missouri, said today.

When Clinton was being accused of renting the Lincoln bedroom in return for political contributions, Gephardt was noticeably silent—a "news story" the *Times* failed to cover.

Again, why the front-page placement for a story that the paper already reported three days earlier? Perhaps the *Times* was more interested in demonstrating that it too can engage in political attack:

> One party official said the briefings had threatened to become "radioactive" after Mr. Thompson was criticized for meeting donors in his office this month.

Recall that the vehicle for such criticism was *The New York Times*.

Turning the tables, how did the *Times* cover political fund-raising by a Democrat president? The Democrats have used the very same fund-raising techniques; however, the *Times* would have everyone believe that these techniques were invented by Republicans and that Democrats were only employing Republican techniques.

In an article run under the headline "CLINTON SHAKES THE MONEY TREE: IN TURNABOUT, HE USES GOP TACTIC TO RAISE POLITICAL FUNDS" (October 1, 1994), the *Times* wrote:

> WASHINGTON, September 30—President Clinton's stock speech on the campaign trail this autumn, in ballrooms and meeting halls, always includes a long recitation of his achievements. But it omits a striking one: in 20 months, he has personally raised $40 million in Democratic political donations—nearly half the national party's reported total.
>
> He has done it mostly by taking a leaf from the voluminous fund-raising manual of the Republicans before him, and using the prestige and power of the White House for Democratic financial gain.
>
> Like George Bush and Ronald Reagan, Bill Clinton has flattered big-money donors with private White House parties and seats at state dinners and momentous events. He has freed Cabinet officers, their aides and White House officials to give private briefings on business and politics to especially generous supporters.

So, the *Times* used its front-page ("BUSH GALA EXPECTED TO NET $15 MILLION," May 20, 2001) to inform the public that campaign donors would get seats at campaign fund-raising dinners but failed to mention that virtually the same practice had been used by President Clinton five years earlier— "virtually," because it appears Clinton would provide "big-money donors" with seats at state dinners (which are all held on the premises of the White House), not just at fund-raising events. Of course, the *Times* would have us believe that Clinton was only copying the nefarious practices invented by his Republican predecessors—which excuses Clinton while disparaging Reagan and Bush— and that Presidents Carter, Johnson, and Kennedy never provided campaign donors with access to cabinet officers or state dinners. While the tone of the *Times'* coverage of Bush's fund-raising activities was accusatory and disparaging, the *Times* gave the impression that it approved of and admired how Clinton approached his fund-raising affairs.

While Clinton "freed" cabinet officers to give private briefings to "generous supporters," Bush cabinet officers were later chided by the *Times* for avoiding the same practice. None of Clinton's cabinet officers had ever feared becoming "radioactive" for meeting with donors, and the *Times* never reported how those donors helped Clinton "engineer" his re-election that year.

"SURPRISINGLY"

When a *Times* editorial position is proven by events to have been wrong, the *Times* acts surprised. For example, in a typical knee-jerk, "Oppose-Bush-On-Every-Issue" editorial entitled "TEARING UP THE ABM TREATY" (December 13, 2001), the *Times* opposed President Bush's proposal to have the U.S. withdraw from the obsolete Antiballistic Missile Treaty:

> With his decision to junk the 1972 Antiballistic Missile Treaty, President Bush is rolling the diplomatic dice. If he is lucky, the Russians will live with the decision and relations with Moscow will continue to improve while Washington freely experiments with new missile defense systems. If he is not, Mr. Bush may alienate the Kremlin and give rise to a dangerous new arms race with Russia and possibly China as well. Why he would choose to take that risk at a moment when he badly needs Russian cooperation in the war against terrorism is baffling.

Of course, according to the *Times*, the president can either be "lucky" or "unlucky"; he can never be "right" or, God-forbid, "smart." Whether lucky, right, or smart, Bush apparently surprised the *Times*, which reported the following news in a story run under the headline "TAKING COMMAND IN CRISIS, BUSH WIELDS NEW POWERS" (January 1, 2002):

> With only cursory consultation of Congress, he announced the American withdrawal from the 1972 Anti-Ballistic Missile Treaty, with surprisingly little backlash from Russia or the allies.

Call it "dumb luck."

"LACED"

Something is usually "laced" with poison, not praise, but to praise the Republicans and their war plans is, to liberals, akin to poison. Thus, in an article run under the headline "ASHCROFT DEFENDS ANTITERROR PLAN; SAYS CRITICISM MAY AID U.S. FOES" (December 7, 2001), the *Times* was not entirely pleased when some Democrats voiced support for the Bush administration's war on terrorism:

> The Democratic critics on the committee were careful in their questioning and most laced their remarks with some support for the administration, even for the proposal thought to be most controversial, the establishment of military tribunals to try terrorists.

Here also we see the use of the adverb "even" to suggest "though it may seem improbable" or "can you believe they actually supported the administration's plan to use military tribunals to try terrorists?" By the way, who said that plan was "thought to be most controversial"? As no one is quoted to that effect, it looks like the *Times* is directly injecting its opinion—"thought to be"—into a news story once again.

"THOUGH"

When a Republican makes an assertion the *Times* doesn't agree with, the paper typically points out that he failed to address or explore what the *Times* believes is a flaw in his argument.

In a "straight" news article run under the headline "ALLIES TELL BUSH THEY'LL ACT ALONE ON CLIMATE ACCORD" (July 22, 2001), the *Times* inserted its own counterpunch to a statement by President Bush when he responded to demonstrators protesting Western free trade policies:

> Mr. Bush has countered the protesters by insisting that ever freer trade is the answer to the problems facing developing nations, though never once here has

he explored the side effects on countries unable to compete with the richest nations.

By reporting on what President Bush did not do—an effort more appropriately reserved for an editorial or "News Analysis" piece—the *Times* here demonstrated how its political bias against the president once again impeded its mission "to give the news impartially without fear or favor." Here the *Times* suggested that free trade puts poor nations at an economic disadvantage to rich nations. But the *Times* itself has been urging for years the lifting of the trade embargo against Cuba, apparently under the impression that free trade between the U.S. and Cuba would benefit the island nation. Even President Clinton actively supported free trade agreements, such as the North American Free Trade Agreement (NAFTA). It should have been no surprise that President Bush "never once" explored the "side effects" of free trade on poorer nations, because it is not likely that he ever seriously considered a notion so contrary to common economic wisdom. It appears the only reason the *Times* suggested what Bush *did not* do at the conference was to undermine the president's response to the protesters.

Having explored how a propagandist uses labels and loaded language to conduct a war against its political opponents, we now turn from cluster-bombing with labels and loaded language to carpet-bombing with entire stories: opinion pieces disguised as "news" articles published as part of a series. In other words, the crusade.

NINE

Distorting with Crusades

We do not crusade in our news columns.

—*Arthur Hays Sulzberger, publisher of the* New York Times, *1935-1961*

lanting a story is not very effective when there is no story to slant. But when the publisher perceives a wrong that requires attention, it may not be enough to merely express the paper's views on the editorial page. It may be necessary to forcibly disguise the entire opinion as a news story and place it on the front page. When a newspaper "floods the zone" with a series of opinion pieces disguised as front-page news stories, the practice is known as *crusading*.

As soon as the Bush administration began to make noises about possible military action against Iraq, the *Times* began an orchestrated campaign to influence the American public against it. When the editors of the *Times* realized that talk of war might help the Republicans during the midterm elections of 2002, the *Times* began turning up the heat.

One of the first volleys in that summer's accelerated crusade appeared as the lead story on the front page of the *Times* under the headline "PROFOUND EFFECT ON ECONOMY SEEN IN A WAR ON IRAQ" (July 30, 2002). A paradigm for employing the Quote-Someone-Who-Agrees-With-Us technique, the article opened with the following "news":

WASHINGTON, July 29—An American attack on Iraq could profoundly affect the American economy, because the United States would have to pay most of the cost and bear the brunt of any oil price shock or other market disruptions, government officials, diplomats and economists say.

This editorial disguised as a news story deserves a Pulitzer Prize for its sheer audacity. To support the headline the *Times* was so desperate to publish, the reporters called up the usual suspects—government officials, diplomats, economists, and other experts who could be counted on to say something to support the *Times'* thesis—but all the reporters could muster are the following feeble quotes (none of which appear until page 9, evidently because they hardly support the lead sentence of the story at all):

"I think a good case can be made that voters will want to understand the case for war or any kind of extended military action better than they do now because the economic considerations are considerable," said Kim N. Wallace, a political analyst for Lehman Brothers in Washington.

Clearly, nothing in that quote even remotely supports the notion that military action against Iraq would have a "profound effect" on the economy. All this analyst said was that the public—a large majority of whom, according to polls taken at the time, were already informed enough to favor the U.S. taking military action against the Iraqi regime—might want to be even better informed as the situation developed. The importance of a better informed public is hardly the stuff of front-page news.

Next quote:

James R. Schlesinger, a member of the Defense Policy Review Board that advises the Pentagon who held senior cabinet posts in Republican and Democratic administrations, said he believed that the president would opt for a significant ground presence in Iraq. He said he did not think that fear of economic instability by itself would cause the United States to refrain from trying to unseat the Iraqi leader.

"My view is that given all we have said as a leading world power about the necessity of regime change in Iraq," Mr. Schlesinger said, "means that our credibility would be badly damaged if that regime change did not take place."

Neither that quote, nor its setup, supports a finding of a "profound effect." If anything, Schlesinger suggested that whatever the effect on economic stability it would seem to be insufficiently profound enough to deter us from removing Saddam Hussein from power.

The next quote is from a House Democrat, from whom you would think the *Times* could wring a juicy quote:

> Representative John M. Spratt Jr. of South Carolina, the senior Democrat on the House Budget Committee and a member of the Armed Services Committee said the United States would come up with whatever money was necessary.

No support for a "profound effect" here, either. All the congressman was saying was that spending trade-offs are the bread and butter of legislation and the House was ready to appropriate the money necessary to maintain national security.

Next quote:

> James A. Placke, a former senior diplomat specializing in the Persian Gulf and now a senior associate of Cambridge Energy Research Associates, said the market reaction to any invasion of Iraq was at best uncertain. "Given the market's lack of enthusiasm for this venture, I wouldn't think the market reaction would be very good," he said.

This expert, to his credit, basically said he didn't know what effect military action would have on the economy. It would certainly be no surprise if an invasion of Iraq caused a short-term drop in the stock market. Nor would a short-term rise in the price of oil, which was what we experienced during the time preceding the first Gulf War against Iraq, support the thesis of a "profound effect" on the economy.

It is clear that despite nothing to support it the fabricated headline and news lead served only one purpose: to support the *Times'* editorial policy against the use of military force against Iraq.

The crusade continued two days later when the *Times* published a similar story under the headline "EXPERTS WARN OF HIGH RISKS OF A U.S. INVASION OF IRAQ" (August 1, 2002).

The next day, August 2, the same reporter wrote another story, also employing the Quote-Someone-Who-Agrees-With-Us technique, which ran under the headline "EXPERTS PUT LARGE PRICE TAG ON REBUILDING OF IRAQ" (August 2, 2002).

The following day, the *Times* continued the campaign against Bush's policies on Iraq with a story under the headline "BACKING BUSH ALL THE WAY, UP TO BUT NOT INTO IRAQ" (August 3, 2002). We made use of this article earlier to illustrate how you can fill a story with quotes from "ordinary Americans" to state your anti-Bush views for you and how a paper can increase the credibility of those quoted by making sure they are Republicans. Here the reporter ventured into Republican country, Arizona, and found, as you may recall, four ordinary people—a jewelry store manager, a Vietnam veteran, a shoe store manager, and a high school teacher—who each said they backed Bush but not his policy on Iraq.

That same day—following three days of articles gravely touting the "profound effects," "high risks," and "large price tag" of waging war with Iraq—the *Times'* editorial staff dropped the other shoe. In one of the many *Times* editorials questioning the Bush administration's intentions regarding Iraq ("A TIME FOR CANDOR ON IRAQ," August 3, 2002), the *Times'* editorial writers suggested that President Bush had been less than candid with the public on the subject of Iraq:

> It is time for Mr. Bush to level with the nation about his intentions and to talk candidly about why he feels military action against Iraq may soon be necessary, and what the goals, costs and potential consequences of a war would be.

To accuse President Bush of being less than candid with the public on the "costs and potential consequence of a war" with Iraq, after three days of taking liberties with the facts on those very subjects on its own front pages, must have strained the credulity of many readers, even devoted readers, of the *New York Times*.

The risk of the *Times*' completely losing its credibility for news reporting took a giant leap forward when the paper was publicly called on the carpet for its front-page coverage of Iraq. You will recall from a previous chapter how the *Times* distorted the published views of Dr. Henry Kissinger to support a front-page attack article under the headline "TOP REPUBLICANS BREAK WITH BUSH ON IRAQ STRATEGY" (August 16, 2002).

Two days later, Charles Krauthammer, the syndicated columnist for the *Washington Post*, wrote in a column entitled "KIDNAPPED BY THE TIMES" (August 18, 2002):

> A story that should be on Page A22, the absence of one Iraqi opposition leader (out of a dozen-odd) at a meeting in Washington, is Page A1, above the fold. Message: Disarray in the war camp. A previous above-the-fold front-page story revealed—stop the presses!—that the war might be financially costly.
>
> Then there are the constant references to growing opposition to war with Iraq—in fact, the polls are unchanged since January—culminating on Aug. 16 with the lead front-page headline: "Top Republicans Break with Bush on Iraq Strategy."

Krauthammer went on to expose how the *Times*, in that August 16 article, distorted the views of Dr. Kissinger, forcing the *Times* later to print a grudging correction. Krauthammer then concluded with a swipe at the *Times*' carelessness:

> It is one thing to give your front page to a crusade against war with Iraq. That's partisan journalism . . . It's another thing to include Henry Kissinger in your crusade. That's just stupid. After all, it's checkable.

Having been so plainly exposed in the *Washington Post*, one would think that the *Times* would have been well advised to step back and re-examine their approach to the front page. On the contrary, the editors of the *Times* brushed off the criticism and continued their campaign against the Bush administration's policies on Iraq, as though nothing had happened.

Within a week, the *Times* again employed the Quote-Someone-Who-Agrees-With-Us technique in a front-page lead article under the headline "IRAQ SAID TO PLAN TANGLING INVADERS IN STREET FIGHTING" (August 26, 2002):

> WASHINGTON, Aug. 25—President Saddam Hussein of Iraq will try to compensate for his armed forces' glaring weaknesses by raising the specter of urban warfare if the Bush administration moves to attack the Iraq government, according to Pentagon officials and former United States government experts.

In an effort to weaken the overwhelming public support for military action against Iraq, the *Times* used the time-honored technique of bringing into the limelight the horrors of war in the most graphic way imaginable—in this case, raising the specter of U.S. forces fighting street-to-street with the Iraqi army:

> In anticipation of an eventual American attack, Iraq has already started military preparations, they say. . . .
> But this time Mr. Hussein's goal is not so much to hold ground as to hold power. That means that Iraq can be expected to use the threat of urban warfare to try to deter the United States from attacking in the first place and to raise the political costs if Washington decides to press ahead with an invasion.

What's most interesting here is that the *Times* was not speculating on the *actual* ability of American forces to deal with "urban warfare," or even on whether Iraq is actually contemplating urban warfare, but merely on Iraq's "threat" of using it to deter the U.S. from taking military action in the first place. Here is what the expert who was quoted to support the *Times*' view actually said:

> "Iraq has no hope of prevailing in a straight military fight, and after Desert Storm the Iraqis probably realize that," said Kenneth K. Pollack, the director of national security studies at the Council on Foreign Relations and a former C.I.A. analyst of the Iraqi military.
> "Their best and most likely strategy will be to try to create the political conditions that would lead the Bush administration to think twice about an attack," Mr. Pollack said. "And one way to do that is to make us believe that we are going to face a Mesopotamian Stalingrad."

This expert was talking about Iraq creating the "political conditions" to *deter* the Bush administration from planning an attack, referring to Iraq's making the U.S. "believe" it's going to face a bloody urban battle. The expert said nothing to suggest that Iraq could *actually* create real conditions that our military could not handle.

As to the actual prospect of a street-to-street battle, the *Times* quoted another expert, retired General Barry McCaffrey of the Army, who led the 24th Mechanized Division against Iraq forces in the Gulf War:

> "My assessment is that if you put enough pressure on them, they will come apart and not fight," General McCaffrey said in an interview. "The notion that they will retreat into the built-up areas and turn them into a kind of Stalingrad is laughable."

General McCaffrey wasn't talking about a scare tactic to bend the resolve of the Bush administration or the American public; he was talking about the actual prospects of a ground war. His point was that, in an actual fight, the Iraqi army would fall apart at the seams.

What the *Times* was attempting to do with this article was something Saddam Hussein could never accomplish on his own (i.e., without the complicity of the most influential newspaper in the world): frighten the American public with the picture of a bloody urban battle in an attempt to deter military action against his regime.

The article also included a section regarding Iraq's weakened military, making the point that it's a "pale reflection" of the force it had when it invaded Kuwait and contrasting it with the U.S., which has "upgraded its military with more technologically advanced reconnaissance systems and precision weapons."

With the body of the story so disconnected from its lead sentence, one could imagine the reporter having originally submitted the article with the following lead:

> WASHINGTON, Aug. XX—Though President Saddam Hussein of Iraq will try [with the aid of the *New York Times*] to raise the specter of urban warfare if the Bush administration moves to attack him, Iraq's forces, which experts say will come apart upon a ground invasion, are no match for the U.S. military, according to Pentagon officials and former United States government experts.

Faced with having to print a headline like "IRAQ NO MATCH FOR U.S. FORCES IN THE AIR OR ON THE GROUND," the *Times* editors, it would seem, would have no choice but to rewrite the lead to better suit their editorial opposition to military action. However it may have evolved, from the reporter's mind to the front page of the *Times*, the resulting piece was nothing more than another thinly veiled editorial. It is remarkable, however, how the *Times* could publish an opinion article in which the main premise was not supported by a single quote.

The *Times* continued its public relations campaign on behalf of Saddam Hussein when it traveled to the Iraqi slums for some independent-minded observations to print on its front page ("IRAQI SLUM VOWS TO FIGHT U.S. BUT IT COULDN'T BE FRIENDLIER," February 1, 2003):

> "We are ready to confront the United States," said Halima Nebi, 57, matriarch of a family forced by poverty to pack 21 people into one apartment in Saddam City. "We will use stones, bricks, guns, our own hands."

FLOODING THE ZONE

The foregoing articles comprised just a small part of the *Times'* campaign to flood the zone, using its vast soft-money operation to influence the American public. Space and propriety do not permit a similar parsing here of each and every slanted article published by the *Times* during the year 2002. But the reader may get a sense of what was going on by glancing at the following headlines, making up the *Times'* political campaign against the Bush administration's policies just on the subject of Iraq:

RUSSIAN AIDE WARNS U.S. NOT TO EXTEND WAR TO IRAQ
(February 4, 2002)

TERROR ACTS BY BAGHDAD HAVE WANED, U.S. AIDES SAY
(February 6, 2002)

CHENEY, IN JORDAN, MEETS OPPOSITION TO MILITARY MOVE IN IRAQ
(March 13, 2002)

SAUDIS WARN AGAINST ATTACK ON IRAQ BY THE UNITED STATES
(March 17, 2002)

IRAQ OFFERS HELP OVER PILOT
(April 11, 2002)

U.S. OFFICIALS DIFFER ON STRATEGY FOR IRAQ
(JUNE 19, 2002)

KURDS, SECURE IN NORTH IRAQ, ARE WARY ABOUT A U.S. OFFENSIVE
(July 8, 2002)

EUROPEANS SPLIT WITH U.S. ON NEED FOR IRAQ ATTACK, CITING
MIDEAST AS PRIORITY
(July 22, 2002)

PROFOUND EFFECT ON U.S. ECONOMY IS SEEN FROM A WAR AGAINST
IRAQ
(July 30, 2002)

AIR POWER ALONE CAN'T DEFEAT IRAQ, RUMSFELD ASSERTS
(July 31, 2002)

EXPERTS WARN OF HIGH RISK FOR AMERICAN INVASION OF IRAQ
(August 1, 2002)

BACKING BUSH ALL THE WAY, UP TO BUT NOT INTO IRAQ
(August 3, 2002)

IRAQ IS DEFIANT AS G.O.P. LEADER OPPOSES ATTACK
(August 9, 2002)

TOP REPUBLICANS BREAK WITH BUSH ON IRAQ STRATEGY
(August 16, 2002)

PRESIDENT NOTES DISSENT ON IRAQ, VOWING TO LISTEN
(August 17, 2002)

OFFICERS SAY U.S. AIDED IRAQ IN WAR DESPITE USE OF GAS
(August 18, 2002)

WHITE HOUSE DENIES TEXAS SESSION IS ABOUT IRAQ
(August 21, 2002)

IRAQ SAID TO PLAN TANGLING THE U.S. IN STREET FIGHTING
(August 26, 2002)

IRAQ SPEECH BY CHENEY IS CRITICIZED BY SCHROEDER
(August 28, 2002)

FRANCE MUTES ITS CRITICISM OF U.S. STANCE TOWARD IRAQ
(August 29, 2002)

IRAQ PUTS BLAIR AT ODDS WITH PARTY
(September 1, 2002)

A BIT AMBIGUOUSLY, RUSSIA BACKS IRAQ OVER U.S. THREAT
(September 3, 2002)

MAIN U.S. GOAL IS OIL, IRAQ SAYS
(September 3, 2002)

CONGRESS NOW PROMISES TO HOLD WEEKS OF HEARINGS ABOUT IRAQ
(September 6, 2002)

WITH FOCUS SHIFTING TO IRAQ, DOMESTIC ISSUES FADE
(September 6, 2002)

ARABS, BY DEGREES, OPPOSE AMERICAN ATTACK ON IRAQ
(September 6, 2002)

POLL FINDS UNEASE ON TERROR FIGHT AND CONCERNS
ABOUT IRAQ
(September 8, 2002)

POWELL DEFENDS A FIRST STRIKE AS IRAQ ACTION
(September 8, 2002)

OPPOSITION IS GROWING TO BLAIR'S STAND ON IRAQ
(September 8, 2002)

WITH FEW VARIATIONS, TOP BUSH ADVISORS PRESENT THEIR CASE
AGAINST IRAQ
(September 9, 2002)

IN SENATE, A CALL FOR ANSWERS AND A WARNING ON THE FUTURE;
FOCUS ON IRAQ
(September 10, 2002)

3 GROUPS ALREADY SQUABBLING OVER OIL-FLUSH NORTH IRAQ
SHOULD HUSSEIN BE TOPPLED
(September 12, 2002)

PAKISTANI WANTS NO PART IN AN ATTACK ON IRAQ
(September 12, 2002)

SHARES MIXED ON VARIED ECONOMIC NEWS AND IRAQ TALK
(September 14, 2002)

SPLIT ON IRAQ IN U.N.
(September 15, 2002)

U.N. DEBATE OVER BUSH'S STANCE ON IRAQ DRAWS FRESH
SKEPTICISM, AND SOME SUPPORT
(September 15, 2002)

OUR TOWNS: LOOKING FOR THE ELUSIVE TWO-THIRDS WHO WANT WAR WITH IRAQ
(September 15, 2002)

JORDAN COULD SUFFER FROM U.S. ASSAULT ON IRAQ
(September 15, 2002)

REPUBLICANS WIELDING IRAQ AS AN ISSUE IN SENATE RACES IN CONSERVATIVE STATES
(September 18, 2002)

BISHOPS ARE WARY OF STRIKE ON IRAQ
(September 18, 2002)

EUROPEANS STRIVE TO TIGHTEN TRADE TIES WITH IRAQ
(September 19, 2002)

GORE CRITICIZES BUSH OVER STANCE ON IRAQ
(September 24, 2002)

3 RETIRED GENERALS WARN OF PERIL IN ATTACKING IRAQ WITHOUT BACKING OF U.N.
(September 24, 2002)

CONDITIONS ARE SAID IMPROVING IN IRAQ
(September 26, 2002)

LIBERALS OBJECT TO BUSH POLICY ON IRAQ ATTACK
(September 28, 2002)

INCREASED ATTENTION ON IRAQ IS RAISING ANXIETIES, TOO
(September 28, 2002)

CHURCHES AND ETHICISTS LOUDLY OPPOSE THE PROPOSED WAR ON IRAQ, BUT DEAF EARS ARE MANY
(September 28, 2002)

U.S. Is Dismissing Russia's Criticism of Strikes in Iraq
(October 1, 2002)

Bush Appears to Soften Tone on Iraq Action
(October 2, 2002)

Iraq Hopes Oil Sways Russian Vote in U.N.
(October 2, 2002)

Turkey, Mindful of Kurds, Fears Spillover If Change Washes
over Iraq
(October 3, 2002)

Maine Race Is Focused on Region, Not Iraq
(October 4, 2002)

Democrats Are Divided in Debate on Force against Iraq
(October 4, 2002)

Candidates in Tough Races Seem Mindful of Political
Repercussions on Stance on Iraq
(October 5, 2002)

Celebrities Known for Their Political Outspokenness Have
Little to Say about Iraq
(October 6, 2002)

Thousands at Central Park Rally Oppose an Iraq War
(October 7, 2002)

Arab Leaders Glumly Brace for Inevitable War, with an Eye to
Anger in the Streets
(October 8, 2002)

C.I.A. Sees Terror after Iraq Action
(October 9, 2002)

CAMEO APPEARANCE BY IRAQ IN NEW MEXICO RACE
(October 9, 2002)

U.S. AIDES SPLIT ON ASSESSMENT OF IRAQ PLANS
(October 10, 2002)

2 CRITICS OF BUSH IRAQ POLICIES SAY THEY'LL BACK RESOLUTION
(October 10, 2002)

THE AFTERMATH: RIFT OVER PLAN TO IMPOSE RULE ON IRAQ
(October 10, 2002)

U.S. FRENCH SPLIT ON IRAQ DEEPENS
(October 15, 2002)

SUPPORT FOR HUSSEIN; A SHOW OF LOYALTY (JUST SAY YES) IN IRAQ
VOTE FOR THE ONE AND ONLY
(October 16, 2002)

BUSH GARNERS LITTLE SUPPORT AT U.N.
(October 17, 2002)

A VULNERABLE KUWAIT READIES ITS DEFENSES FOR A U.S. ATTACK ON
IRAQ AND THE REACTION
(October 20, 2002)

FROM ITS PALACES, IRAQ'S VIEW IS OF A WORLD FILLED WITH ALLIES
(October 20, 2002)

12 AMERICANS STAGE PROTEST HUSSEIN IS HAPPY TO ALLOW
(October 27, 2002)

THOUSANDS MARCH IN WASHINGTON AGAINST GOING TO
WAR IN IRAQ
(October 27, 2002)

TURKEY, IN THE MIDDLE, GROWS MORE WORRIED EVERY DAY ABOUT
A U.S. ATTACK ON IRAQ
(October 28, 2002)

RESERVE CALL-UP FOR AN IRAQ WAR MAY EQUAL 1991'S
(October 28, 2002)

JORDAN, BETWEEN IRAQ AND U.S., WORRIES ABOUT WAR
(November 1, 2002)

WAR ON IRAQ NOT YET JUSTIFIED, BISHOPS SAY
(November 14, 2002)

Our search of headlines containing the word "Iraq" during this period did
not turn up a single one that could be construed as favoring military action.

During December 2002, the *Times* directed its reporters to take a different
tack in the paper's campaign to oppose military action against Iraq. There soon
started to appear feature stories on the front-page of the *Times* covering "a day
in the life of" everyday people in Iraq.

For example, in a front-page feature story entitled "IRAQ ARMS QUEST
COVERS A ZEST FOR DRINK" (December 7, 2002), the *Times* made light of the
UN weapons inspections:

> BAGHDAD, Iraq, Dec. 6—When Dr. Hussein al-Duremi went with his
> friends to the Tiger Eye liquor store on the 14th of Ramadan Street today, they
> had a good laugh with a fellow Iraqi customer called Wali about the United
> Nations weapons inspectors who went looking for nuclear bombs this week in
> three gin factories outside Baghdad.
>
> "It's not an atomic bomb they're putting in there is it, Wali?" one shopper
> asked as a $21 bottle of Johnnie Walker Black Label whiskey was slipped into a
> brown paper bag, the totem of a liquor trade that thrives here as in no other
> Arab country.
>
> Wali, a 24-year-old electrical engineer, chuckled, as have many Iraqis
> since learning about the strange business of the nuclear detectives in the
> booze plant.

With this new front in the crusade against the nation's security policies, the *Times* was doing much more than helping Saddam Hussein make light of American efforts to oust his regime. Psychologists who study the personal dynamics of kidnapping advise kidnap victims to make sure their abductors learn the victim's name and the names of relatives and others associated with the victim. Familiarizing the abductors with such human associations makes the victim less of an object and therefore more difficult to harm. Thus, the *Times* would seem to be preparing the public for another round of opinion polls to determine America's tolerance for civilian casualties in a war against Iraq.

In another front-page article, under the headline "IN BAGHDAD, THERE'S LITTLE ROMANCE IN MUSIC BY CANDLELIGHT" (December 26, 2002), the *Times* wrote:

> BAGHDAD, Iraq, Dec 25—The musicians of the Iraqi National Symphony Orchestra, elegant in black tie or long black skirts, were just settling into their places on the final night of their Christmas week concerts when the electricity failed and the performance hall was plunged into darkness.
>
> For a while afterward, the performance rolled with a dreamlike quality. A note from the oboe floated through the pitch black, guiding the players tuning their instruments, until candles affixed to the music stands illuminated their scores. The musicians played an initial overture and then the tenor soloist, Emad Jamil, sang the Agnus Dei from Bizet's "L'Arlesienne."

To demonstrate the absurdity of this transparent paradigm of propaganda, one would have to imagine the front page of the *New York Times* during the height of World War II featuring a series of articles on the activities of innocent Japanese citizens—performing the traditional tea ceremony or cultivating rice in the field or fishing along the shores of the Pacific—with interviews on their reflections on the prospects of a U.S. invasion. Perhaps the *Times'* behavior here will be deserving of a chapter of its own in a sequel to Ann Coulter's new book, *Treason*.

While the *means* of influencing public opinion includes crusades that "flood the zone" with "news" articles, flanked by like-minded editorials and op-ed pieces, all favoring the *Times'* political views, the *ends* of those efforts are reflected in the public opinion polls which provide the measure of a crusade's success or failure.

When a crusade successfully turns public opinion in favor of the *Times'* position on an issue, the poll results are given first class treatment on the front page. When the outcome proves disappointing, the results are not reported, de-emphasized, or distorted to minimize the embarrassment of rejection. The polls themselves often become part and parcel of a zone flooded with journalistic fraud, as will be shown in the next chapter.

TEN

Distorting with Polls

What a difference a word makes!

— *Dick Morris, writing for the* New York Post

---

classic technique developed in the 1990s and honed to perfection in the new millennium by the *New York Times* involves the use of opinion polls to influence public opinion. The methodology is straightforward.

First, the *Times* employs its massive soft-money machine to influence public opinion through a crusade—a series of slanted front-page "straight" news articles, editorials, and op-ed pieces.

Second, the *Times* commissions a public opinion poll on the issues about which it has been advocating. Well, "commissions" is not exactly the right word. Ignoring the obvious ethical considerations arising from the conflict of interest (i.e., reporting on a poll based on questions over which it has influence), the *Times* conducts the poll itself in a joint venture with CBS News called the *New York Times*/CBS News poll.

Third, because they maintain complete control over the conduct of the poll, the *Times* chooses the subjects of the poll and determines its timing. The poll is often timed to immediately precede an election or an important congressional vote.

Fourth, because the *Times* controls which questions to ask and how to ask them, the poll questions are written in a way to generate a predetermined result, providing the answers the *Times* requires to support its editorial views. This kind of survey is often referred to as a *push poll*.

Fifth, if the results of the poll satisfactorily support the *Times'* editorial position, the results are published on the front page of the *Times* with a suitable headline. If the results are not satisfactory, either the results (1) are not reported at all in the *Times*, or (2) a distorted interpretation of the results are published on the front page with a suitable headline.

Finally, the *Times* publishes an editorial about the "disturbing" results of the poll, and its op-ed columnists are invited to pile on with their erudite analysis and egg-throwing. The cycle soon repeats itself with another front-page crusade, another editorial campaign, and another push poll.

All of this, the *Times* knows, reverberates through the sound chamber of the liberal media with newspapers who subscribe to the New York Times News Service and television news outlets, especially CBS, repeating the poll results. Ultimately, liberal columnists and television commentators use the results—or the *Times'* distorted interpretation of them—to support their left-wing diatribes.

The result is either public opinion bent toward the *Times'* point of view or the *appearance* of a like-minded public opinion—that is, opinion distorted to reflect what the *Times* thinks the public should believe.

Let's take a look at just a few examples.

DISTORTING THE POLLS

It was a month before the 2000 presidential election, and the *New York Times* was in full gear, marshalling all of its resources to get Al Gore elected. The lengths to which the *Times* campaigned for Al Gore in the 2000 election is legendary, and the skillful interpretation of polls played no small part in that campaign. Front-page "objective" news articles, editorials, and op-ed pieces were being written with a determination to boost Gore's election prospects and to belittle George W. Bush as someone not ready for the presidency. A month before the election, the *Times* was finally ready to take a poll.

In a poll that focused on the candidate's experience and readiness to hold the nation's highest office, George Bush performed surprisingly well in answers to questions that would be expected to play to Al Gore's strengths.

Being that Al Gore had been a congressman and senator for sixteen years and vice president of the United States for another eight years, it was not surprising that 71 percent of the public believed Gore "has prepared himself well enough for the job of president," and 68 percent said Gore had the "skills needed to negotiate effectively with world leaders"—questions predetermined to significantly favor Gore over Bush.

The *Times,* however, must have been stunned to learn that about 50 percent of the public also believed that George W. Bush ("the village idiot from Texas") was both prepared to be president and had the skills needed to negotiate effectively with world leaders. Moreover, an impressive 67 percent said that Bush had the ability to be an effective president.

On the question of leadership, Bush actually beat Gore: 67 percent of registered voters said that Bush had "strong qualities of leadership," while 61 percent said that Gore did. Even 40 percent of Gore supporters, according to the poll, believed that Bush would make an effective leader.

Now, let's turn to how the results were reported by the *New York Times.* In a front-page "news" article, under the headline "CANDIDATES GIVEN HIGH MARKS IN POLL ON FITNESS TO LEAD" (October 3, 2000), the *Times* provided this interpretation of the results of the latest *New York Times*/CBS News poll:

> Taken as a whole, the survey had much encouraging news for Mr. Gore and very little for Mr. Bush.

To understand how the *Times* could reach such a conclusion from its own data, you must consider why the poll was conducted in the first place. The poll, and the accompanying article, was a vehicle for the *Times* to accomplish two things: (1) use the power of its front page to transmit its own doubts about Bush's qualifications to be president and (2) succinctly frame the issue to be addressed in the first debate between the candidates—namely, isn't George W. Bush too dumb to be the leader of the free world? The lead sentence of the article does a pretty good job of driving home the first objective:

BOSTON, Oct. 2—On the eve of the first presidential debate here, most Americans say Gov. George W. Bush and Vice President Al Gore are strong leaders, but they consider Mr. Gore far more prepared for the White House and better qualified to deal with world leaders and members of both parties in Congress, the latest New York Times/CBS News Poll shows.

The second objective was driven home later in the article when the *Times* sent the following message to journalists and television news anchors, so that there may be no misunderstanding as to why people would be tuning in to watch the debate:

> A majority of Americans say they will tune in to the debate. In addition to seeing where the two candidates stand on the issues, the poll's respondents say they will be looking to determine whether the nominees seem ready to handle the responsibilities of being president.

Imagine how Gore might have fared if the public had been asked if Gore "had conducted himself ethically enough in public office to have the character and personal integrity to be president?" Had the poll focused on the issue of character and personal integrity—asking questions about the candidates' past political fund-raising activities or how they reacted to President Clinton's moral behavior in the Oval Office—the results would have reflected a bias in favor of Bush, and the *Times* could have instead signaled to the media a Bush-favored debate question: Do we want the moral legacy of the Clintons to maintain control of the White House?

But the agenda of the *Times* was to elect Gore, not Bush, and the *Times,* as we know, has become particularly adept at fearlessly hammering home its editorial views in the form of "objective" news:

> The survey found that as voters start to form detailed impressions of the candidates, even those who say they intend to back Mr. Bush express reservations about his preparedness.

Later, the article included the following curious statement:

The lingering questions about Mr. Bush's preparedness do not seem to have affected his overall standing in the head-to-head competition as reflected in the poll.

If concerns about Bush's preparedness did not affect his standing in the polls, then perhaps Bush's favorable standing in the polls arises from something else. From this data—that a candidate's preparedness to be president will not affect one's vote—one might reasonably conclude that the public is basing their vote upon the character of the candidates and their positions on the issues, and *not* on their preparedness.

Since the *Times* obviously believes that half the public could not possibly agree with Bush, and since it would only hurt Gore to speculate on the character issue, questions about Bush's preparedness, as long as the *Times* has something to say about it, would continue to "linger."

The *Times* continued the assault:

> The most striking finding in the survey is the extent to which voters have reservations about Mr. Bush's preparedness.

Most striking? While disparaging Bush's preparedness seemed to be the very purpose of the survey, the findings didn't support that conclusion at all. In the next sentence, the *Times* almost comes clean about the bias of the poll:

> Their concerns may reflect their knowledge that Mr. Gore has served as vice president for eight years and, before that, was in the House and Senate for 16 years. By contrast, Mr. Bush did not hold public office until he was elected governor of Texas in 1994.

For the *Times*, the lingering questions of Bush's readiness to be president continued through his inauguration and only ended on September 11, at least temporarily.

The *Times'* use of poll data to boost Al Gore's 2000 presidential election campaign when it needed boosting and defend it when it needed defending was not limited to the *Times'* interpretations of the *New York Times/CBS News* polls. For example, in an article that ran under the headline "DESPITE UPS AND DOWNS SURVEY SHOWS RACE IS TIED" (September 28, 2000), the *Times* put the following spin on a *Los Angeles Times* poll that put presidential candidate George Bush at a 48 percent to 42 percent lead over Al Gore:

> After watching his opponent's popularity rise in the polls over the last month, Gov. George W. Bush got a dose of good news over the last few days. The momentum is now his, with three new nationwide polls showing that he has regained some of the ground he lost to Vice President Al Gore. Mr. Bush seems to have the edge in at least two of the polls. But is it real?
>
> The basic fact is, no one is ahead. When the polls are looked at together, the presidential race is so close that it is impossible to give either candidate an edge.
>
> Mr. Bush got his most encouraging news from The Los Angeles Times, which reported yesterday that thanks to a 22-point advantage among men, Mr. Bush was now leading Mr. Gore, 48 percent to 42 percent. But since the margin of sampling error is plus or minus four percentage points, the findings have to be considered a statistical tie.

Thus, the *Times* dismissed Bush's 6 percent lead as a "statistical tie." Consider the likelihood of the *Times* applying the same logic to dismiss a 6 percent lead by a Democrat over a Republican.

A few months after Bush took office, the *Times* and CBS conducted another poll, and the results were predictable. On a front-page story, under the headline "60% IN POLL FAVOR BUSH, BUT ECONOMY IS MAJOR CONCERN" (March 14, 2001), the *Times* continued its theme on Bush's preparedness:

> George W. Bush has drawn encouraging reviews for his presidential debut, but Americans are increasingly nervous about the economy and express concerns about Mr. Bush's ability to steer the nation to sustained prosperity, the latest New York Times/CBS News poll shows.

That may have been the lead on the front page, but it should not be surprising that none of the poll questions listed in the *Times* addressed whether Bush had the ability "to steer the nation to sustained prosperity" (or to any kind of prosperity). Several questions concerned Bush's tax cut proposal, which 57 percent of the public supported. Forty-three percent said his tax cut would be "good for the economy" and 56 percent agreed the tax cut is necessary to keep Congress from spending the surplus.

Absolutely nothing appears in the questions or the answers that would suggest any concern whatsoever about Bush's abilities on economic issues. The other results in the survey all supported Bush's views on the issues. Sixty-six percent of the respondents agreed that it was a good idea for the federal government to give money to religious organizations to provide social services. Forty-nine percent agreed that parents should get tax-funded vouchers that they can use to pay tuition for private or religious schools. End of survey.

Yet, in the second and third paragraphs of the article, the *Times* stated:

> After the most contentious election in the nation's history, many Americans have rallied behind their new president. His job approval rating is 60 percent, which is similar to that of his father, George Bush, and Bill Clinton in the opening months of their presidencies.
>
> Even so, Mr. Bush is burdened by a perception that he is not fully in command. Half the public says that Mr. Bush is not really in charge of what is going on in his own administration.

Here is the actual question upon which the conclusion of that last paragraph was based:

> Do you think George W. Bush is in charge of what goes on in his administration most of the time, or do you think other people are really running the government most of the time?
> Bush: 42%
> Others: 50%

Given the question, it is surprising that as many as 42 percent of the respondents answered that Bush, not other people, is "really running the government most of the time." The question itself is a distorted simplification of how well an executive assembles a quality staff and how effective he delegates his vast responsibilities. The U.S. government has millions of employees, and to suggest any president, and not other people, is "really running the government most of the time" is ridiculous.

The survey results could well have been an indication of how well the public thinks of Bush's cabinet appointees—so well, that *they* are really running the government, leaving the president with time to focus on the strategic issues he should be focusing on. Nevertheless, the *Times* chose to interpret the results to declare in a front-page "straight" news article that President Bush is "not fully in command" and is "not really in charge of what is going on in his own administration."

On April 29, 2001, CBS News announced the results of the latest *New York Times*/CBS News poll on its CBSNews.com website, reporting that President Bush's approval rating stood at 56 percent. CBS described the results of the poll this way:

> POLL: WE LIKE HIM
>
> (CBS) As he approaches the end of his first 100 days in office, President George W. Bush gets generally positive reviews—and the public sees him much the same as it did when he first took the presidential oath in January, a new CBS poll reports.

Given the positive showing for Bush, the *New York Times* had no choice but to employ the slant-by-omission technique: the *Times* didn't run a story on this poll—not on its front page, or anywhere else in the paper.

A few weeks later, however, the *Times* published on its front-page the latest results of another *New York Times*/CBS News poll under the headline "BUSH LOSES FAVOR DESPITE TAX CUT AND OVERSEAS TRIP" (June 21, 2001). The conclusion reflected in the headline was based in part on the following:

> Mr. Bush's job approval rating, which stands at 53 percent, is down seven points from March.

Well, if the *Times* had run the report on the *New York Times*/CBS News poll of April 29, which coincided with Bush's first 100 days in office, the news would have been that Bush's approval rating declined only 3 percent, down from 56 percent. It is not unusual for political honeymoons to fade as presidencies mature, and, in any event, the 3 percent difference was within the "margin of error" of the poll.

But let us assume that Bush's approval rating dropped 7 points according to the poll. According to the *Times'* own standards of interpretation (i.e., a 6 percent difference, given the margin of error, is a "statistical tie"), the drop was hardly statistically significant. Nevertheless, the same day, the *Times* published an editorial that resonated with its front-page distortion. Entitled "DISTURBING NUMBERS FOR MR. BUSH," the *Times* declared that the "poll shows the Bush White House is increasingly and alarmingly out of touch with what Americans are thinking."

Shortly after the September 11 attacks, another *New York Times*/CBS News poll was taken, and CBS announced the results on its website under the headline "POLL: REVENGE AND RETURN" (September 15, 2001):

> (CBS) Americans are rallying around the flag and want revenge, according to a *CBS News–New York Times* poll released Monday. They also believe the U.S. should return to business as usual as soon as possible. Nearly all are willing to endure long lines and security checks to prevent terrorist acts, and there is a growing sense that the U.S. will have to go to war.
>
> Eighty-five percent of Americans say the U.S. should take military action against whoever is responsible for Tuesday's attacks. Only six percent oppose military retaliation.
>
> About seven in ten support military retaliation even if that means innocent people are killed.

The "newspaper of record" chose not to record those results.

Within a month after President Bush declared to the world "either you are with us or you are with the terrorists," the *New York Times* made it clear where they stood. In the lead article on the front-page of the *Times* (October 31, 2001), reporting on that week's *New York Times*/CBS News poll, the *Times* ran the following headline and accompanying lead:

SURVEY SHOWS DOUBTS STIRRING ON TERROR WAR
> Americans for the first time are raising doubts about whether the nation can accomplish its objectives in fighting terrorism at home and abroad, including

capturing or killing Osama bin Laden, saving the international alliance from unraveling and protecting people from future attacks, the latest New York Times/CBS News poll shows.

What did the survey actually find? Here are the actual poll questions:

Do you approve of the military attacks led by the United States against Afghanistan?
Approve: 88%
Disapprove: 8%

Would the war in Afghanistan be worth the cost if several thousand American troops lost their lives?
Yes: 61%
No: 27%

In addition, 88 percent of those polled said they had a fair amount or a great deal of confidence "in the ability of the United States government to protect its citizens from future terrorist attacks." This result was striking, particularly when you consider the circumstances during the time in which the poll was conducted. Some postal workers had lost their lives by inhaling powder laced with anthrax, and anthrax was discovered in letters sent to government leaders and prominent television news journalists.

At the time the poll was taken it was still unclear whether Al Qaeda operatives or some domestic psychopath had caused the anthrax scare. Without further evidence, the Bush administration prudently refused to jump to any conclusions, particularly avoiding making any statement that might have caused widespread panic. Nevertheless, the chilling uncertainty gave the *Times* an opportunity to bottom fish for a headline, and it came up with the following question:

Is the government telling people everything they need to know about the anthrax attacks?
Yes: 47%
No: 50%

Well, if 50 percent of the public believed the government wasn't telling them "*everything* they need to know" about the anthrax attacks then, the *Times* apparently thought, there must be some anxiety, or "doubts stirring," out there.

And what caused those doubts to stir? The anthrax attacks? That would be too simple and would mean passing up a chance to bash the Bush administration, as the *Times* managed to do here:

> There were signs of anxiety in the poll, perhaps because it was conducted at a time when developments have made people feel more vulnerable. In recent days, the Bush administration and leaders on Capitol Hill appeared to lack a coordinated message in responding to the anthrax threat.

This might seem to be a pretty thin basis for a headline declaring "DOUBTS STIRRING ON TERROR WAR," but when a Republican president is maintaining a solid 87 percent approval rating, you have to be resourceful and take what shots you can. Perhaps the only one stirring doubts about the war effort was the *New York Times,* but you don't win Pulitzer Prizes by idly standing by when a Republican president enjoys unprecedented success.

After several months of publishing the results of slanted polls and distorted interpretations of them on their front pages, the *Times* finally started to attract some significant media attention from unwelcome corners. It began when the *Times* decided to take a fresh *New York Times*/CBS News poll on the public's impressions of potential military action against Iraq.

The timing of the poll was no accident. It came after an unrelenting ten-month crusade, described in the previous chapter, waged by the *New York Times* in both its news and op-ed pages to oppose the use of force against Iraq. The poll also preceded, by just a few days, an important congressional vote on a resolution permitting President Bush to use force against Iraq. It was also less than thirty days prior to the 2002 midterm elections.

Once again, the *Times* devoted the lead position on its front page, a place reserved for the most important "objective" news of the day, to report its own interpretation of the results of survey questions that it had a hand in crafting. Under the headline "PUBLIC SAYS BUSH NEEDS TO PAY HEED TO WEAK ECONOMY" (October 7, 2002), the *Times* reported:

A majority of Americans say that the nation's economy is in its worst shape in nearly a decade and that President Bush and Congressional leaders are spending too much time talking about Iraq while neglecting problems at home, according to the New York Times/CBS News poll.

This *Times* article was openly criticized for two basic reasons: (1) the *Times'* interpretation of the results was distorted, and (2) the questions were slanted to begin with.

On the day the article appeared, veteran reporter Brit Hume, on his Fox News program "Special Report," suggested that, in its interpretation of the poll's results, the *Times* actually concocted results to questions that were never asked. Commenting directly on the lead sentence above, Hume said (as reported in MediaResearch.org):

> In fact, the poll shows no such thing. It does show that people by a 56 to 43 percent margin think the economy is bad, and it does show that 70 percent of those asked would like to hear political candidates talk more about the economy. But the poll never asks whether the president is talking too much about Iraq.
>
> The poll found a majority—52 percent—think the president is spending his time, quote "about right," with only 41 percent saying he's too focused on foreign policy. Those numbers, by the way, are not reported in the *New York Times*.

Hume's analysis could likewise be applied to many other statements purporting to interpret the results of the poll. For example, the *Times* also asserted the following in its report:

> Americans said they feared a long and costly war that could spread across the Middle East and encourage more terrorist attacks in the United States.

This would lead one to believe that the American public does not support the use of military action against Iraq. But, according to the same poll, 67 percent of the public said they approved of the U.S. taking military action against Iraq to try to remove Saddam Hussein from power.

If 67 percent support the war with Iraq and 52 percent agree that President

Bush is spending his time "about right," how does the *Times* justify its three-deck headline?

PUBLIC SAYS BUSH NEEDS TO PAY HEED TO WEAK ECONOMY
MANY FEAR LOSS OF JOBS
POLL FINDS LAWMAKERS FOCUSING TOO MUCH ON IRAQ
AND TOO LITTLE ON ISSUES AT HOME

The jump headline on page 14, where the article continued, blasted the following: "PUBLIC SAYS BUSH NEEDS TO PAY MORE HEED TO ECONOMY, LESS TO IRAQ." And the only call-out (i.e., large type appearing in the middle of the column) on that page said, "Many Americans worry that they or a family member will be jobless in a year."

Yet, the actual poll results suggested that the public overwhelmingly supported the president's policy on Iraq and, while the congressional candidates could have been talking more about the economy in their campaigns, the public believed the president had his priorities straight.

In addition to being condemned for distorting the results, the *Times* was also roundly criticized for asking slanted questions. In his opinion column in the *New York Post* ("THE TIMES' PUSH POLL," October 8, 2002), Dick Morris, a former political advisor to President Clinton, made the following observations about the poll:

> The phrasing of the questions is so slanted and biased that it amounts to journalistic "push polling"—the use of "objective" polling to generate a predetermined result, and so vindicate a specific point of view.

Morris suggested that the *Times* framed their questions to generate a particular predetermined result: that voters see the economy as a bigger issue than Iraq. Morris pointedly addressed some of the questions asked in the survey:

> **Slant No. 1:** The *Times* poll asks voters if they would "be more likely to vote for a congressional candidate because of their positions on the economy or foreign policy."
>
> The use of "foreign policy" throws the results way off and allows the *Times*

to report that voters want more focus on the economy by 57 percent to 25 percent. But on Sept. 8-9 *Fox News* asked 900 voters a similar question—comparing not economy v. foreign policy, but economy vs. *national security*. The results: an even split, with the economy pulling 32 percent and national security 31 percent. What a difference a word makes!

Slant No. 2: The *Times* then asked what voters would "like to hear the candidates talk more about, the possibility of war with Iraq or improving the economy." It got the expected outcome: 70 percent for the economy, 17 percent for Iraq. But that phrasing surely masks the impatience of voters who favor war with Iraq but are tired of the endless talk about it. Those who favor action and oppose more debate would register on the "economy" side of this biased question.

Slant No. 3: The poll found voters approving of military action against Iraq by 67 percent to 27 percent. But the *Times* then tried to undermine this finding if voters would still back military action if there were "substantial American military casualties" (support drops to 54 percent) or "substantial Iraqi civilian casualties" (support drops to 49 percent).

So where is the question on how support would change if military action is quick and painless, as in the 1991 war? Or if (again as in 1991) postwar examination of Iraqi sites revealed that substantial work on weapons of mass destruction had been going on?

The day after the *Times* ran on its front page its distorted interpretation of this slanted poll, its editors published an editorial entitled "A NATION WARY OF WAR" (October 8, 2002), suggesting that President Bush hadn't convincingly addressed the "potentially costly consequences of war" against Iraq.

MISSING OR IGNORING THE REAL STORY

The systematic distortion of its own opinion polls has also blinded the *Times* to the few bits of real news that their survey results uncover.

For several months prior to the 2002 midterm elections, the *Times*, in articles and op-ed pieces, had been reporting about the frustrations of the Democratic party who had been lamenting the fact that it had no clear message for the midterm election. Democrats had been openly admitting that, as Senator Evan Bayh (D-Indiana) phrased it, "The majority of the American people tend to trust the Republican party more on issues involving national security and defense than they do the Democratic party" ("ENTHUSIASM BY DEMOCRATS IS ON THE WANE," October 7, 2002).

In an article appearing just a few days before the 2002 midterm elections, the *Times* reported ("IN POLL, AMERICANS SAY BOTH PARTIES LACK CLEAR VISION," November 3, 2002):

> The battle for control of Congress moved into its final stretch with Americans unsettled about conditions at home and threats from abroad, but saying that Democrats and Republicans have failed to offer a clear vision about how they would lead the nation, the latest New York Times/CBS News Poll shows.

On the CBS website, the poll was entitled "THE U.S. ITS ALLIES AND IRAQ." Not one question in the poll used the word "vision," and an analysis of what was actually asked shows a more favorable view of the Republicans than the Democrats. Here are some of the actual questions used in the poll:

> Regardless of how you intend to vote, do you think the Republicans have a clear plan for the country if they gain control of Congress this fall, or don't the Republicans have a clear plan for the country?
> Yes: 42%
> No: 39%

> Regardless of how you intend to vote, do you think the Democrats have a clear plan for the country if they gain control of Congress this fall, or don't the Democrats have a clear plan for the country?
> Yes: 31%
> No: 49%

In other words, assuming the respondents understood the compound question to begin with, the Democrats got trounced on this one. A plurality of respondents thought the Republicans had a clear plan, and nearly one-half believed the Democrats didn't. In any event, the question never asked if both parties lacked (or had) a "clear vision."

Publishing the distortion of the plain results of the poll on the front page of the *Times* two days prior to the midterm elections compounded the inaccuracy of the headline. But, perhaps of greater importance, at least to the Democrats who were stunned by their losses the following Tuesday, the *Times* buried the most significant results of the poll—the results of the answers to the third question (out of a total of forty-eight questions) asked by the survey, what is called a "general ballot question":

> If the election of the U.S. House of Representatives were being held today, would you vote for the Republican candidate or the Democratic candidate in your district?
> Republican: 47%
> Democratic: 40%

Two days later, on the Monday prior to the election, *USA Today* reported that its poll had the Republicans leading its general ballot question 51 percent to 45 percent. It seems the *Times* actually had the data that would have allowed them to predict a dismal election for the Democrats, but in their zeal to skew their headline and influence the election, they completely lost sight of not only the truth but also what mattered.

Where slanting a poll's questions and distorting a poll's results do not produce numbers that support the *Times*' editorial positions, and where the numbers actually show a clear public rejection of the *Times*' views on the subject, the *Times* will resort to loaded language, even sarcasm, to report the results—as if to chastise an "unrepentant" public. For example, in "READING THE POLLS ON IRAQ" (February 23, 2003), the *Times* used the following lead sentence to report the results of a *New York Times*/CBS News poll that showed 66 percent of Americans approved of taking military action against Iraq:

> No president will say that polls drive policy, but the Bush administration must take satisfaction in knowing, for instance, that roughly 66 percent of Americans think taking military action against Iraq isn't an altogether bad idea.

"Isn't an altogether bad idea"? How about "a good idea" or just "approve," which is the word used in the poll question? Moreover, by injecting the supposition that "No president will say that polls drive policy," the *Times* seems to be suggesting that President Bush's policy on Iraq was being driven by poll numbers, rather than being a matter of principle or good public policy. This is particularly ironic given that the *Times* had been actively attempting to show how public opinion disfavored military action against Iraq. What's more, if there is a recent president whose policies were renowned for being "driven by" polls, it was Bill Clinton, not George Bush.

The results of the foregoing poll, showing continuing strong public support of military action against Iraq, came at a time when the *Times* was using its front pages to glorify anti-war protests with lengthy articles and colorful photos. Yet, these positive poll results were buried deep in one of the many sections of the Sunday *Times*, far from the front page. We will explore story placement at greater length in the next chapter.

ELEVEN

Distorting with Placement

Accuracy involves not only the truthfulness of
individual statements but the co-relation of these
statements in such a way as to convey to the
reader fair and unbiased impression of a story.

—*Melville E. Stone, co-founder of the* Associated Press
writing to his correspondents

---

book about distorting the news would not be complete without a
chapter on how the placement of news within a newspaper can be
manipulated to reflect the editorial bias of its editors. There are several
ways in which placement may be slanted: (1) by the placement of facts within
an article, (2) by the placement of articles within the newspaper, and (3) by the
selection of stories about which to write and publish.

PLACEMENT OF FACTS WITHIN AN ARTICLE

A story may be slanted by the emphasis a paper places on particular facts
within the story. The slant may be placed (a) at the beginning of the lead

sentence, (b) at the end of the lead sentence, (c) buried in the article where people are less likely to read it, or (d) for those readers who actually read the entire article, at the end of the article, often called the *kicker,* providing the *last word* which the paper would like the reader to take away from the story.

At the Beginning of the Lead Sentence

There was a time when opening the lead sentence of a news article with a phrase or clause was considered unacceptable. For example, the *Style Book of the United Press* (United Press Associations, 1929) admonished:

> Direct approach is the best way of starting a story; do not begin sentences with participles, subordinate clauses and the like. Make your statements in the natural order of subject first, then the verb, etc.

Professional journalists of that era were keenly aware of how stories may be manipulated when a direct approach to news writing is abandoned. Recall that the most emphatic part of any news article is the lead sentence, and the most emphatic part of the lead is its first few words. Thus, an editor may emphasize one aspect of a story—such as the *Why,* which is often merely the opinion of the paper—by placing it at the very beginning of the lead sentence. Opening the lead sentence of a story with a participle or subordinate clause loaded with bias has become a common practice at the *New York Times.*

We explored several illustrations of this technique in previous chapters. For example, a loaded opening phrase surfaced in the lead sentence of the lead front-page article run under the headline "BUSH, IN SHAKE UP OF CABINET, OUSTS TREASURY LEADER" (December 7, 2002):

> WASHINGTON, Dec. 6—Wrestling with a shaky economy and criticism that his administration projects a muddled message on how to respond, President Bush today . . .

In a front-page article run under the headline "BUSH SIGNS BILL AIMED AT FRAUD IN CORPORATIONS" (July 31, 2002), the *Times* wrote:

WASHINGTON, July 30—In a sign of how profoundly the nation's business scandals and volatile stock market have rocked his administration, President Bush . . .

Similarly, a *Times* front-page lead story entitled "BUSH, AS TERROR INQUIRY SWIRLS, SEEKS CABINET POST ON SECURITY" (Friday, June 7, 2002) began this way:

WASHINGTON, June 6—Responding to widespread criticism of the government's handling of terrorist threats, President Bush called tonight for . . .

In a front page article run under the headline "AIDES SAY BUSH WAS ONE TARGET OF HIJACKED JET" (September 13, 2001), the *Times* failed to quote a single person who was critical of the president's actions on the day of attacks, yet the following "fact" was given prominent emphasis in the opening phrase of the lead:

WASHINGTON, Sept. 13—Stung by suggestions that President Bush had hurt himself politically by delaying his return to Washington on Tuesday, the White House asserted today . . .

At the End of the Lead Sentence

The second most emphatic part of the lead sentence may be its last few words. Where there is no need for an attribution, a paper will often place its editorial slant at the end of the lead. We saw previously how a front-page story entitled "WHITE HOUSE AIDES LAUNCH A DEFENSE OF BUSH TAX PLAN" (January 7, 2003) opened with the following opinion-lead:

WASHINGTON, Jan. 6—White House officials rolled out statistics and new details of President Bush's sweeping tax plan today in an effort to head off criticism that it favors only the rich.

The kicker, "in an effort to head off criticism that it favors only the rich," could not possibly have been a reportable fact—the "criticism" had not yet occurred. It was entirely the *Times'* conjecture that (1) the White House rolled out statistics *for that purpose* and (2) that, before the details of the tax plan were announced, there would be criticism "that it favors only the rich."

Buried in the Article

It is axiomatic—as we have seen from our discussion of the development of the inverse pyramid style of news writing—that the further into the story you go, the fewer readers you have. Portions of a front-page story appearing "above-the-fold" of the paper tend to be read more than portions "below-the-fold."

Very few people read an entire news story, especially when it is continued to another section of the newspaper. Thus, when reporting two sides of a story is called for, often the Republican side appears below the fold or is relegated to where the story jumps inside the paper.

Recall the front-page crusade the *Times* ran to discredit SEC Commissioner Chairman Harvey Pitt. After the *Associated Press* broke the story that proved Pitt blameless for the failures previously reported by the *Times*, the *Times* buried the revelation deep into the article, acknowledging the new facts but not its mistake.

In "GOVERNMENT REPORT DETAILS A CHAOTIC S.E.C. UNDER PITT" (December 20, 2002), the *Times* placed the facts that exonerated Pitt, not on the front page, or even in the same section of the paper, but buried in the tenth paragraph of the story where it continued in another section, the Business section, of the paper:

> But Mr. Herdman, a longtime friend and close adviser to Mr. Pitt, decided that the information was not significant and did not need to be shared with the commissioners.

If you hadn't followed the story closely, you would not necessarily have understood the foregoing sentence to mean what the *Associated Press* reported so clearly: that Pitt was unaware of the problems with the nominee and therefore could not have hidden that information from his fellow commissioners. How the *Times* dealt with this revelation, and the correction of its front-page error, revealed an organization that appears to put its political agenda ahead of its responsibility to print the unvarnished truth.

Contrast how the *Times* dealt with its discovery of the truth about Pitt with how an editor-in-chief of an earlier age, writing to his staff at the *Detroit News* in 1916, would have had his newspaper approach a problem of this nature:

> If you make an error you have two duties to perform—one to the person misrepresented and one to your reading public. Never leave the reader of The News misinformed on any subject. If you wrongfully write that a man has done something that he did not do, or has said something that he did not say, you do him an injustice—that's one. But you also do thousands of readers an injustice, leaving them misinformed as to the character of the man dealt with. Corrections should never be made grudgingly. Always make them cheerfully, fully and in larger type than the error, if there is any difference.

As noted earlier, in September 2000, Howell Raines' predecessor established a policy of writing "full stories" to correct errors where "the mistakes were so serious that the headlines and leads of the originals can no longer be said to have stood up." The obvious question arises: What happened to that policy and, if it still exists, why wasn't it followed here?

At the End of the Article—The Last Word

Another common technique of slanting a story by the strategic placement of important elements is giving the final word to someone who or some fact which puts the paper's editorial views in the most favorable light. It also provides the reader with the slant that the paper would like the reader to take away after reading the story. The best place to provide the take-away is in the last word, or kicker, the last few lines of the article.

As pointed out previously, one of the advantages of using the inverse pyramid style of news writing is that it facilitates page makeup—that is, if the least important details are placed at the end of the story, a makeup editor may cut the article short to fit it within the available space without affecting the essence of the story. The modern newsroom, however, is now equipped with sophisticated page makeup software, which provides the makeup editor with greater flexibility in accommodating a story to the space available. Thus, when a reporter employs a kicker, it is more likely to be preserved. In addition, even if a story needs to be cut, the makeup editor himself can either preserve the kicker or actually create one during the process of pruning the story.

The use of the kicker slanted in favor of the paper's editorial views is so common that it should suffice here to provide just a couple of poignant examples. In "LIEBERMAN ANNOUNCES RUN FOR THE WHITE HOUSE IN '04" (January 14, 2003), the *Times* closed the story with the following kicker:

> Repeatedly, Mr. Lieberman underscored what he described as the partisanship in the White House.
>
> "These are not ordinary times for our country," he said. "Therefore those of us who seek our highest office or hold it can not practice ordinary politics."

Since Lieberman must first win the Democratic primary before he faces Bush, it would make more sense to leave the reader with some statement on how Lieberman differentiates himself from his Democratic opponents. However, Lieberman's opponents are not the same as the *Times*' opponents, and the story ends with a jab at President Bush, engineered as much by the *New York Times* as by Senator Lieberman.

By contrast, an article that appeared on the same page as, and adjacent to, the foregoing article, "ASHCROFT SAYS CHURCH GROUPS SUFFER BIGOTRY" (January 14, 2003), ended with the following kicker:

> Mr. Ashcroft's outspoken views on God and religion, his prayer breakfasts at the Justice Department and remarks attributed to him comparing Christianity with Islam last year have made him a lightning rod for criticism from civil rights advocates who accuse him of crossing the line into religious advocacy.

The *Times*' editorial board might be counted among those "civil rights advocates" not quoted in the article.

In another side-by-side comparison, an article entitled "BUSH TAX PLAN GIVES PELOSI AN OPENING" (January 26, 2003) gave the last word to Democrat Nancy Pelosi, the House minority leader:

> "The advantage of this unfortunate situation is, the Republicans have no place to place blame," she said. "It's all on them. Anything they do is their

responsibility. And if we are not as a party able to convey the difference to the American people, then it's not the Republicans' fault, it's our fault."

Adjacent to that story on the same page of the *Times*, an article run under the headline "HASTERT TO TACKLE ECONOMY IN STAGES" (January 26, 2003) gave the last word to the House majority leader's unnamed critics:

> Democrats and a few Republicans have criticized Mr. Hastert and DeLay for tightening their grip on the House by changing the rules and by passing over senior members to reward junior allies with top committee posts.

That negative kicker was remarkable for the fact that it had absolutely nothing to do with any aspect of the article in which it appeared. The paragraph which it followed concerned Hastert's optimism about passing prescription drug coverage legislation. What the kicker alluded to was an effort by Republican leaders to remove several entrenched big-spenders and replace them with House members more aligned with the party's determination to control government waste and eliminate pork-barrel projects. It was as though the reporter wrote several paragraphs on the subject, but the copy editor saw fit to preserve the negative kicker when cutting the relevant paragraphs to save space.

PLACEMENT OF ARTICLES WITHIN THE PAPER

Decisions as to the placement of articles within the paper—whether a story deserves "play" on the front page or whether it should be buried on page 16 or relegated to another section of the paper—goes to the core of the news reporting judgment of any news division. Determinations about placement are naturally going to reflect a news editor's bias about what he or she thinks is important in the world that day. One can only hope that a news editor makes these judgments in a way that is "impartial, without fear or favor."

Given that it is Arthur Sulzberger Jr.'s disastrous vision to have his paper's editorial page editor and its executive editor work "as partners in the *Times* future"— which first manifested itself when he put his now-disgraced editorial page editor, Howell Raines, in charge of the newsroom—the independence of that judgment has now become entirely suspect. The fear is that news placement decisions at the *Times* are now more influenced by the editorial views of its editors than by the newsworthiness of the stories themselves in the context of world events.

Nevertheless, with respect to specific placement decisions, it is difficult to demonstrate bias without an intimate knowledge of the daily discussions that occur among the *Times'* editors. Even an extensive analysis of the relative placement of news stories in other newspapers might prove misleading. Front-page placement in another newspaper may have been a decision that was derived from the *Times'* placement decision, rather than derived from news judgment independent of the *Times*. Given the influence the *Times* has over the news and editorial agendas of other newspapers, such an analysis is sure to understate what might otherwise prove to be more objective placement decisions.

Accordingly, a fair analysis of the objectivity of placement decisions, without direct insight into the placement decision process for specific editions of the *Times*, is problematic.

Of course, once in a while, the placement of a story is so slanted the question of bias it raises is obvious. For example, recall how the *Times*, as part of its crusade against U.S. military action against Iraq, went out of its way to point out on its front page that taking military action against Iraq could increase the price of oil and that such an increase could plunge the American economy into another recession. Nevertheless, when OPEC announced an agreement to increase production, which was aimed at immediately reducing the price of oil by up to 30 percent, the article reporting that news, "OPEC AGREES TO INCREASE ITS OIL PRODUCTION QUOTAS BY 6.5%" (January 13, 2003), failed to merit front-page coverage in the *Times*.

One possible defense for the muted placement of the article is that the front page was already occupied by more important stories. But that was not the case here. The front page of the *Times* that day included five articles appearing above-the-fold, and only one of those articles was so time-sensitive that it had to appear in that issue of the *Times*: "AOL CHAIRMAN QUITS HIS POST AMID CRITICISM." Each of the five other articles, all but one a feature story (i.e., not a "hard news" story), could have been placed anywhere else in the paper, or the editors could have published them any time later in the week or even later in the month: "MANY COMPANIES FIGHT SHORTFALLS IN PENSION FUNDS," "CHINA GAMBLES ON BIG PROJECTS FOR ITS STABILITY," "KURDS FACE A

SECOND ENEMY: ISLAMIC FIGHTERS ON IRAQ FLANK," and "OFFICIALS REVEAL THREAT TO TROOPS DEPLOYING TO GULF."

Only the *Times'* bias toward downplaying good news for the Bush administration—lower oil prices and cooperation from Iraq's Arab neighbors—could explain the *Times'* second page placement of the story that day. The great importance of the OPEC story was soon betrayed by the *Times'* editorial staff when, in an editorial appearing a week later ("THE AXIS OF OIL," January 21, 2003), it called the decision by OPEC to increase production "this month's most notable stimulus plan for the American economy."

When a drop in jobless claims caused the Dow Jones Industrial Average to rise 180 points in one day, the story, run under the headline "DECLINE IN JOBLESS CLAIMS SPURS 180-POINT CLIMB IN DOW" (January 10, 2003), was buried on page 5 of the Business section. The drop in new claims for unemployment benefits for the previous week was considered a "milestone" because it was the first time in a year that claims dropped below 400,000.

However, just one day later, news of an increase in jobless claims for the previous *month* (which included three weeks of older data) received prominent placement on the front page above-the-fold under the following grave headline: "WITH COMPANIES STILL GLOOMY, PAYROLLS SHRINK BY THOUSANDS" (January 11, 2003).

We have seen how the *Times* reported the "news" in "REPUBLICANS BREAK RANKS WITH BUSH ON IRAQ" (August 16, 2002) when it trumpeted its distorted reading of an op-ed piece that Henry Kissenger wrote for the *Washington Post* and what former national security advisor Brent Scowcroft wrote in an op-ed piece for the *Wall Street Journal.* The news of those op-ed pieces became the lead story on the *Times'* front page. But when eight European leaders, including Prime Ministers Tony Blair of England, Jose Maria Aznar of Spain, and Silvio Berlusconi of Italy and the leaders of Portugal and four Central European nations, wrote an op-ed piece for the *Wall Street Journal* and eight of the leading newspapers of Europe, the *Times'* editors didn't think the story warranted front-page coverage. Why? It appears no one at the *Times* was willing to wake up in the morning to read what would have been a more appropriate headline: "EUROPEAN LEADERS JOIN RANKS WITH BUSH ON IRAQ." The *Times* not only buried the article on page 10, they ran it under a headline that completely obscured the story: "EUROPEAN LEADERS DIVIDE BETWEEN HAWKS AND DOVES" (January 31, 2003).

STORY SELECTION

Another placement technique involves whether to place the story in the paper at all. A news organization can slant the news by aggressively chasing down those stories which conform to its editorial agenda and by ignoring those which do not. For example, conservative critics have charged that the *Times* continually chooses to write stories about studies released by liberal organizations yet ignores those studies conducted on the same or similar topics by conservative organizations.

Story selection is a difficult area of bias to document, much like proving slanting by omission, which, as suggested earlier, is virtually impossible for the casual reader to detect.

As we have seen, a reader of the *Times* would have discovered only by accident the results of a *New York Times*/CBS News poll showing that President Bush's approval rating stood at 56 percent, what CBS News described on its website ("POLL: WE LIKE HIM," April 29, 2001) as "generally positive." The *Times* decided not to report these results—not on its front page nor anywhere else in the paper.

A *New York Times*/CBS News poll that was taken shortly after the September 11 attacks showed that 85 percent of the American public supported military action against whoever was responsible for the attacks. CBS announced the results on its website under the headline "POLL: REVENGE AND RETURN" (September 15, 2001). The *New York Times* chose to ignore the poll.

Probably the most egregious example of bias by story selection concerned a story that the *Times* decided to run *twice*—the second time *with feeling*. This example is remarkable not for what it omitted but for what it reported twice, with two entirely different results.

On Sunday, October 27, 2002, the *Times* reported on a war protest that took place a day earlier in an article appearing on page 8 under the headline "THOUSANDS MARCH IN WASHINGTON AGAINST GOING TO WAR IN IRAQ." The lead stated:

> WASHINGTON, Oct. 26—Thousands of protestors marched through Washington's streets, chanting and waving banners against possible military action against Iraq. The rally was one of several held in American and foreign cities today.

Fewer people attended than organizers had said they hoped for, even though after days of cold, wet weather, the sun came out this morning. Participants said the shootings in and around the city in the last three weeks had kept people from planning to visit Washington.

After some apparent grumbling by the event's organizers over the *Times'* lukewarm coverage of the story, the *Times* decided to write a second story *about the same event.* A full four days after the protest event, the *New York Times* declared, "RALLY IN WASHINGTON IS SAID TO INVIGORATE THE ANTIWAR MOVEMENT" (October 30, 2002), and rewrote history:

> Emboldened by a weekend antiwar protest in Washington that organizers called the biggest since the days of the Vietnam War, groups opposed to military action in Iraq said they were preparing a wave of new demonstrations across the country in the next few weeks.
>
> The demonstration on Saturday in Washington drew 100,000 by police estimates and 200,000 by organizers', forming a two-mile wall of marchers around the White House. The turnout startled even organizers, who had taken out permits for 20,000 marchers. They expected 30 buses, and were surprised by about 650, coming from as far as Nebraska and Florida.

The revised story cured an unintended setback in the *Times'* crusade against the Bush administration's policies on Iraq. Notice, also, the clever use of the passive voice in the headline "RALLY IN WASHINGTON IS SAID TO INVIGORATE THE ANTIWAR MOVEMENT." One political commentator, Glenn Reynolds of Instapundit.com, observed (October 30, 2002):

> As is typical for these pieces in the Times, the quotes are all from demonstrators who say their demonstration was a success. A more accurate headline would be "Rally in Washington is Said by Ralliers to be Success." Coming soon: "Enron Accounting Said to Be Legitimate, Even Noble," in a story interviewing only Enron accountants. Of course these people think their rally was a success. And of course the Times swallows it whole, because it wants the rally to look successful.

The question remains, however: How did the *Times* get from its first report that "Fewer people attended than organizers had said they hoped" to its second that "The turnout startled even organizers"? During his taped interview at U.C. Berkeley on November 18, 2002, just a few weeks after these two articles were published, Howell Raines was asked to explain the inconsistency between the two stories:

> *Mark Danner:* A question from the audience (reading from an index card): "It appeared to me that your coverage of the October 26th Iraq peace demonstration in Washington was quite contradictory. How did two different accounts appear over just a couple of days?" I remember this. I believe there were different numbers given for the number of people who participated and so on—quite different stories in the paper.

> *Raines:* Not really. The first story was incomplete—and I don't mean to be splitting hairs with you—but it said thousands when it should have said tens of thousands.

When the *Times* gets the numbers wrong—"thousands rather than tens of thousands," as Raines says—then it typically corrects the error in a column called "Corrections," appearing on page 2 each day. Recall, when the *Times* discovered that it had misinterpreted Henry Kissinger's views on the Bush administration's policies on Iraq, it didn't write another story with a different version of their coverage; it merely printed a back-handed "Editor's Note" on page 2. He continued:

> When we became aware that we had under-covered the event, we went back and wrote a story that re-examined the number of people who were there and re-examined the organizational framework of the anti-war organization, as they were putting it on.

The room fell silent—perhaps they, too, didn't know what to make of the answer. Perhaps they were searching in their minds for the last time the *Times* rewrote a story because the first version "under-covered" the event. The professor then moved on to the next question, but Raines side-stepped it and abruptly returned to his defense of the protest story, as though he realized he hadn't been entirely persuasive:

> I'd like to respond to this comment about the march coverage. It does make a difference where the reporters are. In this case, we had four people in the field, and they simply didn't get it exactly right. That's why we went back to it.

It should be striking that the *New York Times* dedicated as many as four of its reporters to cover a single protest march. Nevertheless, could four qualified reporters have really gotten the story wrong the first time around? Raines continued with his defense:

> The fact is when you revisit the story, the error was a judgment error, not a "the number was 5 when it should have been 6"—it was a matter of scale and interpretation and scope.

In other words, now taking the opposite tack, Raines said it was *not* about the numbers. The reporters didn't get the numbers wrong; rather, they simply "under-covered" the event itself, its "scale," its "interpretation," its "scope." That is, they didn't make a big enough deal out of it—they "under-covered" its "scale" and "scope," and these four *news* reporters got the "interpretation" wrong: they reported the event as disappointing, rather than startlingly successful.

In making his final defense of his anti-war coverage, Raines concluded:

> And that's what we try to bring to our journalism—the feel for the event, the context, the history, the whole picture.

But it seems incredible that the *Times* would rewrite a story and, in doing so, provide the precise slant desired by those who were not pleased with the first version had not the *Times* consciously made the decision to do so for entirely political, as opposed to newsworthy, reasons.

As difficult as it may be to identify, slanting the news by selective placement of articles within the paper—not to mention facts and quotes within the story—are mainstays for a news organization bent on using its news division to influence public opinion. Identifying how a news organization editorializes in the way it determines what is and what is not important is also the subject for biographers and historians. One would hope that someday a fair-minded *Times* staffer will "blow the whistle" and we'll finally get a colorful account of how this aspect of bias is employed by the *New York Times*.

In the next chapter, we will see how the *Times* systematically, consciously or otherwise, used story selection and placement to obscure "the context, the history, the whole picture" of the war in Iraq in early 2003. The result was a brand of bias that has become the hallmark of the *New York Times*.

TWELVE

Distorting the War Coverage

In the United States today, we have more than
our share of the nattering nabobs of negativism.

—*Spiro T. Agnew, vice president of the United States;
San Diego, California (September 11, 1970)*

fter waging a year-long crusade against the Bush administration's
policies on Iraq, the *Times* watched in horror while a resolute President
Bush, in opposition to the ideological agenda of the paper's editors,
proceeded to wage the war on terrorism as he and his advisors deemed were in
the best interests of those who elected him, the American public. As for the
president, it was a political gamble of historic proportions. As for the *Times*, it
was an opportunity that could only produce upsides for its war against the president and the advancement of its left-wing political agenda.

If events proved the president wrong about Iraq, it would be easy to disparage the military effort as ill-conceived and poorly executed. If the president succeeded, the *Times* could downplay his achievements and even create an illusion
of failure, employing every technique of propaganda and distortion at its disposal. The talking points would be familiar: War was necessitated only by
Bush's diplomatic failure. Victory could be claimed only by the finding of

weapons of mass destruction. Victory may be had, but at what cost? A quick military victory, perhaps, but then comes the hard part.

In this chapter, we will proceed chronologically, beginning with the *Times'* coverage during the days leading up to the launch of the military campaign, followed by the three weeks of warfare, the liberation of a jubilant Iraqi people, and, in the immediate aftermath, the birth of a new nation. The various techniques of distortion, which should be familiar to readers of the previous chapters, will be designated by the section headings that follow. In the end, the *Times* paints for itself an encyclopedic illustration of a "nattering nabob of negativism" and demonstrates a brand of journalism that is blinded to "the context, the history, the whole picture."

SLANTING WITH OPINION

On Tuesday, March 17, 2003, President Bush gave Saddam Hussein his final ultimatum: the dictator had forty-eight hours to leave his country or face a military attack. It was big news—the penultimate prelude to war. The next day, under the headline "BUSH GIVES HUSSEIN 48 HOURS, AND VOWS TO ACT" (March 18, 2003), the *Times* came close to writing a straightforward lead:

> WASHINGTON, March 17—President Bush last night gave Saddam Hussein 48 hours to go into exile or face attack from the United States and a handful of allies.

Of course, characterizing the allies as "a handful," which connotes a small amount, seemed clearly calculated to belittle the size and importance of the coalition supporting the war effort. Never mind the sizable number of British and Australian troops who were directly deployed in military operations, and never mind the unconditional support the president enjoyed from over forty countries, including nearly every country in Europe that didn't have a multibillion dollar financial stake in the survival of Saddam Hussein's regime.

Before the article was printed, a copy editor with proper respect for impartiality could have converted it from an editorial to a news story by simply replacing the slanted characterization with the facts:

WASHINGTON, March XX—President Bush last night gave Saddam Hussein 48 hours to go into exile or face attack from the United States and its allies.

QUOTE-SOMEONE-WHO-AGREES-WITH-US

As the war approached, the *Times* worked to undermine the effort by engineering the front page to reflect a hefty amount of fear and anxiety, as well as ample cynicism about the president's true motives for war. To that end, on the same front page that carried Bush's ultimatum to Saddam Hussein, the *Times* carried a story under the headline (March 18, 2003):

RELIEF ON END TO UNCERTAINTY AND FEAR ABOUT WAR'S TOLL

That article quoted a 36-year-old electrician who felt differently about this latest conflict with Iraq than he did about the Persian Gulf War of 1991: "It's a lot more scary this time." Later in the article, a patron at a lunch counter was quoted saying, "I think our focus is on Iraq because of the president's vendetta against Hussein, because of his father."

That front-page "news" was accompanied by a front-page article entitled "IN IRAQI CAPITAL, PEOPLE PREPARE FOR THE CONFLICT" (March 18, 2003). In that report, we learned the remarkably surprising news that Baghdad, bracing for war, was "a city filled with apprehension and anticipation."

SLANTING WITH PLACEMENT

Granted, there's nothing inherently ideological about covering the fear of the American people or the anxiety of the Iraqis during the days leading up to the war. Nevertheless, to move the themes of fear and anxiety to the front page, while relegating several more newsworthy stories to the interior of the paper, demonstrates an agenda not unlike that of Al Jazeera, the Arabic satellite news channel, which in its war coverage tended to emphasize civilian casualties over the extensive efforts made by coalition forces to avoid them.

The same issue of the *Times* (March 18, 2003) contained several highly newsworthy stories, any one of which would have tended to reduce the amount of fear and anxiety about the war:

TURKEY MAY RECONSIDER VOTE ON ITS ROLE IN IRAQ INVASION
(appearing on page A14)

U.S. BUSINESS WILL GET ROLE IN REBUILDING OCCUPIED IRAQ
(page A16)

STOCK PRICES RISE AS WAR IN IRAQ APPEARS INEVITABLE
(page C1)

SAUDI'S STOCK OIL RESERVE TO MAKE UP FOR IRAQ LOSS
(page C1)

Each of these merited front-page placement, but as they worked against the fear and anxiety theme, they didn't have a chance. Meanwhile, for entirely different reasons, an article on the questions being raised about the relevance of the United Nations, "ECLIPSED BY EVENTS, U.N. OFFICIALS WONDER ABOUT THE PAST AND PONDER THE FUTURE" (page A19), likewise had little chance of getting near the front page.

SLANTING BY OMISSION

The next day, the *New York Times* printed the following front-page headline (March 19, 2003):

A WORRIED WORLD SHOWS DISCORD

While adding "worry" and "discord" to its "fear" and "anxiety" theme, the *Times* had in its possession, but chose not to share with its readers, the results of a new *New York Times*/CBS News poll that showed anything but discord, at least in the U.S., on the question of Iraq. As reported on the CBS News website on March 18, 2003, the *Times* poll demonstrated:

On two key points, the President has broad public support. 72% agree that he should have given the 48-hour ultimatum to Saddam Hussein, and not begun military action without it.

Most Americans also are willing to take military action without a specific United Nations approval of the use of force against Iraq. Less than a third believe the President should have waited for United Nations approval.

CBS also reported that 69 percent of the public supported taking military action against Iraq and 63 percent of the American public approved of the way Bush was handling Iraq. Even more newsworthy, the president's job approval rating jumped significantly, from 59 percent to 64 percent. To report the results of these polls, however, would have undermined the negativism the nabobs apparently sought to convey.

SLANTING WITH PLACEMENT

President Bush launched the war, and the *Times* reported the announcement the following day in a lead front-page article entitled "U.S. BEGINS ATTACK WITH STRIKE AT BAGHDAD AFTER DEADLINE FOR HUSSEIN TO GO RUNS OUT" (March 20, 2003). Now, with the nation at war, the front page also alerted the American public to the news: "MOVE TO WAR LEAVES CALIFORNIANS MORE ALIENATED THAN THREATENED." The only possible front-page relevance of this article was its usefulness in bashing President Bush's decision, which it accomplished by quoting someone who agreed with the *Times*, someone identified as a "San Francisco fundraiser":

"I am hoping the administration has so much more knowledge that it can justify its actions, because on the face of it, I can't see a reason for doing this."

Continuing its fear and anxiety theme, the front page also sported the obligatory story about Iraqi anxiety—"THE QUESTION ON EVERY MIND IN BAGHDAD: WHEN WILL IT BE?"—and American fear—"AS TROOPS WAIT, TIME TO REFLECT AND PRAY," which quoted a soldier:

"My wife, Beth, is scared. We have a 1-year old daughter. Her name is Jade. My wife is really scared."

Meanwhile, buried on page A10 of the same issue was a real news story, one which shed a significant ray of hope for eventual peace in the Middle East: "PALESTINIAN BECOMES PREMIER, DIMINISHING ARAFAT'S POWER." The importance of the story was betrayed by its own language, which described the event as "a move that marks the most significant cut in Yasir Arafat's powers since he became leader of the Palestinian Authority."

Other newsworthy items buried in that day's issue included "BIN LADIN CHOSE 9/11 TARGETS, AL QAEDA LEADER SAYS" (page A20) and "BUSH ADMINISTRATION TO SEEK EMERGENCY MONEY TO PROTECT AGAINST TERRORIST ATTACKS IN U.S." (page A20). Apparently, these stories were relegated to the interior of the newspaper to make room for the "news" about how Californians feel about the war, what a soldier's wife feels about her husband's fate, and when the Iraqi's feel the war will begin.

SLANTING THE *WHY*

That last article—"BUSH ADMINISTRATION TO SEEK EMERGENCY MONEY TO PROTECT AGAINST TERRORIST ATTACKS IN U.S." (March 20, 2003)—which appeared on page A20, would seem to have been an excellent candidate for front-page placement, at least judging by the attention paid to its Bush-bashing. Employing the spin-the-news-first-with-opening-phrase technique, the lead read as follows:

> WASHINGTON, March 19—After months of criticism that the Bush administration had failed to provide enough money to defend against terrorist attacks on American soil, the White House said today that it would ask Congress for an emergency spending package for domestic counterterrorism programs.

Editors could have rendered this lead impartial by removing the slanted cause (i.e., the *Why*) of the administration's action and opening the story instead with the following plain statement of fact:

WASHINGTON, March XX—The White House said today that it would ask Congress for an emergency spending package for domestic counterterrorism programs.

Later in the article, the *Times* actually reported on the *Why*:

Administration officials said the decision to seek the new domestic security money was a result of terrorist threats linked to an apparently imminent American attack on Iraq and recent intelligence suggesting that new terrorist strikes were likely.

SLANTING WITH A KICKER

Even though the article did not quote a single person who was critical of the president's funding for homeland security or who questioned the motivations of the White House for making the request, the story ended with the *Times* itself questioning Bush's motivations, a classic kicker:

Whatever the administration's motivation, however, the decision to seek the money was welcomed by Democratic opponents on the issue.

SLANTING THE FACTS

In a front-page story published on the second day of the military campaign, under the headline "WAVES OF PROTESTS, FROM EUROPE TO NEW YORK" (March 21, 2003), the *Times* reported that "some 5,000 people" chanting "Peace Now" demonstrated in New York's Times Square.

According to the *Associated Press* ("HUNDREDS AT NYC ANTI-WAR PROTEST," March 21, 2003), the *Washington Post* ("WORLDWIDE, CIVIL DISOBEDIENCE," March 21, 2003), and the *New York Sun* ("THE WORLD SPLITS IN REACTION TO AMERICA'S OFFENSIVE," March 21, 2003), the number of people attending the protest was about 300, no where near the *Times'* account of 5,000. *Newsday*, another rival New York newspaper, estimated that the number of protesters attending the demonstration was only 200 ("ABOUT 200 PROTEST IN TIMES SQUARE," March 21, 2003).

What explains the vast difference between the *Times'* account and everyone else's—a figure that was up to 25 times higher than what was actually observed by the other news agencies? "Experience has taught me," said Elmer David, director of the U.S. Office of War information during World War II and former reporter and editorial writer for the *New York Times,* "when the versions of the same story given by two wire services differ materially, to prefer the less exciting."

Only an incurable cynic would attribute the difference to the *Times* having counted the people lined up in Times Square to purchase same-day, half-price theatre tickets. Neither is there any evidence that disgraced reporter Jayson Blair was associated with the story. With the *Times* itself recently acknowledging a "profound betrayal of trust and a low point" in its 152-year history, such speculation, before implausible, would not now seem unreasonable.

But the answer to the question was betrayed by a *University Wire* story carried by college newspapers around the country. One version of the story was published by the *Daily Texan* under the headline "THE THRESHOLD OF WAR: A VIEW FROM NEW YORK" (March 21, 2003). The story revealed the following:

> Organizers estimated more than 5,000 antiwar demonstrators marched to the center of the city near rush hour Thursday.

Thus, the *University Wire* was reporting that the figure reported by the *Times*—5,000—was actually the number being provided to the press by the organizers of the demonstration. It seems, therefore, that while the estimates of 200 to 300 by the *Associated Press* and other New York area newspapers were based on independent observation, the *Times,* whose 43rd Street and Times Square headquarters were just a few steps away from the demonstration, seemed all too ready to accept what they were told by the protest organizers.

SLANTING WITH HEADLINES

Seeing a headline that reads "CRITICS SAY U.S. LACKS LEGAL BASIS FOR ATTACK" (March 21, 2003), one would expect the article it summarized would contain quotes by legal experts supporting a view that, in fact, the U.S. lacks a legal basis for launching the war and perhaps the alleged legal grounds upon which such criticism was based. The article, however, contains nothing of the kind.

The only source of criticism was a brief statement from Russian Foreign Minister Igor S. Ivanov, who merely pointed out his country's view that none of the UN Security Counsel resolutions regarding Iraq "authorizes the right to use force." That is a far cry from suggesting that the U.S. had no legal basis for going to war.

Others quoted in the article included German Foreign Minister Joschka Fischer and French Foreign Minister Dominique de Villepin—but both addressed their comments to the failure of the Security Council process, not the legal basis for the military campaign by the U.S.

SLANTING WITH POLLS

Another *New York Times*/CBS News poll was taken, and CBS News, under the positive headline "POLL: U.S. BACKS BUSH ON WAR" (March 21, 2003), reported it this way:

> On Thursday, CBS News and The New York Times re-interviewed a sample of respondents first interviewed two weeks ago. 74% now approve of the U.S. taking military action against Iraq, up from 64% among these same respondents two weeks ago.

The poll also reported that 67 percent of those surveyed approved of the way Bush was handling his job as president, nine points higher than just a week earlier.

The *Times* reported the same results under the muted headline "A NATION AT WAR: THE POLL" (March 22, 2003). The lead opened this way:

> American support for President Bush's policy in Iraq has surged now that the war has begun . . .

"Now that the war has begun"? If the *Times* hadn't spiked its own opinion poll story of a few days ago, the public would have been informed that American support for Bush's policy in Iraq surged *before* the war had begun. The lead continued:

> . . . but there are deep partisan divisions in the nation's view of the conflict, according to the latest New York Times/CBS News poll.

The slanted story which followed made a sow's ear out of a silk purse by (1) emphasizing the differences between how Democrats and Republicans responded to the survey—a difference the *Times* found "reminiscent of the partisan divide that marked the later years of the Vietnam War" (i.e., the "quagmire"); (2) by comparing President Bush's poll results unfavorably to similar results enjoyed by his father at the onset of the Gulf War in 1991 (when his father wasn't dealing with an economy wracked by international terrorism); and (3) by suggesting the public was "unsure of Mr. Bush's motivations in launching this attack."

About the only motivations the public could be sure of are those of the editors of the *New York Times* in launching a partisan attack—in a front-page "news" story—against the commander in chief within forty-eight hours after the nation had gone to war.

SLANTING WITH OPINION

During the year 2002, *Times* op-ed columnist Frank Rich wrote a total of twenty-five opinion columns for the paper's op-ed page. All but two of those twenty-five columns contained opinions either criticizing the Bush administration and its policies (including charges of "lies," "arrogance," and "dishonesty") or chastising the Democrats for not being critical enough of President Bush or the Republicans. The titles of these op-ed pieces included:

IT'S THE WAR, STUPID
(October 12, 2002)

SLOUCHING TOWARD 9/11
(August 31, 2002)

THE WACO ROAD TO BAGHDAD
(August 17, 2002)

ALL THE PRESIDENT'S ENRONS
(July 6, 2002)

DEPARTMENT OF HOMELAND INSECURITY
(June 8, 2002)

RELIGION FOR DUMMIES
(April 27, 2002)

THE BUSH DOCTRINE, R.I.P.
(April 13, 2002)

THE UNITED STATES OF ENRON
(January 19, 2002)

PATRIOTISM ON THE CHEAP
(January 5, 2002)

Apparently, Rich's diatribe against President Bush so impressed executive editor Howell Raines that Raines promoted Rich to associate editor of the paper. Thus, on January 7, 2003, Rich began serving as an advisor to the *Times'* cultural news editor and soon began writing a cultural essay for the front page of the Sunday *Times* Arts & Leisure section. In announcing Rich's promotion and new responsibilities, Raines said, "I'm delighted to welcome him back to the news pages."

On the same day, Raines also announced that the editor of the *Times'* op-ed page, Terry Tang—Rich's boss—would also be joining the paper's *news* department. In a press release, the *Times* stated that Tang would be assuming "significant new responsibilities in the newsroom." Tang joined the *Times'* editorial page in 1997, after eight years as an editorial writer and columnist with the *Seattle Times*. No recent news reporting experience was evident from the biography of Tang released by the *Times*. Given that Raines himself was recruited from the editorial page of the *Times*, it was becoming increasingly evident that these personnel changes alone were betraying a clear direction for the *New York Times*: journalists with a particular political ideology were being recruited to manage how the news was being reported by the *Times*.

In his new job for the news pages, Rich got off to a roaring start with a piece bashing the commander in chief in the most deplorable terms the very first Sunday after the war begin. As President Bush was sending the men and women of our armed forces into harm's way, and with early reports of American military casualties being reported in the *Times* that very Sunday, Frank Rich devoted his lead column in the Sunday Arts & Leisure section to a comparison of President Bush's press conference of March 6, 2003 with a scene from the motion picture *Chicago*.

In his column, "THEY BOTH REACHED FOR THE GUN" (March 23, 2003), Rich charged that President Bush (referred to as "the former Andover cheerleader") failed to convince America's friends to "come aboard" in supporting military action against Iraq—an accusation that was simply wrong on its face. Then, lamenting that the journalists participating in the president's March 6 press conference showed too much respect for Bush, Rich tossed the following zinger:

> One reporter, April Ryan of American Urban Radio Networks, asked, "Mr. President, as the nation is at odds over war, how is your faith guiding you?"— a God-given cue for Mr. Bush to once more cloak his moral arrogance in the verbal vestments of humble religiosity.

Welcome back to the "news pages," Rich. Leaving aside his lack of propriety, columnist Rich cannot be faulted for merely expressing his opinions. The problem here lies in the decision to recruit an op-ed page columnist with such well-known political views and giving him leave to express those views—insidiously wrapping them in a thin cloak of popular media references—in a section of the paper intended for media and entertainment news and commentary. Must readers of the entertainment section be indoctrinated with the political ideology of the *New York Times* editors, too?

SLANTING WITH PLACEMENT

While Frank Rich was maligning the commander in chief with the most personal line of attack imaginable—questioning the sincerity of the president's religious beliefs—President Bush was saying his prayers and preparing the country for the coming realities of war. In the same issue of the *Times*, buried on page 10 of its Nation at War section, the president issued a specific warning, reported in "BUSH WARNS THAT THE WAR IN IRAQ MAY LAST LONGER THAN ANTICIPATED" (March 23, 2003):

> WASHINGTON, March 22—President Bush gathered his war council at Camp David this morning, while warning that the war in Iraq "could be longer and more difficult than some have predicted."
>
> Mr. Bush's caution reflected a concern within the White House that the relatively quick progress made by forces moving through southern Iraq, and the apparent disarray of the Iraqi leadership in the opening days of the war, could create expectations of a quick victory.

Subsequent events soon proved the prescience of the commander in chief's warnings. The next day, Monday, March 24, 2003, readers of the *Times* were confronted with many of the realities of which the president was speaking. These are the five main headlines that appeared on the front page of the *Times* that morning:

ALLIES AND IRAQIS BATTLE ON 2 FRONTS
20 AMERICANS DEAD OR MISSING, 50 HURT

MARINES MEET POTENT ENEMY IN DEADLY CLASH

AS ALLIED TROOPS RACE NORTH, IRAQ WARNS OF A FIERCE FIGHT

LOWERING EXPECTATIONS

TEMPERED, THE OSCARS GO ON

Bad news for Bush is good news for the *Times*. Now, with plenty of bad news to report, the *Times* temporarily dispensed with its practice of counterbalancing the gravity of the big, hard news of the day with lighter feature stories. Relegating all other domestic and international news to the interior of the paper, the *Times* appeared to favor the sweet smell of blood, the president's blood, reporting all the bad news that's fit to print on its front pages. For the next several days, the front page of the *Times* would be a virtual phalanx of bad news.

For example, the following day, Tuesday, March 25, 2003, the front page of the *Times* bore only the following headlines:

ALLIES CONFRONT BAGHDAD DEFENDERS; U.S. COPTERS REPELLED; ONE IS DOWNED

MARINES, BATTLING IN STREETS, SEEK CONTROL OF CITY IN SOUTH

TV IMAGES CONFIRM FEARS OF PRISONER'S KIN

BUSH IS REQUESTING NEARLY $75 BILLION FOR WAR EXPENSES

EFFORTS TO FORESTALL ILLNESS IN GULF WAR

HUSSEIN RALLIES IRAQI DEFENDERS TO HOLD CAPITAL

THE GOAL IS BAGHDAD, BUT AT WHAT COST?

SLANTING WITH OPINION

In one of the above headlines, "HUSSEIN RALLIES IRAQI DEFENDERS TO HOLD CAPITAL" (March 25, 2003), the *Times* implicitly opined that Saddam Hussein was alive at the time he was purportedly rallying his troops. If the *Times* had used the same level of skepticism that it typically reserves for statements by President Bush, it would never have let such a headline slip onto the front page. In fact, the article itself reads like a press release issued by Hussein's information ministry:

With their confidence visibly bolstered by five days of fighting that has shown Iraqi troops offering stiffer resistance than expected, Iraq's leaders resurfaced today in a contemptuous, even cocksure mood and challenged American forces to push on across the last 50 or 60 miles of desert toward a decisive showdown in Baghdad.

Were the Iraqi leaders really exuding confidence or just feigning it? The *Times* was lending a level of credibility to the Iraqi information minister not seen since their support of President Clinton. This was the same information minister who just a few weeks later was being called "Baghdad Bob" and "Comical Ali," whose sense of humor was being favorably compared to that of Chico Marx: "Who you gonna believe, me or your own eyes?" The article continued:

President Saddam Hussein, silent since shortly after an American bombing raid in the first airstrikes last week, appeared on television in a 25-minute speech aimed at further stiffening Iraqi defenses. He said American and British forces were "in real trouble right now" after soldiers were killed, captured or taken prisoner on the drive north from Kuwait.

The *Times* had already reported that a first strike of multiple cruise missiles at the start of the war may have taken the life of Saddam Hussein, along with the lives of his two sons and perhaps other Iraqi leaders. Whether Hussein survived those initial attacks had been a matter of intense scrutiny by the U.S. intelligence and intense debate in the news media. But by failing at the outset of the article to question the authenticity of the videotape, which may have been made prior to the commencement of hostilities for purposes of propaganda, the *Times* simply accepted the Iraqi perspective on the issue. In doing so, the *Times* gave credence to the following taped statements made by Saddam Hussein, as reported in the next four paragraphs of this front-page article:

"Hold against them," Mr. Hussein told groups of paramilitary fighters who have harassed the allied invaders. "Hit them hard. Hit them with all force and accuracy."

Iraq's aim, Mr. Hussein said, should be to drag out the war, denying the

251

United States and Britain the quick victory they planned and dragging them into "this quagmire."

"Today we are standing in a position that would please a friend and anger an enemy and all the infidels," he said. "But we are going to be victorious and we are causing them to suffer.

"These are your decisive days," he added. "Hit now. According to what? According to what God has ordered you to do—'Cut their throats, and be patient.'"

The only explanation for this blind acceptance of the authenticity of the tape may be that its contents provided potent fuel for the "fear and anxiety" theme the *Times* was keen to present on its front pages. Had the *Times* been mindful of its responsibility for accuracy and objectivity, it would have at least reported the doubts being expressed at that time by the intelligence community about the authenticity of the tape.

SLANTING WITH POLLS

On March 26, 2003, in "OPINIONS BEGIN TO SHIFT AS PUBLIC WEIGHS COSTS OF WAR," the *Times* reported the results of a poll it had begun taking with CBS on a daily basis since the war began:

> Americans say the war in Iraq will last longer and cost more than they initially expected, according to the latest New York Times/CBS News poll. The shift comes as the public absorbs the first reports of allied setbacks on the battlefield.

The poll showed a dramatic drop in the percentage—from 53 percent to 34 percent—of Americans who thought the war would only last a few weeks, as they absorbed the first reports of allied setbacks. The basis of these results was two survey questions asked over a period of three days:

> Regarding the war with Iraq, which is most likely?
> • Quick and successful effort

- Long and costly involvement
- No opinion

How soon do you think the war with Iraq will be over?
- In a few weeks
- In several months
- No opinion

It is said that, in court, a good lawyer never asks a question to which he doesn't already know the answer. It should have been no surprise to anyone that as the public began to absorb the realities of military battle, expectations about the war's length and difficulty were going to change. Further, absolutely no one expected the war to last only three days. It was therefore a virtual certainty that expectations about the length and difficulty of the war during the course of any three days of intense battle would change for the worse. It was also certain that nearly all the major television and cable news networks would report the results of the poll, adding a sense of "fear and anxiety" when "context and history" were needed most from our nation's journalists.

Interestingly, and what was not reported in the article, the poll found that 40 percent of the American public seemed initially prepared for the war to last "several months." Knowing what we know now—that the war ultimately only lasted three weeks—we can certainly say that, for a very large number of Americans, the success and speed of the outcome vastly exceeded their expectations.

But what can we say about the drop in the percentage, from 53 percent to 34 percent, who thought the war would only last a few weeks—during the three day period Americans were absorbing the first reports of allied setbacks? About the only explanation possible for this dramatic drop in expectations is that the news these Americans were receiving failed to adequately carry "the context, the history, the whole picture"—Howell Raines' stated goal of the *Times'* news pages. While this drop in expectations could not be attributed to the *Times'* coverage alone, clearly the influence of the *Times,* the downbeat tone of its coverage and the reporting of setbacks without the proper context, cannot absolve the editors of responsibility, at least as far as their own reporting was concerned.

NEGATIVE STORY SELECTION AND PLACEMENT

The front page of the *New York Times* published on Friday, March 28, 2003 was the cause of a watershed event. The *Times* coverage of the war was getting so bad it prompted one of its rivals to devote a full page editorial denouncing the *Times'* negative coverage. In a courageous editorial entitled "4TH ESTATE: 5TH COLUMN?" (Saturday, March 29, 2003), the *New York Post* wrote the following:

> Is that really The New York Times that's been on the newsstands lately? Judging by the headlines, it reads more like something edited by Saddam Hussein's propaganda ministry.
>
> "New reality, Hard Choices" face the U.S.-led coalition, read a front-page headline yesterday. Another warned of "A Tough Fight" ahead.
>
> Thursday, its front page spoke of the allies trying to "adapt to setbacks" and how two blasts were "Said to Kill 17 [Iraqi] Civilians."
>
> Two days earlier, that page also mentioned coalition "setbacks," with its lead headline citing not the allies' military success but the fact that "IRAQIS REPEL COPTERS; ONE GOES DOWN." It also gave prominent space to Saddam's vow that "the Allies Will Be Dragged Into a 'Quagmire'"—while a separate article warned: "The Goal is Baghdad, but at What Cost?"
>
> And yesterday, on the paper's Web site: "Bush Administration Frustrated by War Doubts."

Underneath the foregoing introduction was a photo of the entire March 28 front page of the *New York Times* and a point-by-point analysis of each headline on that page. For example, pointing to the lead headline of the *Times'* front page that day, "BAGHDAD BOMBED; DESERT SKIRMISHES STRETCH 350 MILES," the *Post* circled the words "Desert Skirmishes Stretch 350 Miles" and commented on what they thought the *Times* wanted its readers to think: "that 'all hell has broken out' when, in fact, fighting didn't 'stretch' anywhere *close* to 350 miles. Coalition troops roam that distance, but they've been attacked only in isolated spots—and they're smashing every Iraqi force that attacks."

The *Post* then pointed to the photo situated squarely in the middle of the *Times'* front page that day, which depicted four uniformed soldiers riding in a truck, smiling for the camera and making "peace signs" with their hands. But these were not coalition soldiers; they were Iraqi Republican Guard Troops who, according to the caption, had "left Baghdad yesterday, bound for a front south of the capital where allied forces are assembling." The *Post* circled the photo and commented, "An upbeat photo—OF THE ENEMY? (Why not show us Saddam's Fedayeen terrorists?)"

The *Post* circled the headline "A GULF COMMANDER SEES A LONGER ROAD" and said:

> **What the Times wants you to think:** Quagmire! Quagmire! Quagmire! (Just in case anyone missed the point in the other three Page One headlines. But here's a quote from the commander that's *not* in the Times' story: "This is about where we'd expected [to be at this point].")

The *Post* circled the headline "IRAQI DEFENSE CHIEF VOWS FIGHT, PREDICTING BAGHDAD CLASH IN DAYS" and commented with its interpretation: "It's going to be ugly. Get scared." Finally, one of the front-page headlines that day in the *Times* declared, "WAR TO KEEP GOING UNTIL REGIME ENDS, BUSH AND BLAIR SAY."

Circling the top line of the three-line headline "WAR TO KEEP GOING," the *Post* commented:

> **The Times wants to you to think:** The war may never end—indeed, it may be unwinnable. Echoes of Vietnam? (Please.)

The combined effect of the *Times*' presentation, the *Post* said, seemed "to work to put the darkest possible spin on Operation Iraqi Freedom." "Just like Vietnam," the *Post* concluded. "Maybe it is déjà vu, after all."

Had the *Post* turned to that day's Nation at War section in the *Times*, it would have found more negativism, including the following ludicrous headline (March 28, 2003):

ENDLESS SUPPLY CONVOY IS FRUSTRATED ENDLESSLY

Needless to say, the convoy of trucks that supplied the troops during the first several days of the war was finite in its length and duration, not endless, and any frustration arising from having to resist the roadside attacks from Iraqi fighters was short-lived. A more objective, less tabloid-like, headline might have been: "IRAQI FIGHTERS CONTINUE TO PESTER SUPPLY CONVOY."

EMPHASIZING THE INSIGNIFICANT

The following day, the *Times* opened a new front on its war against the commander in chief. Portraying Iraqi resistance as stronger and more troublesome than it actually was and blowing out of proportion the logistical challenges of supplying the front lines, the *Times* began to characterize the American military leadership as out of touch with the troops on the ground.

In "2 VIEWS OF WAR: ON THE GROUND AND AT THE TOP" (March 29, 2003), the *Times* reported:

> CAMP SAYILYA, Qatar, March 28—Top American generals and their field commanders have begun to give sharply differing accounts of the war in Iraq, sometimes creating an impression that two different wars are being fought.

To begin with, whether generals and their commanders have sharply different accounts of the war, a difference that creates "an impression two different wars are being fought," is strictly a matter of opinion. What is that opinion doing in a lead sentence on the front page of the *New York Times*? A careful reading of the article, however, reveals a more subtle agenda. Where the article continued on page 10 of section B of the paper, you will find the following:

> General Franks has not appeared in the high tech briefing room since Monday. Instead, the duty has been assigned to Brig. Gen. Vincent Brooks, a telegenic young West Point graduate who has auditioned and rehearsed the role by communication aides assigned to Central Command by the White House. . . .
> The descriptions of the war from Centcom are leading to grumbling here. . . .
> Frustration is building in the media center.

Frustrated that General Franks himself was too busy (and too concerned about security leaks) to give them face-time, reporters stationed in Qatar who covered the briefings at Centcom were preparing for journalistic mutiny. According to the *Times* article, when Michael Wolff, the media critic at *New York* magazine, expressed his frustrations directly to General Brooks, "the room erupted in applause."

Could this article—a front-pager suggesting that the reticent generals at Centcom were clueless about what's happening in the field—have been merely a vehicle for the *Times* reporters to vent their frustrations with Centcom? Allegedly reporting on what was happening in the field, with no apparent support whatsoever—neither quoting nor identifying a single source—the *Times* stated:

Field commanders complain of dire shortages of food, fuel and ammunition.

After that report reverberated through the echo chamber of American media organizations, television news reporters embedded with the troops tried in vain to discover such shortages. However, while some embedded reporters reported a temporary reduction in food rations, no serious or "dire" shortage of food, fuel, or ammunition was confirmed by any other reporter on the scene. Even if one or more field commanders actually suffered a shortage, what evidence was there that the problem was widespread? It seems "the context, the history, the whole picture," if reported, would have undermined the petty agenda that appeared to be behind this article.

More Cluster-Bombing with Negativism

In addition to "2 Views of War: On the Ground and at the Top," the front page of the *Times* on Saturday, March 29, 2003 also bore the following headlines:

Iraq Says Blast in Baghdad Kills Dozens of Civilians; U.S. Blamed

A Pause in the Advance, and Some Time to Reflect

Haunting Thoughts after a Fierce Battle

Either Take a Shot or Take a Chance

In that last article, the *Times* quoted a soldier who said, "We had a great day. We killed a lot of people."

In another article on the same page under the uncharacteristically positive headline "KURDS AND G.I.'S ROUT MILITANTS IN NORTH," the *Times* reported the military success in the following backhanded way:

> In a war that has seen early setbacks and unwelcome surprises, this was an operation in which the immediate outcome exceeded expectations.

SLANTING THE *WHY*

As we discussed in a previous chapter, the *Why*, the cause of an event or motive behind a statement, is rarely a matter of fact and, in the political context, is always a matter of opinion. But that does not seem to deter the *Times* from formulating an opinion, slipping it into a "news" article, and then emphasizing it by placing it in the lead sentence and often in the most emphatic part of the lead, the first few words.

In "WHITE HOUSE SAYS WAR IS 'ON TRACK'; SHOW OF SUPPORT" (March 29, 2003), the *Times* ascribed a motive to several statements by administration officials and put the Bush administration on the defensive at both the beginning and end of the lead sentence of this lead front-page story:

> WASHINGTON, March 28—The Bush administration worked to firm up support for the war today, accusing Saddam Hussein of operating death squads, warning Syria and Iran against interfering with allied operations and mounting a concerted effort to counter the impression that the fighting had gone worse than expected in its first nine days.

This is how an impartial editor could have rewritten the above lead without slanting the story:

> WASHINGTON, March XX—The Bush administration today accused Saddam Hussein of operating death squads and warned Syria and Iran against interfering with allied operations. Critics charged that these actions were part

of a concerted effort to counter the impression that the fighting had gone worse than expected in its first nine days.

It would be inappropriate to include that second sentence if the paper was unable to quote, on the record, at least one of the critics making the charges.

CRUSADING WITH THE RACE CARD

The senior editors of the *Times* seem obsessed with race, taking every opportunity to publish stories that emphasize the difference between the races rather than the humanity and common human rights which all people, no matter what race, share and deserve. In a front-page feature story under the headline "MILITARY MIRRORS A WORKING-CLASS AMERICA" (March 30, 2003), the *Times* took the opportunity to remind us of the racial differences of the brave soldiers who were among the first to make the ultimate sacrifice for their country:

> Of the 28 servicemen killed who have been identified so far, 20 were white,
> 5 black, 3 hispanic—proportions that neatly mirror those of the military as a
> whole.

Leave it to the *New York Times* to assure the American public that the Saddam Fedayeen did not discriminate on the basis of race when it came to killing American soldiers. Then, turning to one of its favorite themes, its fascination with the wealthy and privileged, the *Times* suggested a new reason why we went to war with Iraq:

> But just one [killed American soldier] was from a well-to-do family, and
> with the exception of a Naval Academy alumnus, just one had graduated from
> an elite college or university.

Thus, it was not Saddam Hussein's torture chambers, weapons of mass destruction, or cooperation with Al Qaeda; the real reason we went to war was that Saddam's battlefield death squads, like Bush's tax cut proposals, favored the rich. With America's national security and the prospect of a liberated Iraq at stake, and with the lives of American soldiers in the balance, must even the most profound human actions of our time—real warfare—be reduced by the *New York Times* to the Marxist fiction of class warfare?

SLANTING WITH OPINION

The same issue of the *Times* carried another Frank Rich contribution to what Howell Raines characterized as the "news pages," the Arts & Leisure section. Rich's column, "IRAQ AROUND THE CLOCK" (March 30, 2003), began:

> And so it turned out that "Shock and Awe"—or "shockinaw," in cable parlance—didn't have legs. Less than a week after it pumped up the stock market and gave the country a presentiment of a quick and tidy war, it was all but forgotten.

If anything will be remembered about Gulf War II, it will be the fact that it was "quick and tidy." Rich's column then proceeded to extol the virtues of famed reporter Peter Arnett, whom Rich called "one person on the scene who didn't buy the initial story line." We can thank Rich for documenting one of Arnett's more brilliant observations:

> It's déjà vu all over again, the idea that this would be a walkover, the idea that the people of Basra would throw flowers at the Marines.

History will record (while bearing in mind the hardships endured and the sacrifices made by the brave soldiers who engaged the Iraqi forces) that the war *was* a walkover and that the people of Basra *did* throw flowers at the Marines. Rich's praise for Arnett could not have come at a worse time. The next day, Arnett was fired for appearing as a stooge for Saddam Hussein on Iraqi national TV. During the several weeks that followed his disgrace, commentators and lawyers debated whether Arnett should be prosecuted for treason.

To his credit, however, Rich did offer a profound observation that was to be found nowhere else in the *Times* during this period:

As the pendulum swings, it's fair to ask: could the new quagmire narrative be just as transitory and misleading as the discarded celebratory cakewalk of "Shock and Awe."

By recognizing the "new quagmire narrative," Rich seems to have been keenly aware of the negative account of the war being told by his own newsroom. And, in an odd way, he also acknowledged that, perhaps, Fox News—who, Rich suggested, covered the war "without irony or ambiguity or anything other than good news"—had the story right all along.

NEWS ANALYSIS FOR DUMMIES

A "News Analysis" entitled "BUSH PERIL: SHIFTING SAND AND FICKLE OPINION" by R.W. Apple Jr. graced the front page of the same Sunday issue of the *Times* (March 30, 2003). Since the piece was an editorial, it earns no criticism here as an example of slanted news reporting, but it is worth commenting upon because, in my experience, never has so much prognostication on the front page of a major newspaper been later proven so false. The piece asked, "Is [President Bush's] luck about to turn in the winds and sands of Iraq?"—a question followed by the following observations, which all turned out to be wrong:

> With every passing day, it is more evident that the failure to obtain permission from Turkey for American troops to cross its territory and open a northern front constituted a diplomatic debacle.

Wrong.

> With every passing day, it is more evident that the allies made two gross military misjudgments in concluding that coalition forces could safely bypass Basra and Nasiriya and that Shiite Muslims in southern Iraq would rise up against Saddam Hussein.

Wrong.

Street by street fighting in the rubble of Baghdad and other cities—an eventuality that American strategists have long sought to avoid—now looks more likely.

Wrong.

The war could last so long that the American public loses patience.

Wrong.

This new analyst demonstrated the perils of relying solely on the *New York Times* for the news about the war. And, like the *Times*, he seemed to find more credibility in the comments of "Baghdad Bob," the Iraqi information minister, than the war updates provided by the Bush administration, which the reporter mocked as being made with "metronomic regularity."

SLANTING THE *WHY*

The nattering nabobs of negativity continued their attempts to put the Bush administration on the defensive, conveying in news article after news article the *Times'* opinions about the motives behind statements made by President Bush and officials in his administration about the war effort.

In the front-page article "CALLING TROOP LEVELS ADEQUATE, RUMSFELD DEFENDS WAR PLANNING" (March 31, 2003), the *Times* wrote:

> WASHINGTON, March 30—Defense Secretary Donald H. Rumsfeld, fending off sharp criticism of his wartime management, said today that he and his commanders had not underestimated the number of ground troops needed to defeat Iraq, nor had they slowed deployment of forces to an extent that hampered the offensive.

A favorite ploy of the *Times* is to equate questions asked by reporters as criticism of the Bush administration. It is notable that in a story that began "fending off sharp criticism" the article failed to quote anyone who sharply criticized the Defense Department. Instead, the *Times* reported the primary source of the criticism as follows:

> But in their appearances on the Sunday morning talk shows, Mr. Rumsfeld and General Myers were beset by questions suggesting that they had failed to . . .

If Tim Russert, George Stephanopoulos, Tony Snow, or any of the weekend political talk show hosts were asked whether they "criticized" the person they interviewed during the course of their program, they would have to, in truth, deny it completely. They simply asked questions. Certainly, by no possible definition of the term, could it be said they engaged in "sharp criticism" of the administration. Yet, those questions formed the foundation of a front-page article in the *New York Times* showing the secretary of defense defending the wisdom of his war plans while troops in the battlefield were risking their lives on the basis of that plan.

QUOTE-SOMEONE-WHO-AGREES-WITH-US

The next day, the front page of the *Times* carried a "news" article that turned up the volume, "RUMSFELD'S DESIGN FOR WAR CRITICIZED ON THE BATTLEFIELD" (April 1, 2003). With such a headline, first-page placement, above-the-fold, and a lead that declared there have been a "series of complaints," you would think the body of the article would contain substantial evidence to back up its premise—that Rumsfeld's war plan had been criticized by those fighting the war in Iraq. A careful reading of the article reveals only the following two paragraphs relating to the premise contained in the article's headline:

> One colonel, who spoke on the condition that his name be withheld, was among the officers criticizing decisions to limit initial deployments of troops to the region. "He wanted to fight this war on the cheap," the colonel said. "He got what he wanted."
>
> The angry remarks from the battlefield opened with comments made last Thursday—and widely publicized Friday—by Lt. Gen. William S. Wallace, the

V Corps commander, who said the military faced the likelihood of a longer war than many strategists had anticipated.

Those two paragraphs, both appearing on the front page, comprised the entire case supporting the claim that the war plan was being "criticized by officers on the battlefield." The rest of the article contained journalistic padding, amounting to no more than a rehash of the previously reported differences between Secretary Rumsfeld and certain subordinates at the Pentagon as to how best to transform the military.

Is that the best the *Times* can come up with: one colonel, speaking on condition of anonymity? Here is what the *New York Times Manual of Style and Usage* says on the subject: "Anonymity must not become a cloak for attacks on people, institutions or policies. . . . The vivid language of direct quotation confers an unfair advantage on the speaker or writer who hides behind the newspaper, and turns of phrase are valueless to a reader who cannot assess the source."

What's going on here? The *Times* knows that its reputation, or what's left of it, is being used to lend credibility to an attack against the secretary of defense during a time of war, and no one can check the source out for themselves. It is not even clear whether this anonymous colonel was actually someone "on the battlefield"—a key fact, which raises the emotional tenor of the criticism (i.e., that the brave men and women in uniform under fire are at odds with their leadership). Can an officer stationed at V Corps Headquarters, which is located in Kuwait, really be considered "on the battlefield"?

The article raised the emotional level further by (1) characterizing the remarks from the battlefield as "angry," again with no support, and (2) suggesting that Rumsfeld's planning was analogous to mistakes made in Vietnam, again with no support whatsoever:

> Here today, raw nerves were obvious as officers compared Mr. Rumsfeld to Robert S. McNamara, an architect of the Vietnam War who failed to grasp the political and military realities of Vietnam.

A reference to Vietnam? "Quagmire, quagmire, quagmire," and yet the credibility of those making the accusations cannot be assessed by the reader. This is not the way a responsible newspaper should conduct itself during a war.

VARIATION: MISQUOTE-SOMEONE-WHO-DOESN'T-AGREE-WITH-US

The reference to remarks made by Lieutenant General William S. Wallace, the V Corps Commander, seem benign enough, particularly in light of Wallace's widely publicized quote from the previous week: "The enemy we're fighting is different from the one we war-gamed against."

But the *Washington Post*, who first carried the quote, was forced to print a correction. It seems it misquoted the general, who really stated something more qualified: "The enemy we're fighting is *a bit* different from the one we war-gamed against."

The *Times* never corrected the quote.

ONE-SIDED STORY

The front-page article attacking Secretary Rumsfeld was coupled in the same issue with an article appearing on the front page of the *Times*' Nation at War section, under the headline "BUSH DEFENDS THE PROGRESS OF THE WAR" (April 1, 2003).

This article turned to *anonymous* Republican congressmen whom the *Times* called "jittery" about the war, and the war's potential impact on the next election cycle. Nevertheless, the *Times* seemed to have trouble locating any Democrats who may have been "jittery" about facing re-election—after having voted against a "quick and tidy" war that liberated a repressed people, enhanced national security, and laid a platform for peace in the Middle East.

TIME-OUT FOR EDITORIAL REPOSITIONING

Had Howell Raines gone too far in criticizing the administration during a time the nation was at war? The *Times*' editorial editors seemed to think so. The next day, the editorial page of the *Times* reflected a genuine concern that perhaps the news division overplayed its hand in criticizing the Bush administration.

In its editorial entitled "SECOND-GUESSING THE WAR" (April 2, 2003), the *Times* editors actually came to the defense of Rumsfeld:

> As secretary of defense, Donald Rumsfeld has bruised a lot of egos. Right now, when soldiers' nerves are edgy and the public is concerned about the pace of the war, he can use all the support he can get among the military brass. But many officers—in Iraq and back home—have been stunningly critical. Mr. Rumsfeld tried to fight the war "on the cheap," they say.

Obviously, the editorial editors were trying to distance themselves from the criticism. But was there really any real criticism to begin with? The only quote referenced by the *Times*' editorial was the anonymous "on the cheap" statement made by one solitary colonel, and the editors even seemed to discount the credibility of wartime statements by soldiers whose "nerves are edgy." The editors seemed troubled with the evidence, unable even to point to the "series of complaints" suggested by the front page of the *Times*. Moreover, the editorial recognized that the war was "less than two weeks old and appears to have gone fairly well so far on the ground." (It is fair to ask what newspaper the editorial page writers were reading every morning.) Finally, the editors concluded that "the military strategy worries us far less than what comes next."

It seems the *Times*' editorial editors were beginning to realize that the war was going far better than how it was being portrayed by the *Times*' news division and felt they had better reposition themselves for a "quick and tidy" victory and a new horse to ride—"what comes next"—in their ideological war against the president.

As it turned out, the editorial page had a good sense of when to throw in the towel. As much as the nattering nabobs of negativity in Howell Raines' news division tried to keep the pressure up on the Bush administration, the broad picture, as reflected in each subsequent day's banner headline, was all good news for President Bush.

Could the editorial editors have made an impression on Raines? Here were the lead headlines that appeared in the *Times* over the week that followed the *Times*' editorial defending Rumsfeld:

U.S. GROUND FORCES SWEEP TOWARD BAGHDAD
(April 3, 2003)

U.S. Forces at Edge of a Blacked-Out Baghdad
(April 4, 2003)

U.S. Squeezes Baghdad and Readies Next Step
(April 5, 2003)

U.S. Tanks Make Quick Strike into Baghdad
(April 6, 2003)

Allies Press Baghdad and Thrust into Basra
(April 7, 2003)

U.S. Blasts Compound in Effort to Kill Hussein
(April 8, 2003)

U.S. Tightens Grip; Rockets Rain on Baghdad
(April 9, 2003)

Negative Story Selection and Placement

During the week those positive banner headlines appeared on the front page of the *Times*, the big picture was becoming clear: the military and humanitarian achievements of the coalition forces were gaining momentum and, with each passing day, a picture of a liberated Iraq was coming into focus to a world watching as each victory unfolded. Nevertheless, even as the military campaign was gaining momentum, the nabobs of negativism continued their assault on the American mind. What follows were the grim headlines from the *Times'* front pages and the Nation at War sections during that one week immediately preceding the fall of Baghdad:

Iraq Is Planning Protracted War
(April 2, 2003)

For Arabs, New Jihad Is in Iraq
(April 2, 2003)

MOST BRITONS BACK THE WAR, BUT MISTRUST HOW THE U.S. IS
WAGING IT
(April 2, 2003)

ON THE OUTSKIRTS, ARAB VOLUNTEERS AND BRITISH MIXED
FEELINGS
(April 2, 2003)

A BRIDGEHEAD, AND A THIRSTY WELCOME
(April 3, 2003)

ACCESS FOR NEWS MEDIA BRINGS CHORUS OF CRITICISM AND
QUERIES ON WAR
(April 3, 2003)

IRAQ SHOWS CASUALTIES IN HOSPITAL
(APRIL 3, 2003)

AT WAL-MARTS CLOSE TO BASES, EMOTIONS SPILL INTO AISLE
(April 4, 2003)

AT AIRPORT, BOMBS PROVIDE ONLY LIGHT
(April 4, 2003)

AT DARKENED AIRPORT, A FEELING OF SPOOKINESS
(April 4, 2003)

SOBER REPLIES TO SPECULATIVE QUESTIONS
(April 4, 2003)

IMAGES OF VICTORY OVERSHADOW DOSES OF REALISM
(April 4, 2003)

NEW DANGERS IN FINAL PUSH
(April 5, 2003)

As U.S. Moves In, Iraqi TV Presents a Relaxed Hussein
(April 5, 2003)

For Weary U.S. Troops, End Is Still Elusive
(April 5, 2003)

With Current War, Professors Protest, as Students Debate
(April 5, 2003)

U.S. Forces Have Searched Few Iraqi Weapons Sites
(April 5, 2003)

In Jordan, It's Long Live Iraq, and Woe to King
(April 5, 2003)

Fearing Daily for the Safety of Relatives in Baghdad
(April 5, 2003)

The United States' Message of a Humanitarian War Is Faltering
in the Arab World
(April 5, 2003)

Representatives Disagree on War, but Share Pain of Its
Consequences
(April 5, 2003)

The Rural Opposition: Protesting Where Everybody Knows
Your Name
(April 5, 2003)

U.S. Use of Tear Gas Could Violate Treaty, Critics Say
(April 5, 2003)

Barrage of Fire, Trail of Death in Capital
(April 6, 2003)

DEFIANT IRAQIS SAY U.S. PUSH IS THWARTED
(April 6, 2003)

URBAN WAR BEGINS: IT WAS REAL SCARY
(April 6, 2003)

THERAPY ON THE FLY FOR SOLDIERS WHO FACE ANXIETY IN THE
BATTLEFIELD
(April 6, 2003)

PREPARING FOR POST-HUSSEIN, AND FOR POTENTIAL DANGERS
(APRIL 6, 2003)

DISSONANCE OF GUNS HERALDS GROUND WAR IN IRAQ'S CAPITAL
(April 7, 2003)

BASRA OFFERS A LESSON ON TAKING BAGHDAD
(April 7, 2003)

FOR ONE PASTOR, THE WAR HITS HOME
(April 7, 2003)

BAD ROADS FRUSTRATE PLAN FOR NOOSE AROUND BAGHDAD AS
PRELUDE TO FINAL PUSH
(April 7, 2003)

WHILE MANY ISLAMIC FIGHTERS SURRENDER, KURDS REMAIN WARY
OF NEW TERRORIST ATTACKS
(April 7, 2003)

EVIDENCE CONTRADICTS RUMORS OF TORTURE
(April 7, 2003)

RELATIVES REMEMBER LAST PHONE CALLS FROM THEIR MARINES
(April 7, 2003)

Anti-Americanism in Greece Is Reinvigorated by War
(April 7, 2003)

Telling War's Deadly Story at Just Enough Distance
(April 7, 2003)

Capital Has Look of a Battlefield
(April 8, 2003)

Warm Welcome and Stubborn Resistance for Marines
(April 8, 2003)

So Far, the Public Seems to Tolerate the Level of American
Casualties in Iraq
(April 8, 2003)

Egyptian Intellectual Speaks of the Arab World's
Despair
(April 8, 2003)

Basra Falls, Though Fighting Persists
(April 8, 2003)

Iraq War Sets Bad Precedent, Mbeki Warns
(April 8, 2003)

As Tactics Change and Battle Lines Blur, Risk of Being Killed
by Own Side Increases
(April 8, 2003)

Tormented No Longer, but Wary
(April 9, 2003)

For One G.I., War Becomes Real
(April 9, 2003)

A YOUNG SOLDIER'S FIRST BIG FIGHT
(April 9, 2003)

SOME IRAQIS GRATEFUL TO U.S. BUT WARY OF ANY CHANGES
(April 9, 2003)

DEATH OF JOURNALISTS BRING ACCUSATIONS AND CONCERNS
(April 9, 2003)

A GRENADE ON THE ROAD, THE DEATH OF THE ENEMY: THE HUMAN
SIDE OF WAR
(April 9, 2003)

WHO'LL CONTROL IRAQ'S OIL, TANGLED QUESTIONS ABOUND
(April 9, 2003)

SLANTING WITH HEADLINES—DEEMPHASIZING THE SIGNIFICANT

On Thursday, April 10, 2003, the three-inch tall banner headline in *USA Today* read, "BAGHDAD FALLS: JUBILANT CROWDS SWARM U.S. TROOPS AS 3-WEEK WAR TOPPLES REGIME; 'GAME IS OVER,' IRAQI DIPLOMAT SAYS."

On the same day, using a typeface no larger than any headline appearing on the front page of the paper since the war began, the *Times* mutedly announced:

U.S. FORCES TAKE CONTROL IN BAGHDAD;
BUSH ELATED; SOME RESISTANCE REMAINS

The *Times'* editorial page editors were closer to the target, as their lead editorial that morning was entitled "THE FALL OF BAGHDAD." They also new what was important in the story, emphasizing not an "elated" President Bush but a jubilant Iraqi people:

The murderous reign of Saddam Hussein effectively ended yesterday as downtown Baghdad slipped from the grip of the Iraqi regime and citizens streamed to the streets to celebrate the sudden disintegration of Mr. Hussein's 24-year dictatorship.

Whatever you may think of the political ideologies of the *Times'* editorial page editors, one thing is certain: unlike its news division, they sure know how to write a news lead.

SLANTING WITH LOADED LANGUAGE

Compare the lead sentence of the *Times'* editorial with the lead sentence written by its news division in the paper's lead front-page story in the *Times* that morning:

> KUWAIT, April 9—Much of Baghdad tumbled into American hands today as Saddam Hussein's image was pulled down from pedestals and portraiture in the city. But American and British commanders said the war in Iraq, including the battle for Baghdad, was not over and faced critical days ahead.

The use of the loaded expression "tumbled into American hands" suggests that Baghdad fell into our hands on its own accord, as though our troops and the Bush administration had little to do with the downfall of the regime. For that matter, the entire lead focuses on physical achievements: control of territory (i.e., Baghdad) and the toppling of, not Saddam Hussein, his regime, or his government, but his "image" and "portraiture."

Now, compare the above lead with how *USA Today* carried the news in its lead sentence that day (April 10, 2003):

> BAGHDAD—Saddam Hussein's government lost control of Iraq's capital Wednesday as U.S. forces extended their reach deep into the city. Jubilant crowds tore down a 20-foot statue of the Iraqi leader and dragged its head through the streets in a scene reminiscent of the fall of the Berlin Wall in 1989.

Here, the focus is on the "regime change" and, rather than speaking of Bush as being "elated," *USA Today* referred to the jubilance of the Iraqi people, an observation completely ignored by the *Times* in its headline and lead sentence.

Other leading newspapers got the story right, too.

In Baghdad: Iraqi crowds rejoice; attacks on U.S. troops persist

BAGHDAD, Iraq—President Saddam Hussein's 24-year rule appeared at an end Wednesday, toppled as surely as one of his statues. Cheering, dancing Iraqis swarmed city streets, and Iraq's U.N. ambassador declared, "The game is over."

—Atlanta Journal-Constitution

Baghdad Falls
Iraqis flood streets to greet U.S. troops

WASHINGTON—U.S. forces wrenched Baghdad from the grip of Saddam Hussein's regime with surprising ease, as Iraqi resistance melted away and crowds of Iraqis surged into the streets yesterday to greet U.S. troops and deface images of their president.

—Baltimore Sun

Baghdad Falls

CAMP SAYLIYAH, Qatar—Saddam Hussein's rule in Baghdad ended yesterday. After three weeks of war, the US Army and Marines punched through fast-fading resistance and captured the city center as looters dismantled the remnants of the regime's authority. Cheering Iraqis surrounded a Hussein statue in Firdos Square and, with the help of Marines, yanked the monument to the ground, symbolically smashing the 23-year regime.

—Boston Globe

Baghdad Falls
Iraqis dance as Saddam topples

(The headline was accompanied by photographs of U.S. troops helping pull down the statue of Saddam Hussein in Baghdad's Paradise Square and depicting an Iraqi woman beating it with her slippers while others danced atop it in celebration).

—Chicago Sun-Times

Saddam's Regime Toppled in Baghdad
Iraq's envoy at U.N. admits 'game is over'

CAMP AS SALIYAH, Qatar—Exuberant defiance created an indelible image of liberation Wednesday, when thousands of Iraqis in a Baghdad square beheaded and toppled a giant statue of Saddam Hussein.

—Houston Chronicle

U.S. IN CONTROL; BAGHDAD IN U.S. HANDS;
SYMBOLS OF REGIME FALL AS TROOPS TAKE CONTROL

BAGHDAD—U.S. troops broke Saddam Hussein's 24-year grip on the Iraqi capital Wednesday as cheering, dancing crowds shouted, "Oh, Iraq!" and, with help from the Marines, toppled a four-story statue of the president, dragging its head in the streets while children pelted it with garbage.

"Victory! We are free!" the crowds called out. "Thank you, President Bush!"

—Los Angeles Times

BAGHDAD FALLS; COLLAPSE
HUSSEIN LOYALISTS GIVE WAY TO U.S. TROOPS—AND LOOTERS

BAGHDAD—Saddam Hussein's dictatorship crumbled with the crash of metal on concrete Wednesday as a U.S. armored vehicle brought down a towering statue of the Iraqi president and a jubilant crowd roared its approval.

"Victory! We are free!" people yelled. "Thank you, President Bush!"

—San Francisco Chronicle

HUSSEIN'S BAGHDAD FALLS
U.S. FORCES MOVE TRIUMPHANTLY THROUGH CAPITAL STREETS,
CHEERED BY CROWDS JUBILANT AT END OF REPRESSIVE REGIME

BAGHDAD, April 9—Swept aside by U.S. troops who drove through the streets of Baghdad, President Saddam Hussein's government collapsed today, ending three decades of ruthless Baath party rule that sought to make Iraq the champion of a modern Arab world but left a legacy of fear, poverty and bitterness.

—Washington Post

The *Times* stood strangely alone with its muted coverage of Bush's triumph, the liberation of the Iraqi people, and a military victory which was so stunning that it is challenging traditional views on how future wars will be fought.

NEGATIVE STORY SELECTION AND PLACEMENT

A week earlier the *Times'* editorial page editors declared that what "worries" them is "what comes next." Howell Raines'—"you provide the pictures, I'll provide the war"—news division was ready to deliver just what the editorial editors were eager to write about, and they didn't waste any time. The banner headline the very next day (April 11, 2003) read:

ALLIES WIDEN HOLD ON IRAQ; CIVIL STRIFE ON RISE

By virtue of the military action by coalition forces, the Iraqi people just shed one of the most brutal dictators the world has seen since Stalin, yet the *Times* declares in a banner headline that, as they see it, civil strife in Iraq is *on the rise*!

In the same issue, the *Times* declared, "LOOTING AND A SUICIDE ATTACK AS CHAOS GROWS IN BAGHDAD" and "KIRKUK'S SWIFT COLLAPSE LEAVES A CITY IN CHAOS" (April 11, 2003). No doubt, thought the *Times*, the Iraqis were already pining for the good old days of order enforced under threat of torture.

Then, just when the Iraqis thought it was safe to loot a government building, readers woke up the following morning to read this irresponsible headline strewn atop the six-columns of the *New York Times* (April 12, 2003):

IN BAGHDAD, FREE OF HUSSEIN, A DAY OF MAYHEM

Mayhem? The dictionary defines the word as "the intentional mutilation of another's body" or "injury inflicted on another so as to cause loss of a bodily part or function necessary for self-defense." Mayhem is what happened to Iraqi citizens who criticized the Baath party or who simply brought bad news to Saddam Hussein or one of his pathologically violent sons. A front-page article, "LAST, DESPERATE DAYS OF A BRUTAL REIGN" (April 20, 2003), broadly described the real "mayhem":

> For years, Mr. Hussein's security agents had been breaking into Iraqi's homes, arresting people at will, and taking them away to the gulag of torture centers and prisons. Some emerged weeks, months, or years later, many of them

disfigured, with eyes gouged out, hands and fingers mangled. But tens of thousands never returned, dying under torture, or being summarily executed.

In "SOCCER PLAYERS DESCRIBE TORTURE BY HUSSEIN'S SON" (May 9, 2003), the *Times* described some of the devices of torture used by Hussein's regime:

> This building was equipped with torture contraptions that included a sarcophagus, with long nails pointing inward from every surface, including the lid, so victims could be punctured and suffocated.
>
> Another device, witnesses said, was a metal framework designed to clamp over a prisoner's body, with footrests at the bottom, rings at the shoulders and attachment points for power cables, so the victim could be hoisted and subjected to electric shocks.

Informed *Times* readers already knew precisely how those electric shocks were administered. "FORMER CAPTIVES RECALL HORRORS OF HUSSEIN'S PRISONS" (April 9, 2003) provided the graphic detail:

> BASRA, Iraq, April 8—In an empty interrogation room deep in the prison that was long this city's epicenter of fear, a man explained the purpose of two thick black electrical cables that snaked through a high barred window.
>
> "Here," he said, holding a cable to each ear, "and here," he added, holding them to his groin.

Granted, a secondary meaning of the word "mayhem" is "deliberate destruction or violence," but the fact that the paper used the word in a front-page banner headline to describe the destruction by a few civilians of mere property— mostly the property of the fallen regime—in the aftermath of a sudden liberation from over thirty-years of repression marked by the horrifying bodily torture of untold numbers of innocent Iraqi citizens, reveals the true depth of the perversion that has clouded the news regime at the *New York Times*.

The same kind of perverted cynicism could be the only explanation for the following headline that appeared on the same front page (April 12, 2003):

SNIPER FIRE GREETS G.I.'S IN BIG CITY IN NORTH

While downplaying what everyone else was calling the "jubilant" welcoming of American troops, the *Times* snidely turned the story on its head, letting us know just how some soldiers had been "greeted" upon their entry into an Iraqi city.

The negative story selection continued in other parts of the paper: "SHAKY GROUND IS AHEAD AND BEHIND IN THE NORTH" (April 12, 2003) and "MARINES IN NOWHERE LAND: SENTRY DUTY IN THE DESERT (April 12, 2003).

GETTING THE STORY WRONG, AND THEN SOME

The following day the *Times* reported, "PILLAGERS STRIP IRAQI MUSEUM OF ITS TREASURE" (April 13, 2003). Simply getting the story wrong—even very wrong—does not amount to ideological bias, but when you put an emotional spin on the facts—like equating "mayhem," under these circumstances, to the looting and destruction of property—you risk getting the proverbial egg-on-your-face. And that's exactly what happened to the *Times* (which has still never quite wiped it off). This sad chapter in wartime journalism began with the following melodramatic lead:

> BAGHDAD, Iraq, April 12—The National Museum of Iraq recorded a history of civilizations that began to flourish in the fertile plains of Mesopotamia more than 7,000 years ago. But once American troops entered Baghdad in sufficient force to topple Saddam Hussein's government this week, it took only 48 hours for the museum to be destroyed, with at least 170,000 artifacts carried away by looters.
>
> The full extent of the disaster that befell the museum came to light only today, as the frenzied looting that swept much of the capital over the previous three days began to ebb.

The *Times* then opined, in this "news" story, that the loss was "likely to be reckoned as one of the greatest cultural disasters in recent Middle Eastern history." Yet, in an apparent admission that what had just been dramatized may be entirely incorrect, the article warned:

A full accounting of what has been lost may take weeks or months. The museum had been closed during much of the 1990's, and as with many Iraqi institutions, its operations were cloaked in secrecy under Mr. Hussein.

So what officials told journalists today may have to be adjusted as a fuller picture comes to light. It remains unclear whether some of the museum's price-less gold, silver and copper antiquities, some of its ancient stone and ceramics and perhaps some of its fabled bronzes and gold-overlaid ivory, had been locked away for safekeeping elsewhere before the looting, or seized for private display in one of Mr. Hussein's myriad palaces.

With that background in the body of the article, how could the lead sentence of the story have possibly been couched in such certainty? And how could the *Times* so prematurely conclude that what appeared to have happened was "likely" to be one of history's "greatest cultural disasters"? It is fair to ask whether the opening sentences of this article was the work of the reporter or the reworking of a copy editor seeking to raise the article's newsworthiness to merit front-page placement.

Moreover, the certainty projected in the lead provided an opportunity for the *Times* to further dramatize the circumstances by closing the article with the following Bush-bashing kicker (quoting an Iraqi archeologist):

> Mr. Muhammad, the archaeologist, directed much of his anger at President Bush. "A country's identity, its value and civilization resides in its history," he said. "If a country's civilization is looted, as ours has been here, its history ends. Please tell this to President Bush. Please remind him that he promised to liber-ate the Iraqi people, but that this is not a liberation, this is a humiliation."

We now know, as we'll soon detail, that only a handful of artifacts were miss-ing from the museum, not 170,000, but as few as 25! The reporter who wrote the original April 13 article was prudent to qualify his report with the suspicion that the museum's artifacts may have been "locked away for safekeeping elsewhere before the looting." But the inflammatory headline, melodramatic lead, and anti-Bush kicker of the story—all completely unnecessary and entirely political—overshadowed the truth and set off a firestorm of criticism in the media about the military's failure to protect the museum from looting.

The media firestorm—which spread to television news programs, newspaper editorials, and the archeological community around the world—was fueled by the burning pages of the *New York Times* itself, whose own reporters and columnists also appeared to be victims of the sensational head-fake staged in the original article.

QUOTE-SOMEONE-WHO-AGREES-WITH-US

For example, the above original front-page story was accompanied by an article run under the headline "ART EXPERTS FEAR WORST IN THE PLUNDER OF A MUSEUM" (April 13, 2003):

> The looting of the National Museum of Iraq, a repository of treasures from civilization's first cities and early Islamic culture, could be a catastrophe for world cultural heritage, archaeologists and art experts say.
>
> "Baghdad is one of the great museums of the world, with irreplaceable material," said Dr. John Malcolm Russell, a specialist in Mesopotamian archaeology at the Massachusetts College of Art in Boston.

The thought of losing tens of thousands of ancient artifacts recovered from the cradle of civilization is naturally upsetting, particularly to anyone whose life has been devoted to the preservation and study of such objects. But where is "the context, the history, the whole picture"? Does not this tragedy weigh in at all against the elimination of the horrific torture and threat of such torture over the lives of millions of people? And upon whom do we lay blame for this thievery? Upon the looters or the military? Or President Bush for starting this war to begin with? Do we routinely blame our government for the crimes of petty criminals?

NEGATIVE STORY SELECTION AND PLACEMENT

The lead headline on the front page that day was "U.S. TROOPS MOVE TO RESTORE ORDER IN EDGY BAGHDAD" (April 13, 2003). The Marines may have had reason to be edgy, but they weren't there to *restore* anything. They had just successfully uprooted an oppressive regime, and they were now part of the process of building something that didn't exist: a government of the people, by the people, and for the people, where nothing of the kind had ever existed there before. The troops didn't bring disorder; they brought freedom.

Another story on the same front page, under the headline "IN THE U.S., ELATION WRESTLES WITH ANXIETY" (April 13, 2003), contained absolute nonsense. The U.S. military, as a result of some brilliant planning and near flawless execution, avoided a chemical or biological attack (or both) that would have cost potentially tens of thousands of American lives, successfully prevented a missile attack that could have killed thousands of Israelis and spread the war to other parts of the Middle East, saved the Iraqi oil fields, and liberated millions of Iraqis from one of the most brutal dictators in modern history. Such was "the context, the history, the whole picture."

Yet, editors of the *New York Times* decided, apparently, that it is more important to stoke the "fear and anxiety" theme.

As one of the greatest military and humanitarian actions in the history of the world was winding down, making way for one of the most dramatic constructions of democracy ever undertaken, the *Times* larded its front page with an anxiety story of a traveling businessman enjoying a drink at a college bar. The man expressed his concern that the "image" of the United States as a powerful country was somehow "obnoxious" to him. Then, the *Times* stated what was on its mind:

> And admirers and detractors of the Bush administration ask whether it considered all the possible consequences of the war beforehand.

Other headlines that appeared in the April 13, 2003 issue of the *New York Times* included:

IN U.S. OCCUPIED MOSUL, U.S. COLONEL FACES 1.7 MILLION ADDED RESPONSIBILITIES

TURKS AND KURDS MAINTAIN A MUTUAL SUSPICION

MARINES READY FOR ANYTHING IN A HOLDOUT CITY

ON THE DRIVE TO BAGHDAD, DOUBT AND DEATH

IN THE HEART OF FRANCE, ANTI-U.S. MOOD SOFTENS

The nabobs continued. The next day, April 14, 2003, the *Times* published a story which finally stated in direct terms what the paper's editors must have been thinking all along: Are the Iraqi's better off today than they were four weeks ago? In "LACKING NECESSITIES, MANY IRAQIS CAN'T FOCUS ON FUTURE" (April 14, 2003), the *Times* told a story of "a town gathering for a remarkable democratic display—a town hall meeting." The *Times* made its point:

> They want to know what is being done about the lack of water, security and jobs—three things they say they had under Saddam Hussein's rule.

Other headlines that day included:

G.I.'S LOOK FOR FEDAYEEN; FIND PLEADING CIVILIANS

GREEN BERETS FIGHT CHAOS AND CALLOUSNESS IN A CITY GONE BAD

AS CHAOS CONTINUES, U.S. SENDS AID TO IRAQ

FOR THOSE WHO QUESTION THE WAR, COMPLICATIONS AMID THE PAIN OF LOSS

The following day's front page of the *Times* bore another "fear and anxiety" story: "A COUPLE SEPARATED BY WAR WHILE UNITED IN THEIR FEARS" (April 15, 2003). Then on the front of that day's Nation at War section: "SYRIA FEARS THE UNKNOWN: WHAT'S BEHIND U.S. THREAT."

The news was too positive to earn front-page placement, but the *Times* did carry the story in the Nation at War section: "AMERICANS SEE CLEAR VICTORY IN IRAQ, POLL FINDS" (April 15, 2003). According to the latest *New York Times*/CBS News poll, a majority of Americans believed that "the victory will stand even if Saddam Hussein remains at large or if the United States fails to unearth chemical or biological weapons." Moreover, the poll found that 73 percent of those polled, including

61 percent of Democrats, approved of President Bush's job performance, and a remarkable 79 percent approved of the way the president handled Iraq.

Then, the article reported the larger story, reflecting, finally, American feelings concerning "the context, the history, the whole picture":

> The poll, taken over the weekend, found for the first time since 2001, a majority of Americans, 62 percent, believed that the nation was winning the war on terrorism.

Unfortunately, the big picture didn't warrant front-page coverage. The editors, apparently, felt there were more important stories that merited front-page attention that day: "NEW JERSEY OPENS FILES SHOWING FAILURES OF CHILD WELFARE SYSTEM," "COUNTY SAY IT'S TOO POOR TO DEFEND THE POOR," and, of course, "A COUPLE SEPARATED BY WAR WHILE UNITED IN THEIR FEARS."

THE ARTIFACTS FIRESTORM GOES BIG TIME

With the *Times* now reporting that 62 percent of Americans believe the nation was winning the war on terrorism, what did the *New York Times* choose to focus its editorial capital on? The stolen artifacts, of course. In an editorial entitled "SACKING THE PAST" (April 15, 2003), the *Times'* editorial editors bought Howell Raines' head-fake—lock, stock, and barrel:

> Until this past weekend, one of the most important collections of Iraqi antiquities could still be found in Baghdad. But that was before the looters came.

The following day, the *Times* continued to beat the Bush administration over the head with the alleged museum looting with two more stories. First, "EXPERTS' PLEAS TO PENTAGON DIDN'T SAVE MUSEUM" (April 16, 2003) began:

> WASHINGTON, April 15—The plunder last week of Iraq's national museum, one of the Middle East's most important archaeological repositories, occurred despite repeated requests to the Pentagon by experts and scholars that the site be protected when American troops entered Baghdad.

A senior Pentagon official said the military had never promised that the buildings would be safeguarded.

On the same page appeared "CURATORS APPEAL FOR A BAN ON PURCHASE OF IRAQI ARTIFACTS" (April 16, 2003), reporting that the world's museum officials and archaeologists were calling on the American government to take stronger steps to prevent "further pillaging" in Baghdad. The article included a quote from Secretary of State Colin Powell, who stated, "The United States understands its obligations and will be taking a leading role with respect to antiquities in general but this museum in particular." Yet the article concluded with the following kicker:

"The museum has been ransacked, and nothing has been done to make it safe and secure," Dr. Gibson said in a telephone interview from Chicago. "The mob will come back."

The Arts section of the same issue contained a brief story ("RESTORING IRAQ'S MUSEUMS," April 16, 2003), repeating the misinformation for an audience of readers who may have missed the coverage in other sections of the paper:

Looting across the country has devastated Babylonian, Sumerian and Assyrian collections reflecting 7,000 years of civilization in ancient Mesopotamia.

Where there is fire, there's smoke. *Times* columnist Maureen Dowd finally (what took her so long?) demonstrated that even a Pulitzer Prize-winning columnist can be bamboozled by the front page of the *New York Times*. In her column "HISTORY UP IN SMOKE" (April 16, 2003), Dowd scoured her sources and reported the following:

The coalition forces were guarding the Iraqi oil ministry while hundreds of Iraqis ransacked and ran off with precious heirlooms and artifacts from a 7,000-year-old civilization.

Meanwhile, the front page of the *Times* noted other complaints about the U.S., this time from Iraqis: "FREE TO PROTEST, IRAQIS COMPLAIN ABOUT THE

U.S." (April 16, 2003). Not "many Iraqis," not "some Iraqis," not a "small minority of Iraqis" (not even "Iraqis prodded by radical religious factions in the country")—just "Iraqis." Contrary to the impression given by the headline, the article stated that the protest was relatively small and "there's no sense that these complaints—in which ordinary Iraqis have begun insistently buttonholing any Westerner who wanders by—are degenerating into violence or an unwillingness to cooperate with the Americans." Moreover, the article quoted a sergeant on the scene: "It seems like people are pretty happy to see police on the streets again" and "they are always happy to see us." In light of what was reported, why did the story of these apparently isolated complaints merit such a broad headline and front-page placement? Later in the article, the *Times* printed a choice quote on a familiar theme (quoting an Iraqi on the scene):

> "As an educated man, I see that the future will be worse than the past," he said. "The British and the United States are here for the oil, and even Israel is getting its cut. They all want to destroy Islam."

How about including a quote from one of the Iraqis who "are always happy to see" the American soldiers?

THE TRUTH TRIES TO SURFACE

The first report that the loss of antiquities from the Baghdad Museum may not have been as bad as first reported appeared the following day in a *Times* article under the headline "MUSEUM PILLAGE DESCRIBED AS DEVASTATING BUT NOT TOTAL" (April 17, 2003):

> BAGHDAD, Iraq, April 16—Curators surveyed the damage at the National Museum of Iraq today, and expressed both worry at how much might have been stolen in the looting last week and tentative hope that thousands of years of Iraq's cultural heritage might not have vanished completely.
> "It's not a total loss," Donny George, the director of research for the Iraqi Board of Antiquities, said in an interview today.

George went on to say that "part of the collection had been stored in vaults in the basement just before the war, though some of the heavier and more fragile items remained in the galleries. Some items were also taken elsewhere for storage." Sound famliar? As of that time, George knew of only *three* treasures that were missing. The article also pointed out:

> In one possible encouraging sign, several people in the Al Awi neighborhood that surrounds the museum said they did not see looters leave with any antiquities, even amid gun battles and looting that lasted two days.

Another witness who lives behind the museum reported that:

> [T]he only items from the collection he saw stolen were several old rifles. Mostly, he said, he saw looters take chairs, typewriters, ceiling lamp fixtures and other items from the museum's offices, as happened at nearly every other government office in the capital.

By now, you would think the *Times* would back off a little to determine whether the original suspicion—that most of the antiquities were safely packed away—was correct. But the *Times* ignored the warnings and continued to use the issue to bash the Bush administration's handling of the situation. The op-ed page of the same issue published three more pieces on the alleged looting of antiquities at the Baghdad Museum.

First, in "MISSING IN ACTION" (April 17, 2003), two Yale professors of literature and art history added little more than the name of their school and the false information they read in the *New York Times* to their op-ed piece which began:

> When looters descended upon the Iraq Museum in Baghdad last week, they despoiled one of the world's pre-eminent collections of artifacts from the Tigris and Euphrates Valleys.

Second, in "AN ARMY FOR ART," an art-ownership consultant and a visiting lecturer at Princeton added the credibility of Princeton University to their studied opinion:

The looting of Iraq's national museum in Baghdad could have been prevented. The American and British forces are clearly to blame for the destruction and displacement of its cultural treasures.

Finally, in "A JOB FOR UNESCO," a former U.S. representative to the United Nations made the following contribution to the op-ed trilogy:

How do we repair the damage done? The meeting to be convened today by UNESCO, the United Nations cultural arm, is a good start.

Incidentally, each op-ed piece was accompanied by a captioned drawing of an ancient artifact purportedly lost in the looting. It will be interesting to see whether the *Times*' op-ed staff provides an update to their readers as to whether these artifacts were, in fact, ever lost.

The following day, UNESCO announced that it agreed to send an "emergency" mission to Iraq to assess the damage suffered by the National Museum in Baghdad. ("ART EXPERTS MOBILIZE TEAM TO RECOVER STOLEN TREASURE AND SALVAGE IRAQI MUSEUMS," April 18, 2003). While a UN spokesman speculated, "It looks like part of the theft was a very planned action," those interviewed by the *Times* conceded that

the only information about the damage to the Baghdad museum had come from sporadic satellite telephone calls, news reports and what they can glean from photographs and television film.

QUOTE-COMMON-FOLK-WHO-AGREE-WITH-US

Meanwhile, keep those cards and letters coming. The next day, under the heading "ART LOST TO IRAQ, AND TO THE WORLD" (April 19, 2003), the *Times* printed six letters to the editor, nearly all critical of the Bush administration's handling of what by then was portending to become one of the most botched stories of the war. If there were a Pulitzer Prize for journalistic incompetence, the *New York Times* would soon find itself on the short list. Here are some excerpts from these letters to the editor:

Blame for the disaster at the National Museum of Iraq lies not with the Army but with the priorities and directives of the Bush administration.

The American military did nothing to protect the priceless artifacts of ancient civilizations at the National Museum of Iraq and the House of Wisdom, the country's main library. The sins of omission may be less than the sins of commission but still represent appalling negligence.

The sacking of the museum and burning of the library in Baghdad bespeak our lack of civilization, and of respect for civilization.

The pillaging of the National Museum in Baghdad was not just a loss for Iraqi history. It was also a devastation of world culture akin to the destruction of the library in Alexandria, Egypt, and will be lamented for ages.

The author of this last excerpt—and for that matter, the *New York Times*—might have detailed the ironic historical context. The great destruction of ancient books at the library at Alexandria was by the order of a Muslim, Caliph Omar. In January of the year 641, Omar, upon learning of the library's treasure of forty thousand books, commanded, "If the books contain matter not in accordance with the book of Allah, there can be no need to preserve them. Proceed, then, and destroy them." The books were subsequently distributed to the public baths of Alexandria where they were used to fuel the fires which warmed the baths. One ancient historian reported that it took six months to burn all that mass of material. Only the books of Aristotle were spared. (The discovery of documents supporting this history dispelled the myth that the great library of Alexandria was destroyed by the Romans.)

SLANTING WITH LOADED LANGUAGE

The lead story that day on the front page, "COMPETING GROUPS DISPLAY INFLUENCE IN IRAQ'S CAPITAL" (April 19, 2003), presented a sharp contrast between how the *Times* portrayed, on the one hand, "Shiite and Sunni Muslims united in a demonstration that railed against the United States" and, on the other, "an Iraqi exile backed by the Pentagon" who "emerged from well-guarded seclusion in an exclusive club to stake a claim to a role in Iraq's future."

While the protesters showed "a rare demonstration of solidarity" in their chants of "no to sectarianism, one Islamic state," the *Times* reported:

> A very different tone was struck at the news conference of Ahmad Chalabi, the 58-year old scion of a wealthy Shiite clan who returned to his native Baghdad this week for the first time in 45 years.
>
> Mr. Chalabi is protected by American soldiers on a mansion-lined street in Baghdad's richest neighborhood. One of his supporters, Muhammad Zobaidi, was installed as city administrator at a chaotic meeting called by American officers on Sunday.

A very different tone, indeed: "exile," "well-guarded seclusion," "exclusive club," "scion," "wealthy," "clan," "mansion-lined," "richest neighborhood," "chaotic"? Be prepared to read about the "embattled Mr. Chalabi" and the results of a *New York Times*/CBS News public opinion poll asking whether the American public trusts this scion to do the right thing.

THE ARTIFACTS FIRESTORM CONTINUES

Maureen Dowd apparently glossed over some of the more recent articles regarding the artifacts before penning her next op-ed piece. The self-professed expert in military affairs and police security opined in her Sunday op-ed piece entitled "A TALE OF TWO FRIDAYS" (April 20, 2003):

> The Pentagon could easily have saved the national museum and library if they had redeployed the American troops assigned to guard Ahmed Chalabi, the Richard Perle pal, Pentagon candidate and convicted embezzler who is back in Iraq trying to ingratiate himself with the country he left 40 years ago.

It seems the *Times*' op-ed and editorial staff were still under the impression created by the news division's original story that 170,000 ancient artifacts had been lost as a result of looting. As long as the Bush administration was being blamed for not stopping the looting, it appeared this issue was going to have some legs.

So, if you liked Dowd's piece, you would just love what you'd see by simply turning the page, where you would find the entire back page of the *Times'* Week in Review section devoted to "Lost in Iraq" (April 20, 2003)—the subject heading for three articles concerning what the *Times* called one of history's "greatest cultural disasters."

The first, entitled "Our First Words, Written in Clay, in an Accountant's Hand," charged:

> The tablets in the National Museum, the volumes in the National Library and in the National Archives, the exquisite collection of Korans kept at the Ministry of Religious Endowment have practically all now disappeared. Lost are the manuscripts lovingly penned by the great Arab calligraphers, for whom the beauty of the script must mirror the beauty of the contents. Vanished are the collections of tales, like "The Arabian Nights" . . .
>
> Trust in the survival of the word, as well as the urge to destroy it, is as old as the first clay tablets.

The second, entitled "Missing: A Vase, a Book, a Bird and 10,000 Years of History," recounted a number of other treasures, "the hundreds of thousands of artifacts and texts . . . that can never be replaced." The piece was punctuated with the following pathos:

> Above all, scholars acted as mourners struggling with an overwhelming loss. In Boston, Dr. Russell fought back tears as he described a sculpture from the museum he had seen in the 1980's: a small carving of a bird, one of the earliest stone sculptures in existence, from around 8,000 B.C. "The archeologists had found it literally in the hand of its ancient owner, who had been crushed to death when the roof of his burning house fell in on him, evidently as he tried to save this piece," he said. "In light of what's happened in the past week, that's very hard to think about right now."

The third article, "Did Lord Elgin Do Something Right?" asked what we learned about protecting historical treasures and echoed Maureen Dowd's views with the following observation:

The first lesson, of course, is to station troops at a museum in a war zone.

Then, a full week later, to be certain that the Arts & Leisure audience wasn't missing out on all the fun, Frank Rich finally joined the pile-on with "AND NOW: OPERATION IRAQI LOOTING" (April 27, 2003):

> Let it never be said that our government doesn't give a damn about culture. It was on April 10, the same day the sacking of the National Museum in Baghdad began, that a subtitled George W. Bush went on TV to tell the Iraqi people that they are "the heirs of a great civilization that contributes to all humanity." And so what if America stood idly by while much of the heritage of that civilization—its artifacts, its artistic treasures, its literary riches and written records—was being destroyed as he spoke?

THE TRUTH EMERGES

Several days later, the *Times* finally broke the story that had been evident from the start: someone looted the truth from the original *Times* story about the artifacts. The front page of the *Times*, in "LOSS ESTIMATES ARE CUT ON IRAQI ARTIFACTS" (May 1, 2003), reported:

> BAGHDAD, Iraq, April 30—Even though many irreplaceable antiquities were looted from the National Museum of Iraq during the chaotic fall of Baghdad last month, museum officials and American investigators now say the losses seem to be less severe than originally thought.
>
> Col. Matthew F. Bogdanos, a Marine reservist who is investigating the looting and is stationed at the museum, said museum officials had given him a list of 29 artifacts that were definitely missing. But since then, 4 items—ivory objects from the eighth century B.C.—had been traced.
>
> "Twenty-five pieces is not the same as 170,000," said Colonel Bogdanos, who in civilian life is an assistant Manhattan district attorney.

The story also included accounts of Iraqis returning artifacts to the museum, in some cases by people who said they had taken the treasures to keep them out of the wrong hands. In addition, the article reported that 50,000 Islamic and Arab manuscripts, dating back fourteen centuries, were saved from the Saddam House of Manuscripts. While looters made off with furniture and other office items, the entire library of the museum was bricked up before the war began and escaped vandalism.

Despite all the good news, the *Times* still couldn't resist a parting shot at the American forces in Iraq. The kicker of the story quoted an Iraqi cultural official who said that the U.S. forces and tanks that were near the museum "could have done as they did at the Ministry of Oil. Why didn't they? I don't know. We asked them. They said they were in the middle of a war."

The article concluded with this line: "The American response since then has been to try to fix what has been broken." Ironically, the *Times'* very purpose here was to fix what the paper had engendered during the prior three weeks: false reports and amplifications apparently designed to embarrass the United States and its military. In correcting the record, however, the *Times* made no direct reference to any of its prior news stories, editorials, op-ed pieces, or Arts & Leisure pieces— collectively, the *Times'* crusade that gave credence to the widespread accusations that the Bush administration was responsible for a catastrophic cultural disaster.

A few days later, the world received further confirmation that most of the artifacts had avoided looters. In "MOST IRAQI TREASURES ARE SAID TO BE KEPT SAFE" (May 6, 2003), the *Times* reported:

> A top British Museum official said yesterday that his Iraqi counterparts told him they had largely emptied display cases at the National Museum in Baghdad months before the start of the Iraq war, storing many of the museum's most precious artifacts in secure "repositories."

The article pointed out that Baghdad Museum officials had listed only twenty-five artifacts as definitely missing.

A more definitive confirmation came two days later. In "U.S. SAYS IT HAS RECOVERED HUNDREDS OF ARTIFACTS AND THOUSANDS OF MANUSCRIPTS IN IRAQ" (May 8, 2003), the *Times* reported:

> WASHINGTON, May 7—Teams of American investigators searching in Iraq have recovered more than 700 artifacts and tens of thousands of ancient

manuscripts that had been missing from the collection of the National Museum in Baghdad, some of them stored in underground vaults before the American invasion, American officials said today.

Later in the same article, the *Times* reported circumstances that could cast suspicion on certain archeologists in Iraq:

> American investigators have complained that their work has been hindered by a lack of cooperation from museum workers, who have so far been unable to provide a full inventory of the museum's collection, and by uncertainty over how many objects were on open display when the looting began. American officials say there is a growing suspicion that insiders within the museum's administration were to blame for much of the thefts.

Nevertheless, a week of revelations didn't stop other *Times* writers from furthering the myth of a "cultural disaster" in Iraq. The next day, an art review entitled "WAY, WAY BACK, TO THE DAWN OF THE BEGINNING" (May 9, 2003), covering three-fourths of the front page of the Weekend/Fine Arts section, the *Times* made light of the subject this way:

> Who knows, as of now, what's lost from the Iraq Museum in Baghdad. But as if to illustrate the value of the collection, "Art of the First Cities" opened yesterday at the Metropolitan Museum of Art—the most timely exhibition in years as well as diplomatically dexterous and beautiful.

THE FINAL CRUSADE?

In a final irony, some of the best observations about the press coverage of the war came from the White House. According to a *Times* story under the headline "ADDRESSING NEWSPAPER EDITORS, BUSH'S POLITICAL ADVISOR FAULTS SOME WAR COVERAGE" (April 12, 2003), Karl Rove, speaking to a gathering of newspaper editors in New Orleans, observed that the news media's coverage of the war in Iraq confused people by subjecting them to reporters' "mood swings" and the results of endless polling about the military's progress. The euphoria of April 9, when news coverage was dominated by a statue of Saddam Hussein being pulled to the ground in Baghdad, did not match the earlier "flood of commentary that the military was bogged down and the strategy flawed." "Ultimately," said Rove, "we must have the capacity to stand back and see the deep currents and the important shape of events."

During the war, someone at the *Times* should have read their own newspaper every morning and asked, "Hey, aren't we being entirely too negative here? Are we missing something?" As the *Times* was printing its "quagmire narrative," nearly all the retired army generals on television news outlets were describing what they were observing as the most successful military advance in the history of the world. During the time when things were going pretty well, the *Times* was engaging in a "fear and anxiety" crusade and printing front-page "news analyses" that have since become the butt of jokes.

Recall what Howell Raines said at U.C. Berkeley on November 18, 2002:

> And that's what we try to bring to our journalism—the feel for the event, the context, the history, the whole picture.

"The context, the history, the whole picture"—that is exactly what the *Times* was missing during these tense days of the war. The *Times* only presented a narrow slice of the story—the horrible realities of war, but none of its historical context. The *Times* missed out on the "whole picture" completely. Few were in doubt of the eventual outcome: the liberation of the Iraqis and a mission accomplished for the Americans. But the *Times* seemed singularly focused on promoting its ideological agenda by opposing the administration, downplaying Bush's achievements, and emphasizing the costs of the war—and all the fear, anxiety, and discord that's fit to print on its front page.

By allowing its political ideologies to color its reporting, the *Times* did a huge disservice to the American public. "Every violation of the truth," said Emerson, "is a stab at the health of human society." The *Times*' coverage of Gulf War II put a stake in the heart of its readership. With its reputation now on life support, only one thing is certain: its cure will require a vigorous remedy. In the next chapter, we will explore what actions that remedy might entail while we reflect upon the fate of the *New York Times*.

THIRTEEN

The Future of the New York Times

The best Things, when perverted, become the
very worst: So, Printing, which in it self is no
small Advantage to Mankind, when it is Abus'd
may be of most Fatal Consequences.

—*From an Anonymous Pamphlet, 1712*

From the moment Adolph S. Ochs published his famous dedication
in 1896—"to give the news impartially, without fear or favor"—the
reputation of the *Times* for professional news reporting rose along
with the public's increasing thirst for information about a changing world.
Over the years, the *Times* aggressively leveraged that reputation to "see wrongs
corrected" by fearlessly stating its positions regarding fundamental political,
social, and economic issues on its editorial pages. However, making one's views
known is not enough to incite action; to influence real change, one's views must
carry weight—that is, one must have a certain level of credibility to begin with.
For the *Times*, that credibility had been earned by a long tradition of unbiased
reporting—reporting the news "impartially, without fear or favor."

Ochs seemed to instinctively understand that the effectiveness of the *Times'*
editorial pages as an agent of change was directly proportional to its reputation

for impartial reporting. In other words, should the *Times'* coverage of hard news lose its reputation for being fair and balanced, its editorial positions on fundamental issues of the day would, rightfully, fail to serve those who the *Times* hoped to benefit.

As previously mentioned, this is a principle that Ochs' colleagues at the *American Society of Newspaper Editors* seemed to understand well when they wrote in 1923:

> Sound practice makes clear distinction between news reports and expressions of opinion. News reports should be free from opinion or bias of any kind.

Ochs' successor, his son-in-law, Arthur Hays Sulzberger, understood it too when writing in the 1950s:

> We are anxious to see wrongs corrected, and we attempt to make our position very clear in such matters on our editorial page. But we believe that no matter how we view the world, our responsibility lies in reporting accurately that which happens.

Times, indeed, have changed. Today, Ochs' great-grandson, the current publisher of the *Times*, has turned the family tradition of impartial reporting on its ear. While critics—mainly right-leaning "media watch" organizations—have long charged the *Times* with employing a decidedly left-wing slant to its news reporting, the belief that nothing less than a revolution is taking place at the *Times* has now become widespread.

With the revelations of widespread falsification and plagiarism that have polluted tens, if not hundreds, of the paper's articles, the reputation of the *Times*—already blemished by biased reporting—has plummeted. The nosedive appears to have directly coincided with Arthur Sulzberger Jr.'s first strategic organizational move: the appointment in 2001 of the paper's *editorial editor*, Howell Raines, to oversee its *news reporting* activities. Prior to his taking charge of the newsroom of the *Times*, Raines had been the paper's chief editorial editor for eight years.

The "arrogance," "inaccessibility," and "fear"—using the words of Raines' own employees—that pervaded the executive editor's management style cultivated an environment where the catastrophic Jayson Blair could thrive, but the paper's credibility gap runs much deeper and extends far beyond the lies and stolen news copy of one young reporter.

The furor over the Blair scandal being the terminus of Raines' career actually deflects attention from the real journalistic fraud at the *Times*—the pervasive, deceptive practice of passing off left-leaning opinion as straight news. While an existing problem when Raines ascended, it flourished under his supervision and care.

With Raines gone, the publisher has a real opportunity to reverse the fraudulent reporting practices of the *Times*. If they are not reversed, the *Times* runs the risk of irretrievably losing its reputation and eventually its relevancy. Simply, as the *Times* loses its reputation for reporting accurately what happens, it will suffer two significant consequences: (1) the loss of its relevancy as a credible source of news, and (2) the loss of its relevancy as a means for correcting societal wrongs.

New York Times publisher Arthur Sulzberger Jr. is in danger of destroying the asset his forefathers worked so hard to build. The only question that remains is this: Can the publisher of the *Times*, or anyone else, pull the paper out of its tailspin, or is it just too late to save a great institution from the shortsightedness of its current publisher?

To that question, there would seem to be three possible scenarios:

1. Arthur Sulzberger Jr. fails to act and the *Times* irretrievably loses its relevancy.

2. The *Times* is saved by an internally or externally mounted drive to deliver control of the newspaper from Arthur Sulzberger Jr. to a more responsible publisher.

3. Arthur Sulzberger Jr. finally recognizes how gravely the *Times* has been blemished during his stewardship and, on his own accord or by virtue of advice or pressure from others, reverses course and makes the tough decisions necessary to restore the integrity of the *New York Times*.

FIRST SCENARIO: ARTHUR SULZBERGER JR. FAILS TO ACT

As stated at the outset, this book has been largely derived not from interviews or a careful study of historical correspondence but from what is openly printed within the four corners of the daily editions of the *New York Times*. Little attempt has been made to investigate the secret motivations of the publishers or editors of the *Times*, an exercise best left to biographers and historians. For our purposes, we can only assume that the editorial approach that Arthur Sulzberger Jr., through Raines, has chosen with respect to reporting the news is a well-intentioned effort to serve the professional and financial success of his newspaper and the general welfare of the citizenry.

Leaving motivations aside, however, if the consequence of the approach is the demise of the *Times* as a credible source of news, then, however well-intentioned, his actions will have failed their purpose. From the readers' perspective, something must be said about their approach, not just for the good of the *New York Times* but, in a narrow sense, for the good of those consumers who have come to enjoy the *Times* as a source of news and entertainment and, in a broader sense, for the good of our democracy, which thrives upon a healthy press.

Joseph C. Goulden, in his book *Fit To Print* (Lyle Stuart, 1988), observed:

> The *New York Times*, for better or for worse, has a dominant voice in setting the agenda for America. The *Times* does so because it is respected, and it takes its job of gathering news seriously.

The premise of this book is that the *Times* is quickly losing its respect because it appears to no longer take seriously its job of gathering news and reporting it accurately, without fear or favor. With the loss of that respect, the *Times* is not simply losing its ability to influence public opinion. It is, at best, providing a disservice to its customers; at worst, it is committing an unconscionable form of *journalistic fraud*.

To be clear, the fraud has nothing to do with the editorial positions taken by the *Times*, either on its editorial or op-ed pages, or even within the paper's appropriately labeled "News Analysis" articles.

Our focus has been on providing indisputable proof of the passing off of editorial opinion in the form of straight news stories. This artifice the *Times* has used to influence public opinion is particularly insidious because it derives it power from the paper's reputation for impartial reporting—a reputation built on the ink, sweat, and tears of thousands of professional news reporters since Adolph S. Ochs purchased the paper in 1896.

By the same token, the effectiveness of the fraud, and thereby its usefulness as a means of influencing people, is limited by the extent to which people believe that the news as reported by the *Times* is impartial. As we have demonstrated, the *Times* is being steadily stripped of its will to maintain the integrity integrity of its news reporting, particularly since Arthur Sulzberger Jr.'s fateful decision to place the paper's news division under the control of Howell Raines, the "fire-breathing, take-no-prisoners editorial editor" whose liberal ideologies matched those of the young publisher.

Raines might proffer in his defense the Pulitzer Prizes bestowed upon the *Times* for its reporting of the September 11 attacks, but the credibility of the Pulitzer organization as an objective source of professional accolade is the subject of another book.

Instead of responding to criticism by refuting specific claims of bias, Raines' modus operandi was mainly the casting of ad hominems against his attackers. As we have seen, he publicly suggested that Charles Krauthammer had "taken leave of his senses" and attacked the *Weekly Standard* magazine as a mere mouthpiece for Rupert Murdoch.

More recently, Raines added a new tactic in the defense of his brand of journalism. When attacking his attackers, he charged them with the same criticism being cast against him. According to Raines, his critics were engaged in a "disinformation effort" and were actually advocating biased journalism.

In accepting the "Editor of the Year Award" at the National Press Foundation's awards dinner held on February 20, 2003 in Washington, D.C., broadcast live on C-SPAN, Raines seemed to feign innocence with the following remarks:

> The most important development of the post-war period among American journalists was the acceptance throughout our profession of an ethic that says we report and edit the news for our papers, but we don't wear the political collar of our owners, or the government, or any political party.

Conveniently, he left out himself. He continued:

> It is that legacy we must protect with our diligent stewardship. To do so means we must be aware of the energetic effort that is now underway to convince our readers that we are ideologues.

Here, Raines finally admitted awareness of the criticism that the *Times'* news division had become, under his stewardship, a zealous advocate of its editorial board's ideological agenda. But, instead of accepting that criticism, as he would have his readers accept the criticism of, say, President Bush's tax cuts, presented on his own editorial pages, he went on the attack:

> It is an exercise of disinformation of alarming proportions—this attempt to convince the audience of the world's most ideology-free newspapers that they are being subjected to agenda driven news reflecting a liberal bias.

If Raines' audience were not shocked to hear him speak of the *Times* as "ideology-free," then Bernard Goldberg was absolutely right about the common worldview of mainstream journalists. As for his use of the term "disinformation," readers of this book will have recognized by now that nearly all of the "information" contained herein was taken directly from the pages of the *New York Times*. Being direct quotes, it will be hard for Raines to accuse us of distorting the facts. Readers will have to judge for themselves whether what has been presented here is an exercise of "disinformation" or constructive analysis.

Raines next set up the straw man:

> I don't believe our viewers and readers will be in the long-run misled by those who advocate biased journalism.

Of course not. A sophisticated readership would never allow themselves to be misled by those who would "advocate biased journalism." Nor, by the same token, should it be misled by Raines' attempt to paint his legitimate critics as advocates of the very practices those critics abhor. Attacking his critics with the very charge they are making against him is a childish game unbecoming of a person in Raines' position, yet he developed the theme further:

> But perhaps those of us who work for fair-minded publications and broadcasters have been too passive in pointing out the agendas of those who want to use journalism as a political tool, while aiming an accusing finger at those who practice balanced journalism. I believe as Coach Bryant used to say, "The fourth quarter belongs to us."

Only a few months before he would fumble the ball and leave the game in disgrace, Raines, in an effort to defend his brand of journalism, attempted to kick off a "fourth quarter" public relations offensive against his critics. His strategy, it seems, was not to respond to legitimate criticism with facts and arguments but to simply proclaim himself a practitioner of "balanced journalism" and throw eggs at his detractors. As Andrew Sullivan observed, in Raines' eyes, "it's the critics of the *New York Times'* bias who are the enemies of good journalism."

Within six weeks after receiving the National Press Foundation's "Editor of the Year Award," the Blair scandal stripped Howell Raines bare of his pretentiousness. The contrite executive editor began his repentance with apologies and promises to fix the damage that his own inadequacies had inflicted. Yet, if the *Times'* reporters were waging whether "the tiger could change his stripes," few were taking Raines' side of the bet.

Sulzberger's and Raines' failed attempt to deflect criticism away from themselves at the onset of the Blair scandal should have been a valuable lesson. While Sulzberger waited like Hamlet to finally make up his mind and do the inevitable, the future of a 100-year-old venerable American institution hung in the balance.

Even when he finally accepted Howell Raines' resignation, there were no signs that Sulzberger would reverse the course that he and Raines set for the *Times*. Howell Raines reeled in a big fish when he assumed stewardship of the *New York Times*. But, like Hemingway's memorable character in *The Old Man and the Sea*, "blemished" may be too kind a word to describe what Raines turned over to the Sulzberger family when his journey was done.

As this book goes to press, things do not look good. Wrote Mickey Kaus in *Slate* the day of Raines' departure, "It's not as if the *NYT* is going to stop being a liberal paper. But maybe the *Times'* annoying tendency to *unashamedly* equate Upper West Side liberal sentiments with 'objective' reporting . . . will temporarily abate." But Kaus wasn't too optimistic. "It always seemed to me, however, that the trend became apparent under the editorship of Joseph Lelyveld, who has now been brought back as interim editor" (June 5, 2003). By appointing a man who represents a lighter touch of Raines-style news distortion, all Sulzberger shows is that he accepted Raines' resignation because he was increasingly inconvenient, not because he recklessly mishandled the credibility of the *Times*' news pages. Without a radical change in vision from the top, the same mishandling—the same advocacy journalism—seems a sure, albeit subtler, routine in the newsroom.

If the "low point" marked by the Blair scandal and its attendant fallout was not enough to persuade Arthur Sulzberger Jr. to return the news reporting policies of the paper to the ideals of his great-grandfather, then what will persuade him? Who does Arthur Sulzberger Jr. listen to? These are questions that the board of directors of the New York Times Company must confront before it is too late.

SECOND SCENARIO: ARTHUR SULZBERGER JR. IS REPLACED

The second possible scenario is that Arthur Sulzberger Jr. is forcibly removed as publisher of the *New York Times*, and his replacement embraces a vision of impartiality and appoints an executive editor more suitable to an organization that prides itself on objective reporting.

It would seem that replacing the publisher of the *Times* would be a rather simple affair. After all, the New York Times Company is a public company, listed on the New York Stock Exchange (ticker symbol: NYT), and Arthur Sulzberger Jr. serves as publisher at the pleasure of the company's board of directors.

If the Times Company's directors are not disposed to remove him, the company could be taken over, it would seem, like any other public company. Through a corporate takeover, the board of directors of the Times Company could be replaced, and Arthur Sulzberger Jr. could be given his walking papers.

Currently, the total value of the New York Times Company is about $8 billion. In comparison to the cost of several other recent media acquisitions— AOL acquired Time-Warner for $165 billion; Viacom purchased CBS for $37 billion; Vivendi acquired Universal for $34 billion—an acquisition of the Times Company for $8 billion (or even $12 billion, reflecting a 50 percent premium on its current value to assure a successful acquisition) would not seem insurmountable, at least from a financial perspective. Any number of companies, such as Rupert Murdoch's News Corporation, which is currently valued at about $38 billion, could mount a takeover of the Times Company.

The financial perspective, however, is only one piece of the control puzzle. The Times Company is governed like no other public media company, and a financial takeover would by no means assure a change in control over the *New York Times*. This is because the Ochs/Sulzberger family long ago took great care to retain a lock over the management of the *New York Times*, even if their share of its stock should dwindle to an extremely small minority.

Ellis Cose, in his book *The Press* (William Morrow, 1989), described the *Times* as "shrouded by the densest cloud of mystery; a change in its masthead is scrutinized by journalists in a manner usually reserved for leadership change at the Kremlin." If Cose was referring to the Kremlin under the Soviet Union, then, for the analogy to hold, the last Soviet premier would not have been Mikail Gorbechov but rather the great-grandson of Lenin. In truth, the leadership of the *Times* is controlled more like that of czarist Russia—by a few descendants of Arthur S. Ochs, who purchased the *Times* in 1896, twenty years before the czar was dethroned by a brutal revolution (which is not being suggested here). It would seem that nothing short of a rancorous family brawl is likely to change the *Times*' leadership.

We can unveil the mystery by taking a close look at the corporate scoreboard—that is, the Times Company shareholdings of the Ochs/Sulzberger family and what it means. Information about the Ochs/Sulzberger family shareholdings and how it relates to their control over the *New York Times* is fully disclosed every year in statements the Times Company is required to file with the Securities and Exchange Commission.

As we have said, the key to replacing the publisher of the *New York Times* is to replace those who have the right to hire (and fire) him—a majority of the board of directors of the New York Times Company. With respect to nearly all of the corporations listed on the New York Stock Exchange, the board of directors serves at the pleasure of a majority of the company's owners, its shareholders. Normally, at the annual meeting of the shareholders of a company, the shareholders who control a majority of the stock will get to elect the members of the board. Upon their election, the board appoints their chairman and their officers. This is not how it works at the New York Times Company. The numbers will explain.

There are slightly more than 150 million shares of stock in the New York Times Company. About 150 million shares are Class A shares, and slightly more than ¾ million shares are Class B shares:

Class A	149,939,710 shares
Class B	847,020 shares

A vast majority of the Class A shares—about 85 percent—is owned by the public. (The other 15 percent is controlled by the Ochs/Sulzberger family.) More significant, nearly *all* of the Class B shares are controlled by eight members of the Ochs/Sulzberger family.

Here's the math: There are thirteen members of the board of directors of the New York Times Company. Class B stockholders get to elect nine of them. Class A stockholders only get to elect four of them. Thus, while holding only about 15 percent of the company's stock, several members of the Ochs/Sulzberger family forever maintain an ironclad lock on the composition of the board of directors of the Times Company. Even if the family sold all of its Class A stock, it would still have the right to elect 70 percent of the board by virtue of its control of all of the Class B stock, or about 1/2 percent of the company's stock.

Thus, even a corporate takeover of the New York Times Company—i.e., the acquisition of a controlling interest in the Class A stock—would not change the power that Class B stockholders have over the management of the *New York Times*. By virtue of their written arrangements with the corporation, the Ochs/Sulzberger family would always maintain the right to elect nine of the thirteen board members.

Most of the Class B stock—749,976 shares of it—is owned by eight members of the Ochs/Sulzberger family and a family trust established in 1997 (the "1997 Trust") by the four grandchildren of Adolph S. Ochs. The ownership breaks down this way:

Owner	# of Class B Shares
1997 Trust	738,810
Arthur Ochs Sulzberger	3,570
Arthur Sulzberger Jr.	960

Cathy J. Sulzberger	960
Daniel H. Cohen	1,620
Lynn G. Dolnick	1,118
Jacqueline H. Dryfoos	600
Arthur S. Golden	1,118
Michael Golden	1,12
Total	749,976

Control of the 1997 Trust—and the voting control over Class B shares owned by the trust—is in the hands of the same eight individuals listed above. Arthur Ochs Sulzberger, affectionately nicknamed "Punch" Sulzberger, is the former chairman of the Times Company and former publisher of the *New York Times*. Upon his retirement, Punch was replaced by his son, Arthur Sulzberger Jr. (52). Cathy J. Sulzberger (54), who was adopted by Punch Sulzberger, is Arthur's sister. Daniel H. Cohen, Lynn G. Dolnick, Jacqueline H. Dryfoos, Arthur Sulzberger Golden, and Michael Golden are all cousins.

In honor of the style of the *Times'* columnist Maureen Dowd, we'll call these people, who are the eight trustees who control the 1997 Trust, the "Gang of Eight" (an appellation they don't necessarily deserve, but it serves a satiric purpose). As this book goes to press, the following thirteen people comprised the board of directors of the New York Times Company:

Voted by Class A	Voted by Class B
Raul E. Cesan	John F. Akers
William Kennard	Brenda C. Barnes
Henry B. Schacht	Jacqueline H. Dryfoos
Donald M. Stewart	Michael Golden
	Russell T. Lewis
	David E. Liddle
	Ellen R. Marram
	Arthur Sulzberger Jr.
	Cathy J. Sulzberger

Thus, four of the Gang of Eight sit on the board of the Times Company. The other four Class B directors were elected by the Gang of Eight. As for the four Class A directors, though they were elected by Class A stockholders, they were nominated by a committee controlled by the Gang of Eight.

Let's take a closer look at how this control works. Every board of directors of the New York Stock Exchange is required to appoint a number of committees, each responsible for some aspect of the governance of the corporation. Two of the more important committees include the Compensation Committee and the Nominating & Governance Committee.

The Compensation Committee of the Times Company is responsible for, among other things, overseeing the compensation arrangements of all of the company's executive officers and senior management. It is also responsible for annually evaluating the performance of the chairman of the company. The Compensation Committee, as of the end of 2002, was comprised of the following directors:

Director	Voted by
Brenda C. Barnes	Class B
John F. Akers	Class B
David E. Liddle	Class B
Henry B. Schacht	Class A
Donald M. Steward	Class A

Thus, a majority of the Compensation Committee—the committee responsible for evaluating the performance of Arthur Sulzberger Jr., the publisher of the *New York Times*—is comprised of those directors who sit on the board at the pleasure of the Gang of Eight. Should the Times Company be successfully taken over by another organization, the Gang of Eight, controlling a majority of the board, would maintain the power to elect a majority of the Compensation Committee, and thus the evaluation of the performance of Sulzberger would remain in their control.

The Nominating & Governance Committee of the board of the Times Company is responsible for recommending "candidates to the Board for election to the Board at the Annual Meeting." This includes recommending not only future Class B directors, but Class A directors, as well. As of the end of

2002, the Times Company's Nominating & Governance Committee was comprised of the following directors:

Director	Voted by
Arthur Sulzberger Jr.	Class B
Cathy Sulzberger	Class B
John F. Akers	Class B
William E. Kennard	Class B
Ellen R. Marram	Class A
Donald M. Stewart	Class A

Thus, like the Compensation Committee, the majority of the Nominating & Governance Committee—the committee responsible for recommending future Class A and Class B board directors—is comprised of those directors elected by the Gang of Eight, including Arthur Sulzberger Jr., the current publisher, his father, Punch, and his sister, Cathy.

In February 2003, the board of directors of the Times Company announced that it intended to comply with new New York Stock Exchange rules that require a company's Nominating & Governance Committee to be comprised entirely of "independent directors" as that term is defined by the NYSE. Thereupon, Arthur Sulzberger Jr. and his sister Cathy, who the board determined were not "independent," resigned from the committee. Yet, two of the Class B directors on the Nominating & Governance Committee remained on the committee. They were elected solely by the Gang of Eight, which includes Arthur and Cathy. In addition, the full board, which is controlled by the Gang of Eight, could add any of the other Class B directors to the Nominating & Governance Committee at any time.

In a stunning display of hypocrisy, the Times Company announced that while the NYSE rules carved out an exception to its independence rules for companies, like the Times Company, that have more than 50 percent of its voting power held by a single entity (i.e., the 1997 Trust), the Company's board of directors announced that it decided not to take advantage of the exception and, instead, comply "in all respects with the NYSE rules." Thus, with the resignation of Arthur and Cathy from the Nominating & Governance Committee, the board gave the appearance of independence by technically complying with independence rules that didn't apply to them, but in reality, the Nominating & Governance Committee remained under the tight control of the Gang of Eight.

In a press release dated February 20, 2003 to announce these changes, Arthur Sulzberger Jr. stated:

> In many cases, we simply formalized our current procedures, while in others we went beyond the guidelines to introduce changes that we believe will strengthen the oversight role of the Board. In doing so, it was our intention to satisfy not just the letter, but also the spirit of the new corporate governance requirements.

At the end of the day, despite the corporate window-dressing, should the Times Company be successfully taken over by another organization, the Gang of Eight would maintain the power to elect a majority of the Nominating & Governance Committee, and thus the election of at least nine of the thirteen directors would remain under the direct control of the Gang of Eight.

Moreover, according to the terms of the 1997 Trust, the trustees are directed (a) to retain the Class B stock and to not sell, distribute, or otherwise convert such shares and (b) to vote the Class B stock against any merger, sale of assets, or other transaction pursuant to which the control of the *New York Times* passes from the trustees, unless they *unanimously* agree to such a transaction. In other words, any *one* of the Gang of Eight (including Arthur Sulzberger Jr.) can keep control of the *New York Times* from being transferred to anyone other than the Gang of Eight.

No suggestion is being made here that there is anything legally wrong with the corporate governance structure of the New York Times Company. Of course, one might imagine the "unrepentant" Ralph Nader taking a suspicious glance at circumstances under which 1/2 percent of the shareholders of a public company can forever control its management or at the fact that one single person owning just a few thousand shares of stock can prevent a corporate takeover of a public company against the wishes of the majority of the shareholders. But the purchasers of the Class A shares knew what they were getting into—or, by virtue of the required public disclosure filings of the Times Company with the SEC, they should have known.

Owners of stock in the New York Times Company have effectively no say over the composition of the managers who run it or over how much those managers pay themselves. Ironically, this is a favorite theme of the *Times'* editorial page ("THE EXECUTIVE PAY SCAM," April 14, 2002).

Perhaps an all-time height of hypocrisy was reached in a *Times* editorial that ruthlessly attacked President Bush's nominee for the next treasury secretary. Entitled "C.E.O.'S AND THEIR PAYMASTERS" (December 23, 2002), the *Times* began the editorial this way:

> The year of the corporate scandal may be coming to a close, but corrupting boardroom cronyism lives on. As reported in last Wednesday's Times, chief executives at 420 of 2,000 major public corporations have a sweet deal going. Their boards' compensation committees—the folks who determine their pay— include relatives or individuals with ties to them or to the company.

The article to which that editorial referred ran in the *Times* under the headline "DECIDING ON INDEPENDENCE PAY: LACK OF INDEPENDENCE SEEN" (December 18, 2002). The article summarized a study of the compensation committees of 2,000 of the largest American corporations. Incredibly, the article did not list the New York Times Company among those whose Compensation Committees contained a potential conflict of interest. At the time the article was published, Arthur Sulzberger Jr. and his sister both sat on the board's Compensation Committee. Even if the reporters were told of their intention to resign and though none of the Gang of Eight sat directly on the Times Company's Compensation Committee, the committee's independence could surely come into question given a cursory analysis of the circumstances. The fact that a majority of the Compensation Committee was elected by a board controlled by Arthur Sulzberger Jr., his father, his sister, and just one more vote from only one of his four cousins would seem fitting enough for comment by the *Times'* reporters.

Moreover, recall that Arthur Sulzberger Jr., his father, his sister, and a couple of their cousins control the company's Nominating & Corporate Governance Committee. According to its charter, that committee's responsibilities include making "recommendations to the Board regarding the composition of the Board *and its Committees*, including size and qualifications for membership" (emphasis added). Thus, the Gang of Eight directly control the membership of the Times Company Compensation Committee—this by virtue of their control of 70 percent of the board *and* the committee that makes recommendations on Compensation Committee membership.

Again, there is nothing legally wrong with the Times Company's corporate governance structure—everything seems to be fully disclosed and those who purchase Class A shares in the company should know what they are getting into.

Leaving aside the hypocrisy exhibited by the *Times* on corporate governance and executive pay, the point made here is this: the corporate structure of the New York Times Company does not provide, to put it mildly, a very realistic platform upon which to force a change in the editorial policies of the *New York Times* by means of a corporate takeover.

Sulzberger may be removed forcibly, but only by the will of his family members who control the 1997 Trust. According to the trust, it would require a vote of six of the eight trustees to depose him. Thus, to maintain his job Arthur Sulzberger Jr. would only have to convince his father and his sister to vote with him.

THIRD SCENARIO: ARTHUR SULZBERGER JR. WAKES UP

As we have seen, since the purchase of the *New York Times* newspaper by Adoph S. Ochs in 1896, control over the *Times* has rested entirely with his family and will remain so for the foreseeable future. But changes necessary to save the *Times* may not have to wait for an heir of Ochs' great-grandson to assume control of the paper. Arthur Sulzberger Jr. can become enlightened and save the paper himself.

It remains to be seen, however, what or who will persuade him to take the action necessary to pull the paper out of its current tailspin. Absent an epiphany to motivate him to action, who will Arthur listen to? His father? His sister? His cousins, close friends, or the New York intelligentsia with whom he socializes? Do any of them recognize the real damage Raines inflicted on the *Times*—the great institution Sulzberger's family has built over the last century—by his opinion-tainted news agenda? If they do understand, who among them has the influence or the strength to tell the chairman of the board of the New York Times Company the truth?

With a corporate takeover pretty much out of the question, and with apparently no one willing to approach Arthur Sulzberger Jr. directly, there would appear to be two final prospects for change: (a) the rise of a serious competitor or (b) the embarrassment of widespread criticism.

The Rise of a Serious Competitor

Competition from a New York-based newspaper serious about its news reporting could pose that which is necessary to at least gain the attention of the *Times'* publisher. Unfortunately, none of the tabloid-shaped newspapers currently circulating in New York, even the *New York Post*, which is backed by Rupert Murdoch's News Corporation, would seem to have the gravitas necessary to take on the "newspaper of record."

One hopeful prospect, however, is the *New York Sun*, which began publication on April 16, 2002 with a serious mission. While striving for "honest, objective news" reporting, the paper's editorial page promised to provide an interesting contrast to that of the *Times,* taking positions supporting "lower taxes and school choice" and "limited, constitutional government of integrity." The managing editor of the *Sun*, Ira Stoll, was the founding editor of SmarterTimes.com, which from June 2000 to April 2002 posted on the Internet a daily critique of *The New York Times*. "Reports have it," wrote *Forbes* magazine, "that Stoll is getting under the skin of *Times* editors who are accustomed to basking in the paper's enormous prestige."

The *Sun* is starting with a legendary namesake on its masthead. The original *Sun* debuted on September 3, 1833, eighteen years before the original *New York Daily Times* hit the streets. The *Sun* soon evolved into one of the nation's most influential and revered publications. It was the city editor of the *Sun*, John B. Bogart, who told a young reporter for the first time, "When a dog bites a man, that is not news; but when a man bites a dog, *that* is news." It was *The Sun* that, in 1897, received a letter to the editor from 8-year-old Virginia O'Hanlon inquiring if there really was a Santa Claus. She had been told by her father, "If you see it in *The Sun*, it is so." The newspaper's reply, which ran under the headline "Yes, Virginia, There Is a Santa Claus," became what may be the most widely reprinted column in newspaper history.

Of course, the odds of succeeding against the venerable *New York Times* seem to weigh against the *Sun,* which is starting with over a $3 billion disadvantage. Yet, two developments should give hope to the founders of the *Sun:* (1) the success of the Fox News channel in overtaking CNN in the market for cable news, as a model for what is possible, and (2) Sulzberger's continuing mutilation of the *Times'* reputation for fair and accurate news reporting.

The Embarrassment of Widespread Criticism

Failing a corporate takeover that persuades the Sulzberger family to unanimously agree to relinquish their control or the rise of a qualified newspaper that becomes serious competition for the hearts and minds of troubled readers of the *Times,* there would appear to be only one remaining hope: criticism of the *Times* becomes so widespread that the publisher will be embarrassed into making the changes necessary to change the tone of the newspaper and save it from extinction.

It is earnestly hoped that this book has provided a sufficient degree of focused criticism to spark the awareness necessary to prompt the changes that are essential to return the *Times* to its original greatness. It is written not by a journalist or a media critic but by a loyal consumer of the *New York Times,* someone who actually admires the paper and wants it to succeed. The tack the paper has taken over the past year has threatened a way of life: the pleasure of sitting down each morning with a cup of coffee and an old friend. When that old friend started growing a cancer, the prognosis was predetermined: denial, followed by depression, then anger, acceptance, and finally—resignation.

Thousands of readers, however, are not quite ready to surrender their hope. A genuine change in the editorial attitude of the publisher remains possible, and the promise of an impartial *New York Times,* reporting the news "without fear or favor," may yet again be embraced by a new generation.

ACKNOWLEDGMENTS

I have several people to thank for their assistance in the preparation and publication of this book. I first wish to express my special thanks to my wife, Lori Kohn, my father, Al Kohn, and my friends, Richard and Debbie Lindberg, Steve Brower, and Jim Seltzer, who made critical readings of this work and provided very helpful suggestions for its improvement. My sincerest thanks and gratitude are also due to those who have contributed to the knowledge, skills, and experiences that have found their way into this book, especially Max Berkovitz, my high school language skills and journalism teacher.

I also wish to gratefully acknowledge the thoughtful comments and assistance I received in the preparation of the final manuscript from Joel Miller and Wes Driver, my editors at WND Books. I also thank Mike Hyatt, David Dunham, and Jerry Park at WND Books for their faith in the project and their highly professional support and swift execution. A special thanks is also due to my agent David Brokaw, who hooked me up with the wonderful people at WND and laid the foundation for this project's public introduction. And, of course, I owe one to Rusty Humphries, whose friendship and thoughtfulness really helped drive this book to completion and publication.

After working on the book for several months, I discovered the Internet "blogging" community, whose participants have provided some rather profound commentary on world events and media coverage of those events. Chief among these web-bloggers, and other commentators, include Ira Stoll (SmarterTimes.com), Andrew Sullivan (AndrewSullivan.com), Jack Shafer (*Slate*), Mickey Kaus (KausFiles.com), Jim Romenesko (Poynter.org), Glenn

Reynolds (InstaPundit.com), Robert J. Samuelson (WashingtonPost.com), and L. Brent Bozell III whose staff at the Media Research Center (MediaResearch.org) have worked tirelessly since the 1980s to document many of the artifices used by the mainstream media to distort the news. The analytical skills of Rush Limbaugh, the political genius of Dick Morris, the common sense of Sean Hannity, the timeless values of Robert Bennett, the compassionate understanding of Jack Kemp, the historical perspectives of Newt Gingrich, the raw intelligence of William F. Buckley Jr., the economic analysis of Milton Friedman, the political courage of Senator Mitch McConnell, the pioneering efforts of L. Brent Bozell III, Bernard Goldberg, and Ann Coulter, and the straightforward chutzpah of Michael Savage have all been sources of great inspiration. None, though, have influenced me more than the works of Aristotle, Shakespeare, and Dr. Samuel Johnson.

Errors appearing in prior issues of the *New York Times* are continually brought to the attention of the editors, and the *Times* prints seven or eight corrections each day. These errors, on occasion, can be quite embarrassing. For example, on January 20, 2001, the *Times* reported the following correction: "A front page news analysis article about the nomination of John Ashcroft as attorney general referred incorrectly to Mr. Ashcroft's views on a civil rights issue. He has deplored segregation, not desegregation." As tempting as it may be, imputing typographical errors as evidence of bias is something I have avoided. Though it has been a challenge to divine an *art* from objective evidence, I have not attempted to analyze the *subconscious*.

On this account, I prefer to take Howell Raines at his word when he stated, "The volume of information that we handle in any given day mean that there are going to be errors." Should he find errors in this book, I expect him to take me at mine. More important, it is traditional for authors to accept responsibility for *all* errors, and that tradition shall not be broken here. I will also endeavor to publish corrections at the following Internet site dedicated to that end: **JournalisticFraud.com**.

Finally, I thank my wife, Lori, and my children, Katie and Joey, for their patience and support of this endeavor. Above all, I wish to acknowledge the encouragement and support I received from my parents, to whom this book is lovingly dedicated.

ABOUT THE AUTHOR

Bob Kohn is an attorney and seasoned executive with experience in both the entertainment business and high-tech industries. Mr. Kohn co-authored with his father the legal treatise, *Kohn On Music Licensing* (Aspen Law & Business, 3rd Edition 2002), which *USA Today* called "the bible of legal issues in the music world." The treatise was recently cited by the U.S. Supreme Court in *Eldred v. Ashcroft* (2003), a major decision regarding Congress' power to extend the duration of copyright protection for existing works of authorship.

In 1994, Mr. Kohn won the prize offered by the Encyclopedia Britannica for his essay, "Mind and Brain: The Genius of Fortune," published in the 1994 edition of Britannica's *The Great Ideas Today*. The essay was judged the best solution for a philosophical problem by Mortimer J. Adler, the former editor-in-chief of the Encyclopedia Britannica.

Mr. Kohn was founder of EMusic.com, Inc., the pioneering MP3 music-download subscription service, where he served as chairman until the company was sold to Vivendi/Universal in June 2001. He was an associate attorney at the law offices of Milton A. "Mickey" Rudin in Beverly Hills, California, an entertainment law firm whose clients included Frank Sinatra, among others. Mr. Kohn also worked as associate editor of the *Entertainment Law Reporter*, for which he continues to serve as a member of its Advisory Board.

Mr. Kohn is currently vice chairman of the board of Borland Software Corporation and chairman of Laugh.com, Inc., a comedy record label. A graduate of Loyola Law School in Los Angeles, Mr. Kohn is a member of the California Bar and has taught corporate law at Monterey College of Law, Monterey, California.

INDEX

WND BOOKS

The pen is indeed mightier than the sword. In an age where swords are being rattled all over the world, a new voice has emerged.

You can find WND Books at your favorite bookstore, or by visiting the Web site www.WorldNetDaily.com.

In *Center of the Storm: Practicing Principled Leadership in Times of Crisis,* former Florida Secretary of State Katherine Harris discusses the behind-the-scenes negotiations and backroom bartering that everyone suspected, but no one dared to disclose, during the infamous 2000 presidential election vote recount. Through never-before-revealed anecdotes, she explains twelve essential principles that helped her not just survive but thrive. She clearly illustrates how we, too, can learn these skills that help us in times of crisis. ISBN 0-7852-6443-4

The Savage Nation: Saving America from the Liberal Assault on our Borders, Language, and Culture warns that our country is losing its identity and becoming a victim of political correctness, unmonitored immigration, and socialistic ideals. Michael Savage, whose program is the fourth largest radio talk show and is heard on more than three hundred stations coast to coast, uses bold, biting, and hilarious straight talk to take aim at the sacred cows of our ever-eroding culture and wages war against the "group of psychopaths" known as PETA, the ACLU, and the liberal media. ISBN 0-7852-6353-5

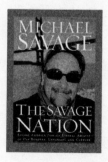

Taking America Back
ISBN 0-7852-6392-6

"Joseph Farah has written a thought-provoking recipe for reclaiming America's heritage of liberty and self-governance. I don't agree with all the solutions proposed here, but Farah definitely nails the problems."

—**Rush Limbaugh**
Host of America's #1 Talk Program,
The Rush Limbaugh Show

"I don't agree with everything Joseph Farah says in *Taking America Back,* but he has written a provocative, from-the-heart call to action. It's a must-read for anyone who wonders how we can expand liberty and reclaim the vision of our founders."

—**Sean Hannity**
Author of *Let Freedom Ring* and Cohost of *Hannity and Colmes* on FOX News

"Joseph Farah and I share a fierce passion for protecting children and a belief that without the Ten Commandments there would be no U.S. Constitution or Bill of Rights. Every American who shares our convictions should read this book."

—**Dr. Laura C. Schlessinger**
Author of *The Ten Commandments*

First Strike
ISBN 0-7852-6354-3

September 11, 2001, did not represent the first aerial assault against the American mainland. The first came on July 17, 1996, with the downing of TWA Flight 800. First Strike looks in detail at what people saw and heard on that fateful night. With an impressive array of facts, Jack Cashill and James Sanders show the relationship between events in July 1996 and September 2001 and proclaim how and why the American government has attempted to cover up the truth.

Seen and Heard
ISBN 0-7852-6368-3

You've heard the saying "Children should be seen and not heard." But teen political writer Kyle Williams is challenging that adage and making a name for himself in the process. As the youngest columnist for WorldNetDaily.com, he has tackled subjects such as abortion, homosexual rights, separation of church and state, and the public school system. In *Seen and Heard,* Williams again takes on the establishment, offering clear evidence that a leftist agenda is at work in our nation. His lively, energetic analysis of current events will leave readers with an understanding of the attack on traditional family values that is taking place daily. Williams's writing style—sound logic infused with passion and conviction—makes *Seen and Heard* both informative and entertaining.

Available September 2003 from WND BOOKS

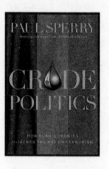

In *Crude Politics,* WorldNetDaily.com's Washington bureau chief Paul Sperry presents alarming evidence that the Bush administration diplomats resumed talks with Pakistani officials over a gas and oil pipeline in Afghanistan while the United States was still reeling from the horror of September 11, 2001. Paul Sperry contends that, true to America's foreign policy of the last century, the Bush administration seized the opportunity to use the attacks as reason to oust the Taliban—the major obstacle blocking plans for the pipeline. ISBN 0-7852-6271-7

Pick it up at your favorite bookstore
or through <u>www.WorldNetDaily.com</u>.